CREATED BY **JOSS WHEDON**

GREG **PAK**   DAN **McDAID**   MARCELO **COSTA**

THE UNIFICATION WAR PART TWO

Published by

BOOM!
S T U D I O S

Designer
Scott Newman with **Marie Krupina**

Assistant Editor
Gavin Gronenthal

Editor
Chris Rosa

Executive Editor
Jeanine Schaefer

Special Thanks to **Sierra Hahn**,
Becca J Sadowski, **Nicole Spiegel**
and **Carol Roeder**.

Ross Richie CEO & Founder
Joy Huffman CFO
Matt Gagnon Editor-in-Chief
Filip Sablik President, Publishing & Marketing
Stephen Christy President, Development
Lance Kreiter Vice President, Licensing & Merchandising
Bryce Carlson Vice President, Editorial & Creative Strategy
Kate Henning Director, Operations
Spencer Simpson Director, Sales
Scott Newman Manager, Production Design
Elyse Strandberg Manager, Finance
Sierra Hahn Executive Editor
Jeanine Schaefer Executive Editor
Dafna Pleban Senior Editor
Shannon Watters Senior Editor
Eric Harburn Senior Editor
Sophie Philips-Roberts Associate Editor
Amanda LaFranco Associate Editor
Jonathan Manning Associate Editor
Gavin Gronenthal Assistant Editor
Gwen Waller Assistant Editor
Allyson Gronowitz Assistant Editor

Ramiro Portnoy Assistant Editor
Kenzie Rzonca Assistant Editor
Shelby Netschke Editorial Assistant
Michelle Ankley Design Lead
Marie Krupina Production Designer
Grace Park Production Designer
Chelsea Roberts Production Designer
Samantha Knapp Production Design Assistant
José Meza Live Events Lead
Stephanie Hocutt Digital Marketing Lead
Esther Kim Marketing Lead
Breanna Sarpy Live Events Coordinator
Amanda Lawson Marketing Assistant
Morgan Perry Retail Sales Lead
Holly Aitchison Digital Sales Coordinator
Megan Christopher Operations Coordinator
Rodrigo Hernandez Operations Coordinator
Zipporah Smith Operations Coordinator
Jason Lee Senior Accountant
Sabrina Lesin Accounting Assistant
Lauren Alexander Administrative Assistant

FIREFLY Volume Two, April 2021. Published by BOOM!
Studios, a division of Boom Entertainment, Inc. © 2021
20th Television. Originally published in single magazine form
as FIREFLY No. 5-8. © 2019 20th Television. BOOM!
Studios™ and the BOOM! Studios logo are trademarks of
Boom Entertainment, Inc., registered in various countries and
categories. All characters, events, and institutions depicted
herein are fictional. Any similarity between any of the
names, characters, persons, events, and/or institutions in this
publication to actual names, characters, and persons, whether
living or dead, events, and/or institutions is unintended and
purely coincidental. BOOM! Studios does not read or accept
unsolicited submissions of ideas, stories, or artwork.

BOOM! Studios, 5670 Wilshire Boulevard, Suite 400, Los
Angeles, CA 90036-5679. Printed in USA. First Printing.

ISBN: 978-1-68415-661-0, eISBN: 978-1-64668-146-4

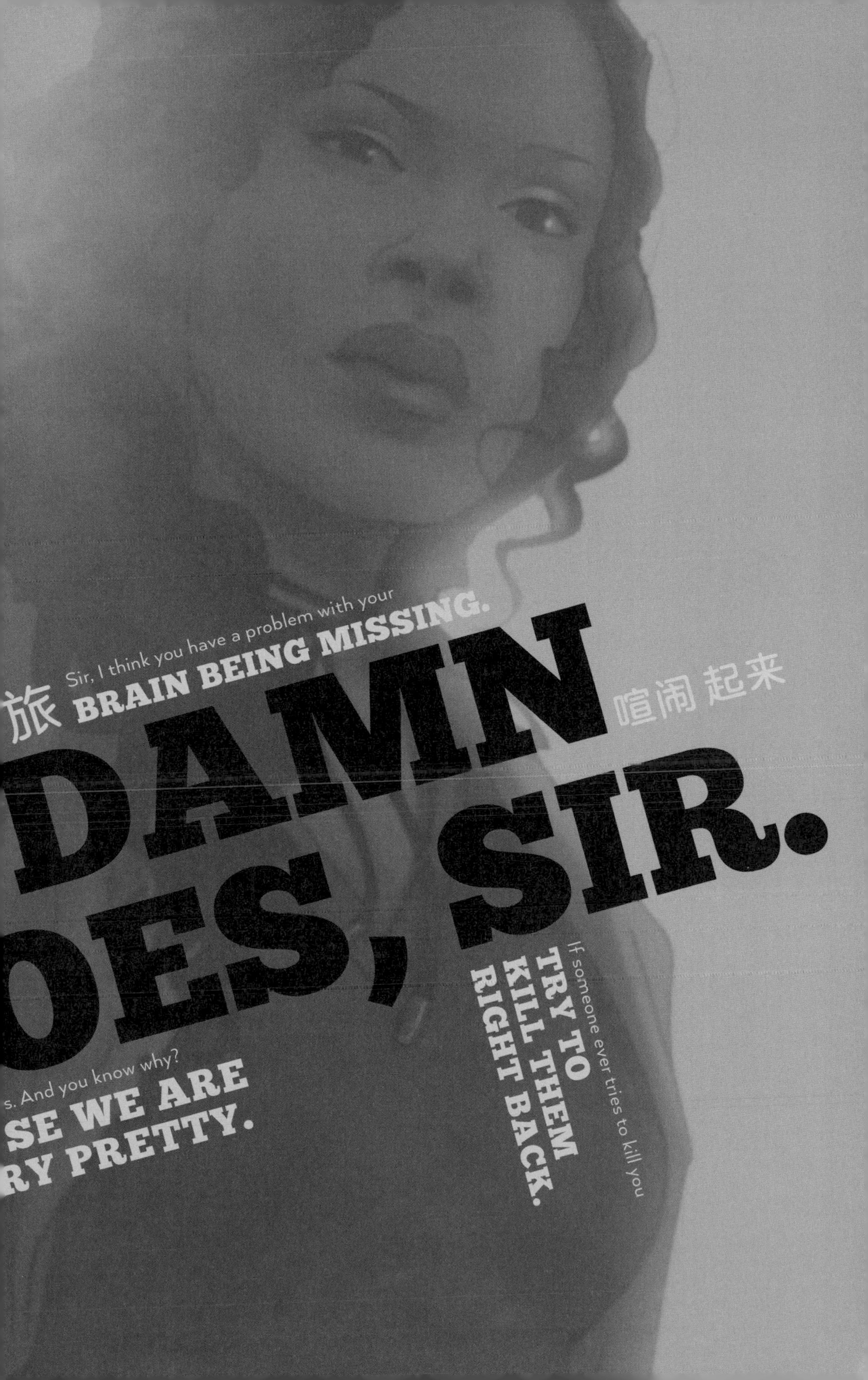
旅
Sir, I think you have a problem with your
BRAIN BEING MISSING.
DAMN
喧闹 起来
OES, SIR.
s. And you know why?
SE WE ARE
RY PRETTY.
If someone ever tries to kill you
TRY TO
KILL THEM
RIGHT BACK.

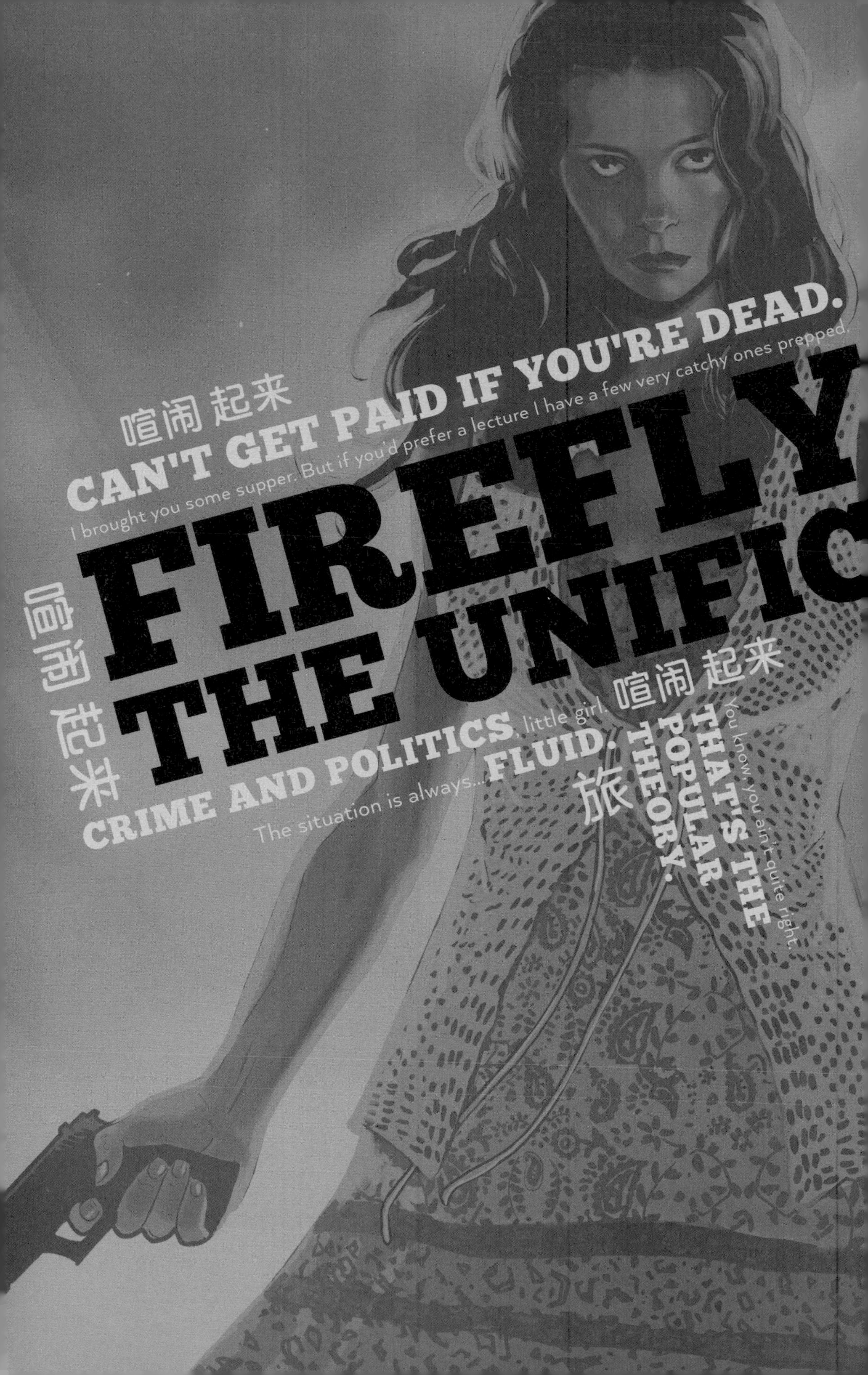
喧闹 起来
CAN'T GET PAID IF YOU'RE DEAD.
I brought you some supper. But if you'd prefer a lecture I have a few very catchy ones prepped.
FIREFLY
THE UNIFIC
喧闹 起来
喧闹 起来
CRIME AND POLITICS, little girl.
The situation is always... FLUID.
旅
THAT'S THE POPULAR THEORY.
You know, you ain't quite right.

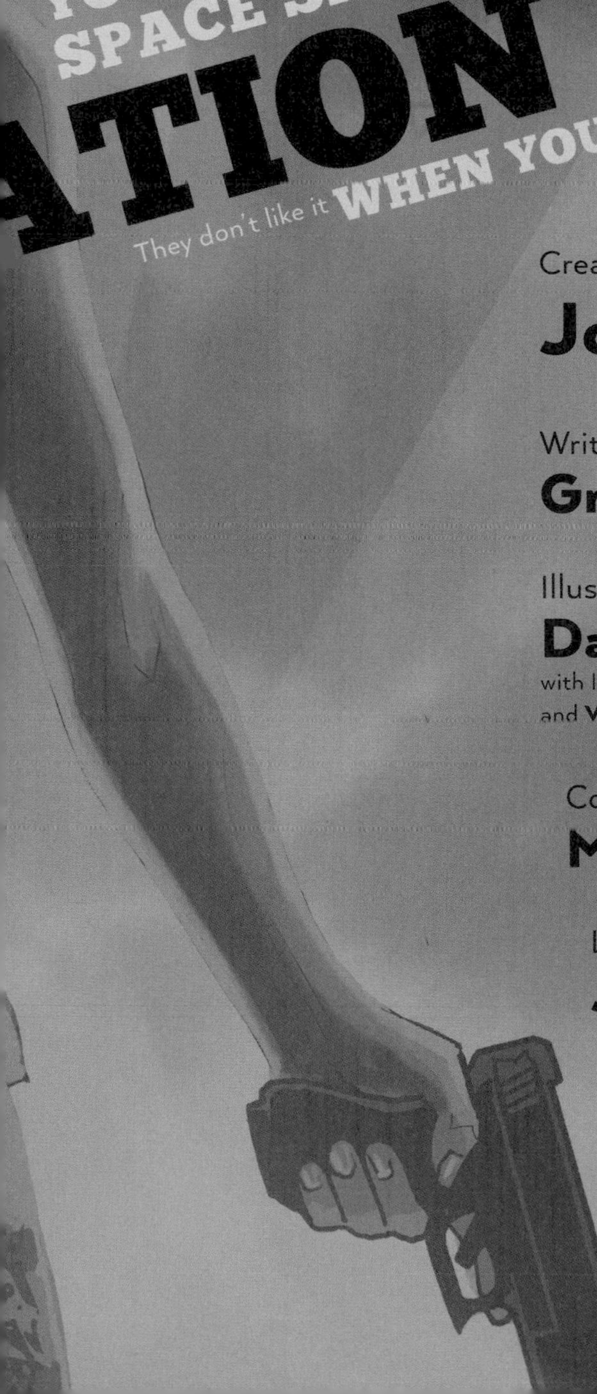

That sounds like something out of science fiction.
YOU LIVE ON A SPACE SHIP, DEAR.

ATION WAR

They don't like it **WHEN YOU SHOOT AT 'EM.** I worked that out myself.

Created by
Joss Whedon

Written by
Greg Pak

Illustrated by
Dan McDaid
with Inks by **Anthony Fowler, Jr.**, Chapter Five
and **Vincenzo Federici**, Chapters Six and Eight

Colored by
Marcelo Costa

Lettered by
Jim Campbell

Cover by
Lee Garbett

CHAPTER FIVE

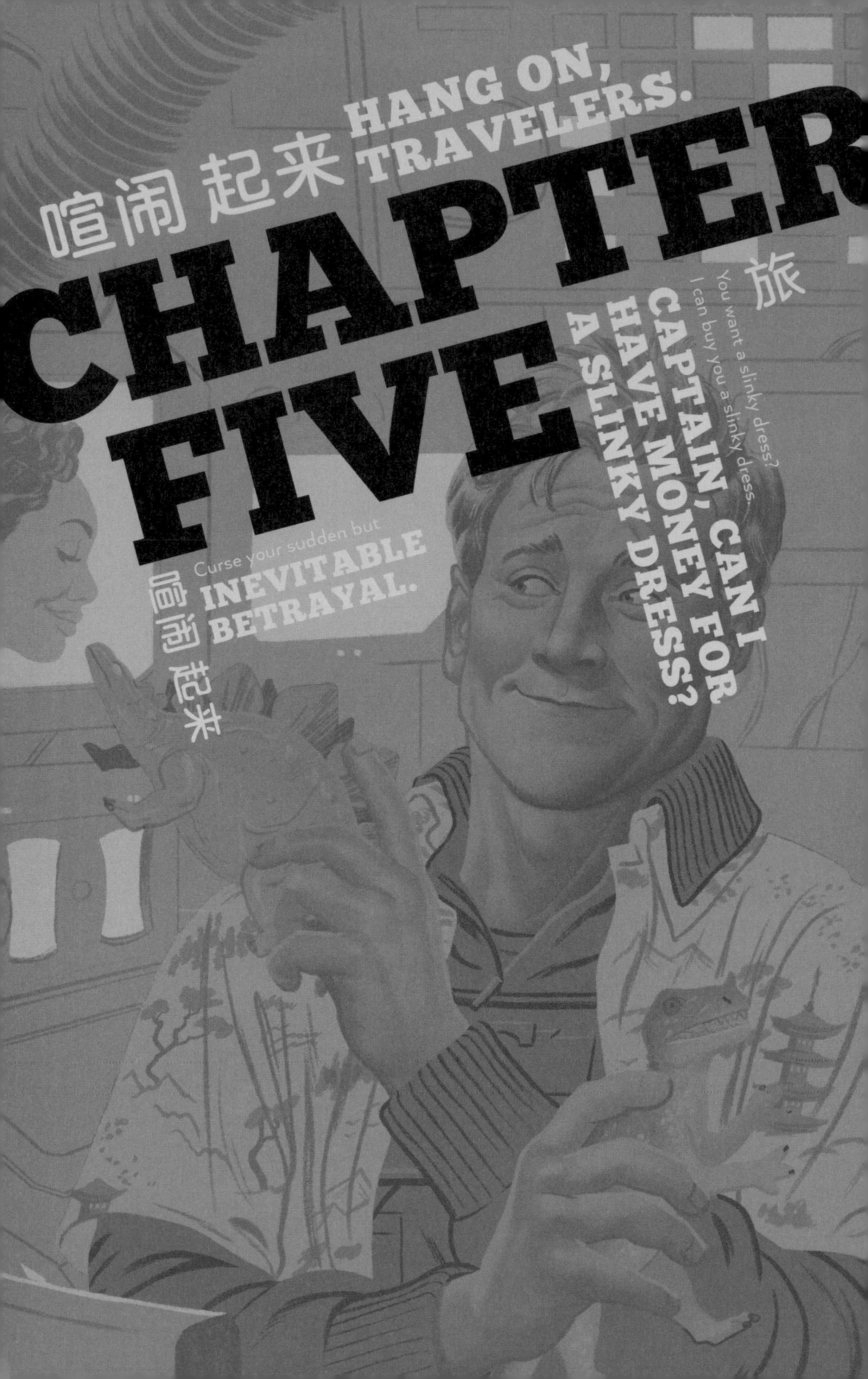
HANG ON, TRAVELERS.
喧闹 起来
旅
You want a slinky dress? I can buy you a slinky dress.
CAPTAIN, CAN I HAVE MONEY FOR A SLINKY DRESS?
Curse your sudden but INEVITABLE BETRAYAL.
喧闹 起来

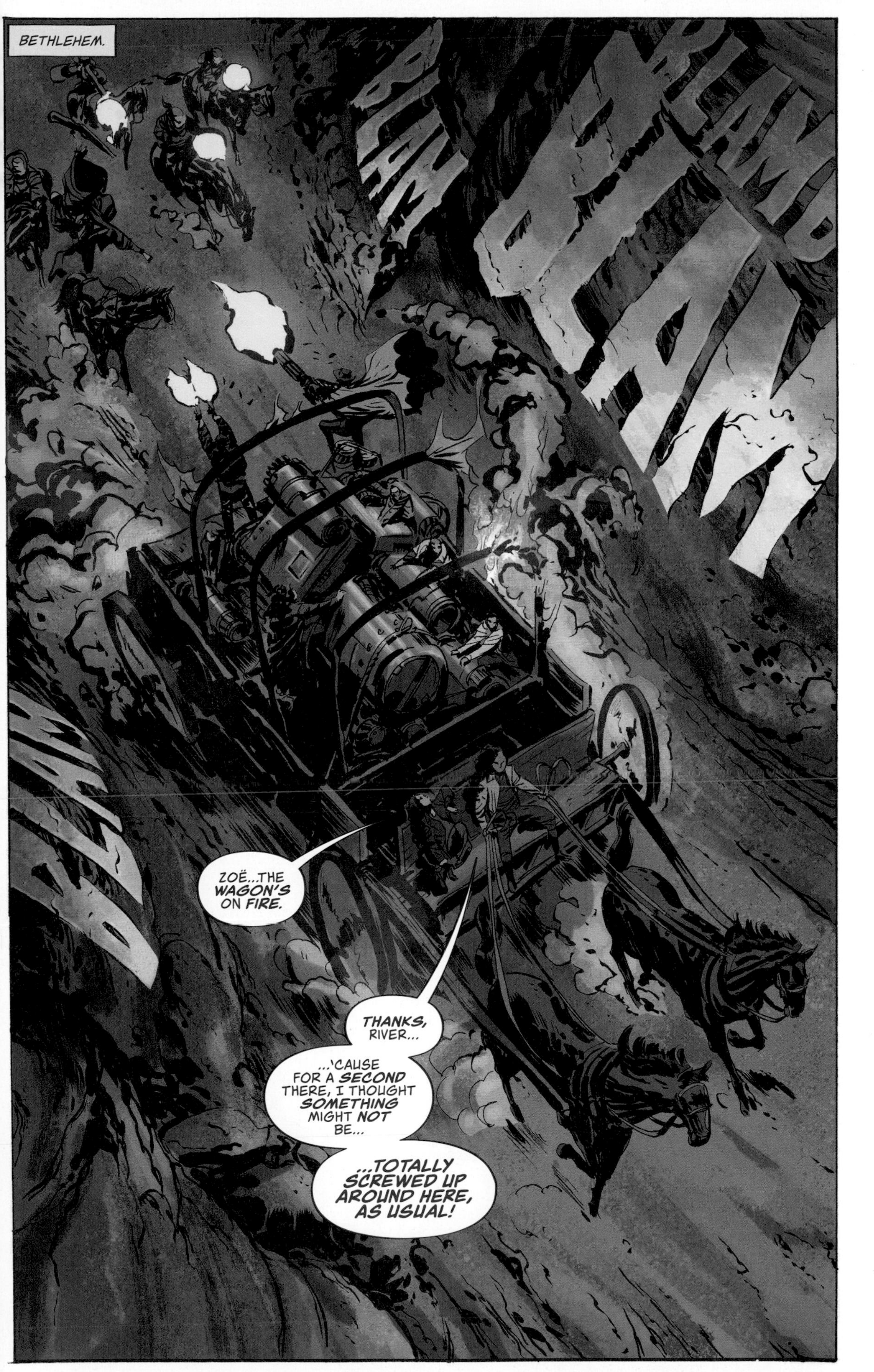
BETHLEHEM.
ZOË...THE WAGON'S ON FIRE.
THANKS, RIVER...
...'CAUSE FOR A SECOND THERE, I THOUGHT SOMETHING MIGHT NOT BE...
...TOTALLY SCREWED UP AROUND HERE, AS USUAL!

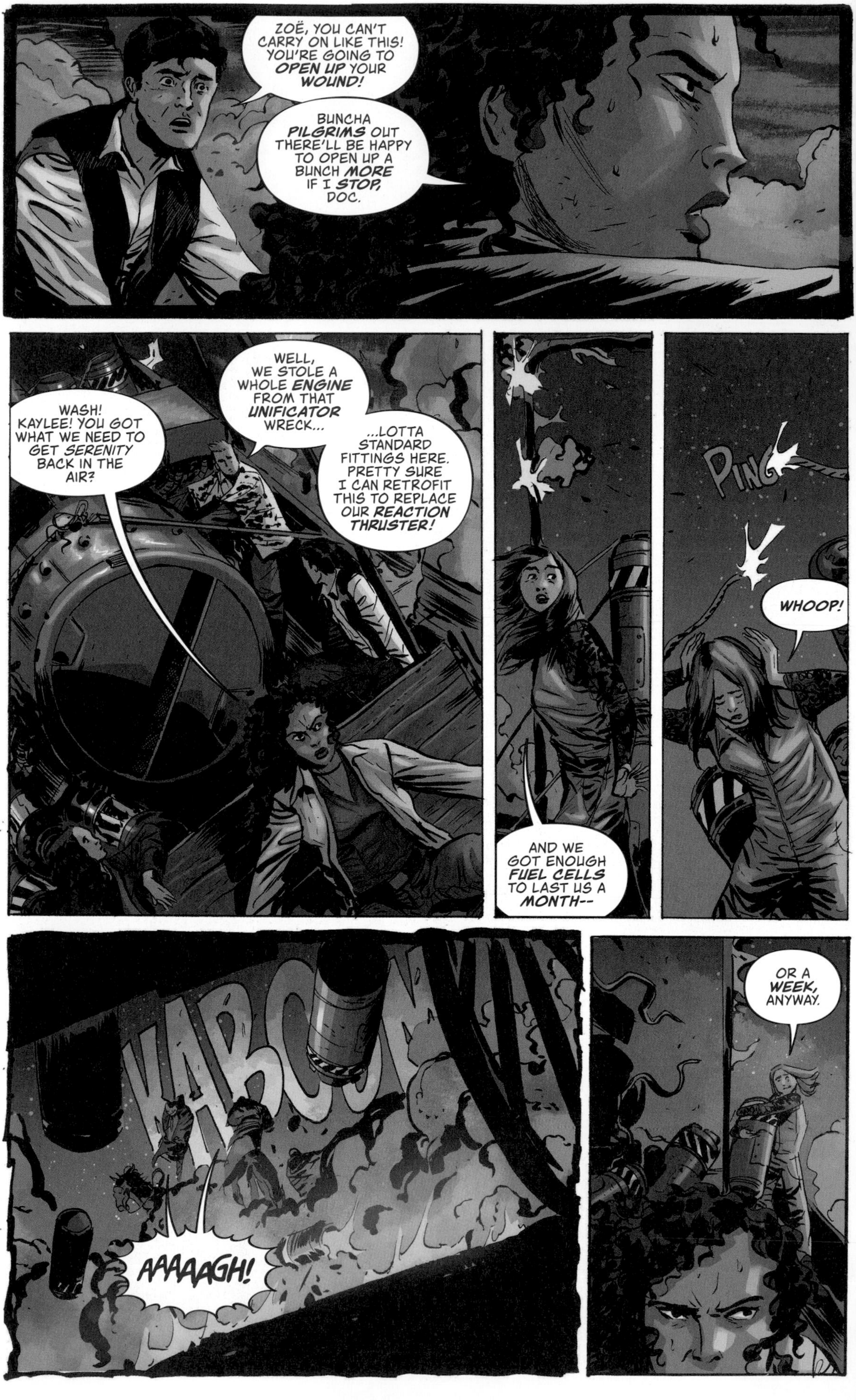

ZOË, YOU CAN'T CARRY ON LIKE THIS! YOU'RE GOING TO OPEN UP YOUR WOUND!
BUNCHA PILGRIMS OUT THERE'LL BE HAPPY TO OPEN UP A BUNCH MORE IF I STOP, DOC.
WASH! KAYLEE! YOU GOT WHAT WE NEED TO GET SERENITY BACK IN THE AIR?
WELL, WE STOLE A WHOLE ENGINE FROM THAT UNIFICATOR WRECK...
...LOTTA STANDARD FITTINGS HERE. PRETTY SURE I CAN RETROFIT THIS TO REPLACE OUR REACTION THRUSTER!
AND WE GOT ENOUGH FUEL CELLS TO LAST US A MONTH--
PING
WHOOP!
KABOOM
AAAAAGH!
OR A WEEK, ANYWAY.

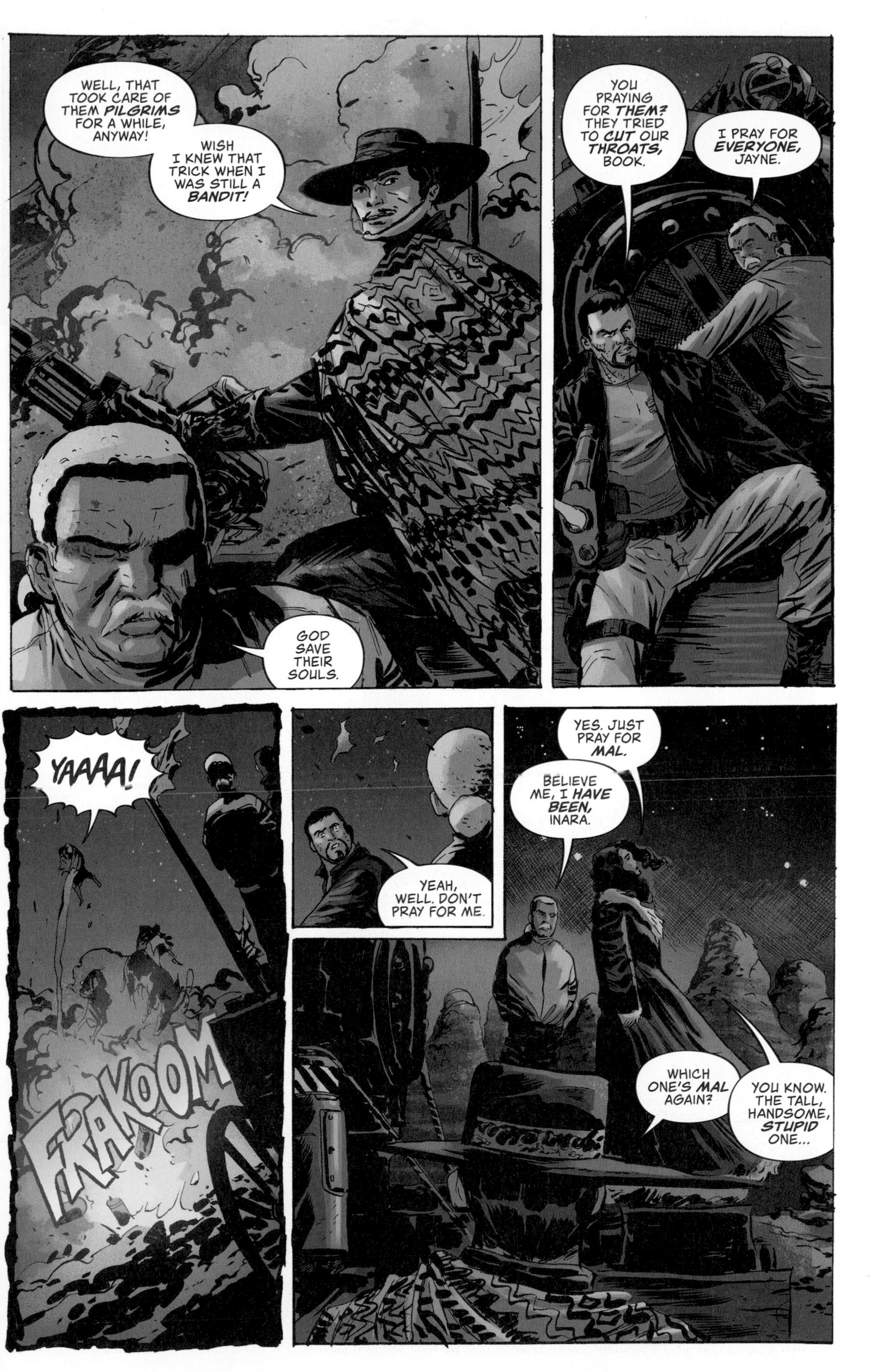
WELL, THAT TOOK CARE OF THEM PILGRIMS FOR A WHILE, ANYWAY!
WISH I KNEW THAT TRICK WHEN I WAS STILL A BANDIT!
GOD SAVE THEIR SOULS.
YOU PRAYING FOR THEM? THEY TRIED TO CUT OUR THROATS, BOOK.
I PRAY FOR EVERYONE, JAYNE.
YAAAA!
FRAKOOM
YEAH, WELL. DON'T PRAY FOR ME.
YES. JUST PRAY FOR MAL.
BELIEVE ME, I HAVE BEEN, INARA.
WHICH ONE'S MAL AGAIN?
YOU KNOW. THE TALL, HANDSOME, STUPID ONE...

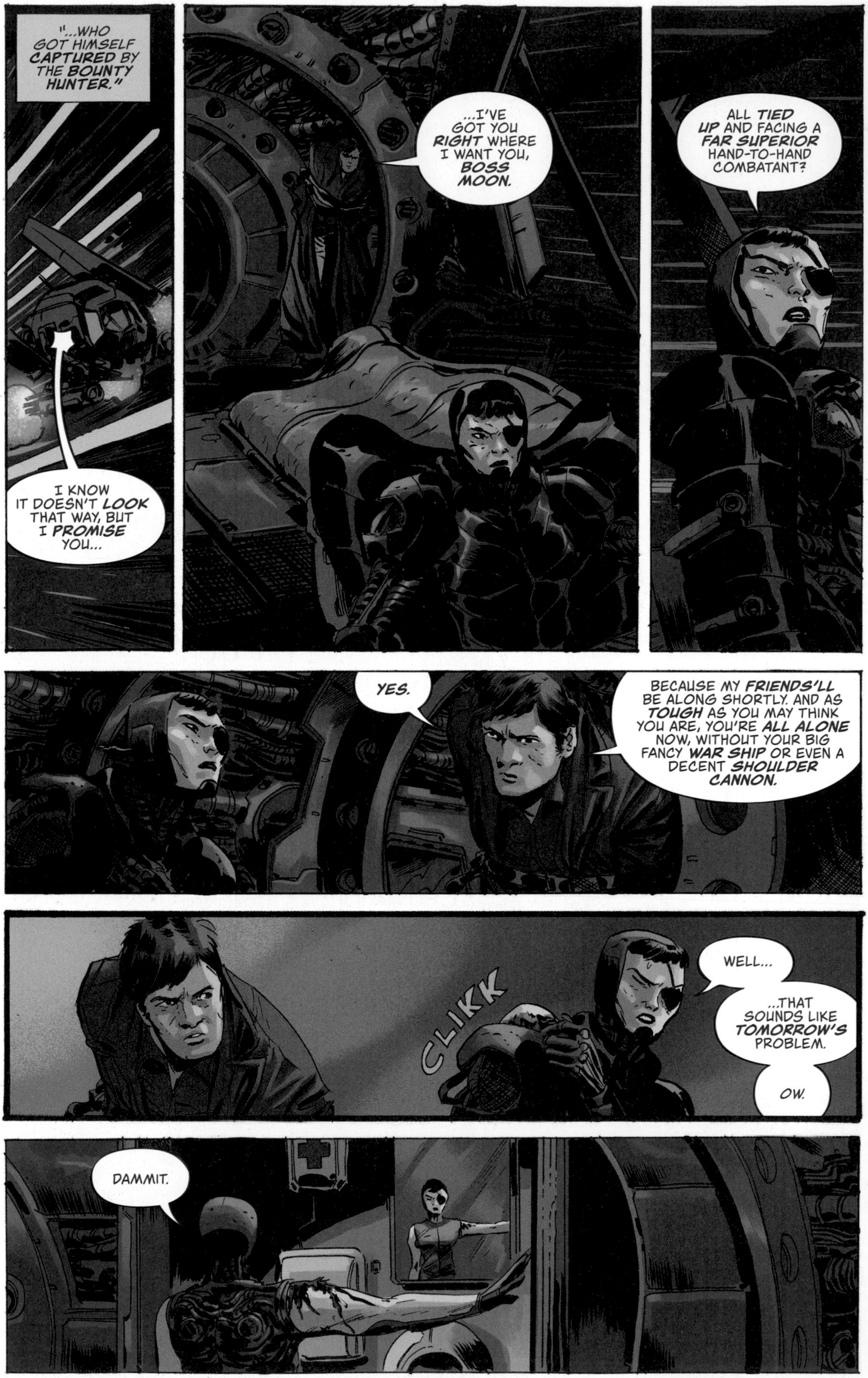
"...WHO GOT HIMSELF CAPTURED BY THE BOUNTY HUNTER."
I KNOW IT DOESN'T LOOK THAT WAY, BUT I PROMISE YOU...
...I'VE GOT YOU RIGHT WHERE I WANT YOU, BOSS MOON.
ALL TIED UP AND FACING A FAR SUPERIOR HAND-TO-HAND COMBATANT?
YES.
BECAUSE MY FRIENDS'LL BE ALONG SHORTLY. AND AS TOUGH AS YOU MAY THINK YOU ARE, YOU'RE ALL ALONE NOW, WITHOUT YOUR BIG FANCY WAR SHIP OR EVEN A DECENT SHOULDER CANNON.
CLIKK
WELL...
...THAT SOUNDS LIKE TOMORROW'S PROBLEM.
OW.
DAMMIT.

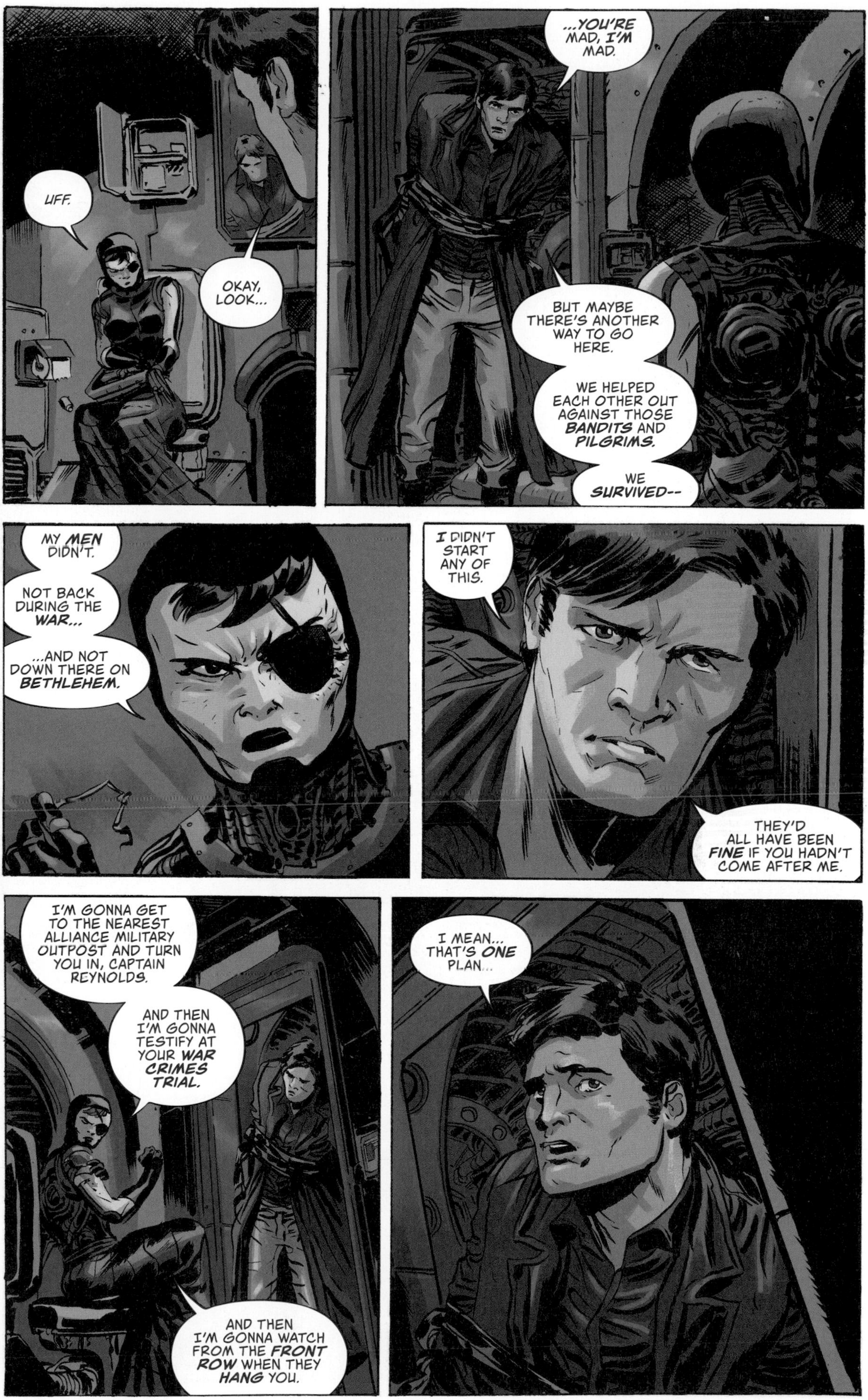
UFF.
OKAY, LOOK...
...YOU'RE MAD, I'M MAD.
BUT MAYBE THERE'S ANOTHER WAY TO GO HERE.
WE HELPED EACH OTHER OUT AGAINST THOSE BANDITS AND PILGRIMS.
WE SURVIVED--
MY MEN DIDN'T.
NOT BACK DURING THE WAR...
...AND NOT DOWN THERE ON BETHLEHEM.
I DIDN'T START ANY OF THIS.
THEY'D ALL HAVE BEEN FINE IF YOU HADN'T COME AFTER ME.
I'M GONNA GET TO THE NEAREST ALLIANCE MILITARY OUTPOST AND TURN YOU IN, CAPTAIN REYNOLDS.
AND THEN I'M GONNA TESTIFY AT YOUR WAR CRIMES TRIAL.
AND THEN I'M GONNA WATCH FROM THE FRONT ROW WHEN THEY HANG YOU.
I MEAN... THAT'S ONE PLAN...

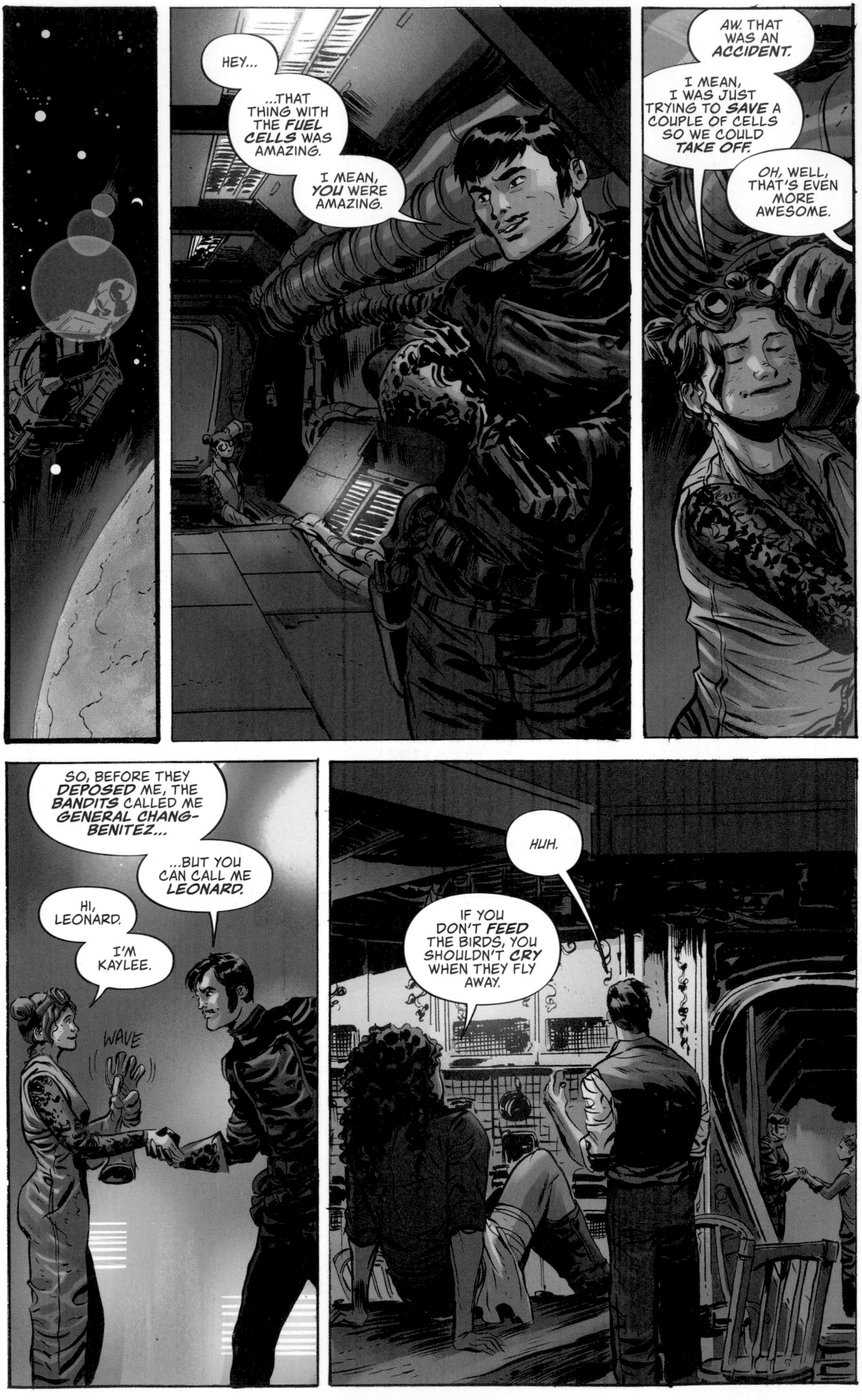
HEY...
...THAT THING WITH THE FUEL CELLS WAS AMAZING.
I MEAN, YOU WERE AMAZING.
AW. THAT WAS AN ACCIDENT.
I MEAN, I WAS JUST TRYING TO SAVE A COUPLE OF CELLS SO WE COULD TAKE OFF.
OH, WELL, THAT'S EVEN MORE AWESOME.
SO, BEFORE THEY DEPOSED ME, THE BANDITS CALLED ME GENERAL CHANG-BENITEZ...
...BUT YOU CAN CALL ME LEONARD.
HI, LEONARD.
I'M KAYLEE.
WAVE
HUH.
IF YOU DON'T FEED THE BIRDS, YOU SHOULDN'T CRY WHEN THEY FLY AWAY.

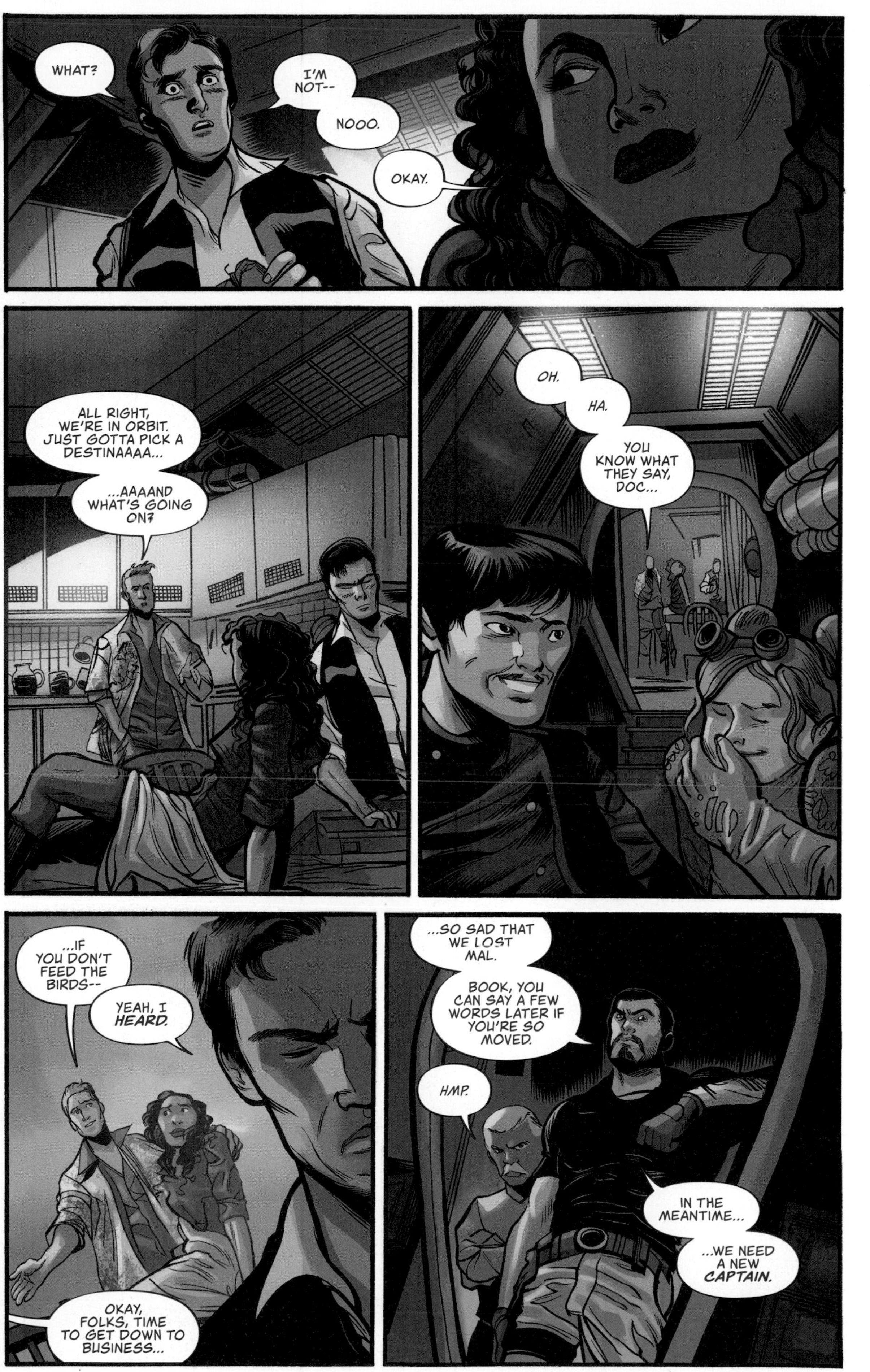
WHAT?
I'M NOT--
NOOO.
OKAY.
ALL RIGHT, WE'RE IN ORBIT. JUST GOTTA PICK A DESTINAAAA...
...AAAAND WHAT'S GOING ON?
OH.
HA.
YOU KNOW WHAT THEY SAY, DOC...
...IF YOU DON'T FEED THE BIRDS--
YEAH, I HEARD.
OKAY, FOLKS, TIME TO GET DOWN TO BUSINESS...
...SO SAD THAT WE LOST MAL.
BOOK, YOU CAN SAY A FEW WORDS LATER IF YOU'RE SO MOVED.
HMP.
IN THE MEANTIME...
...WE NEED A NEW CAPTAIN.

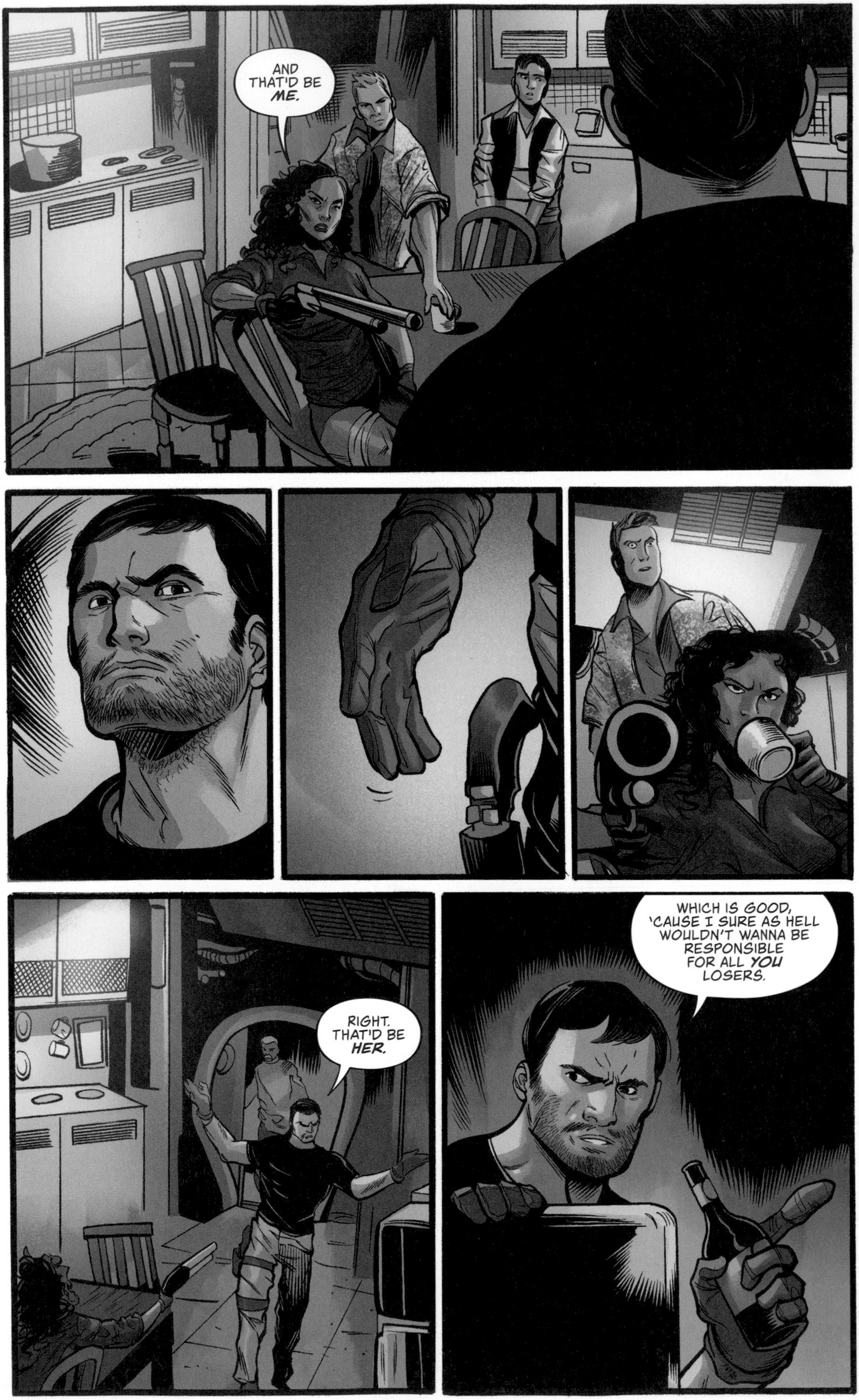

AND THAT'D BE ME.
RIGHT. THAT'D BE HER.
WHICH IS GOOD, 'CAUSE I SURE AS HELL WOULDN'T WANNA BE RESPONSIBLE FOR ALL YOU LOSERS.

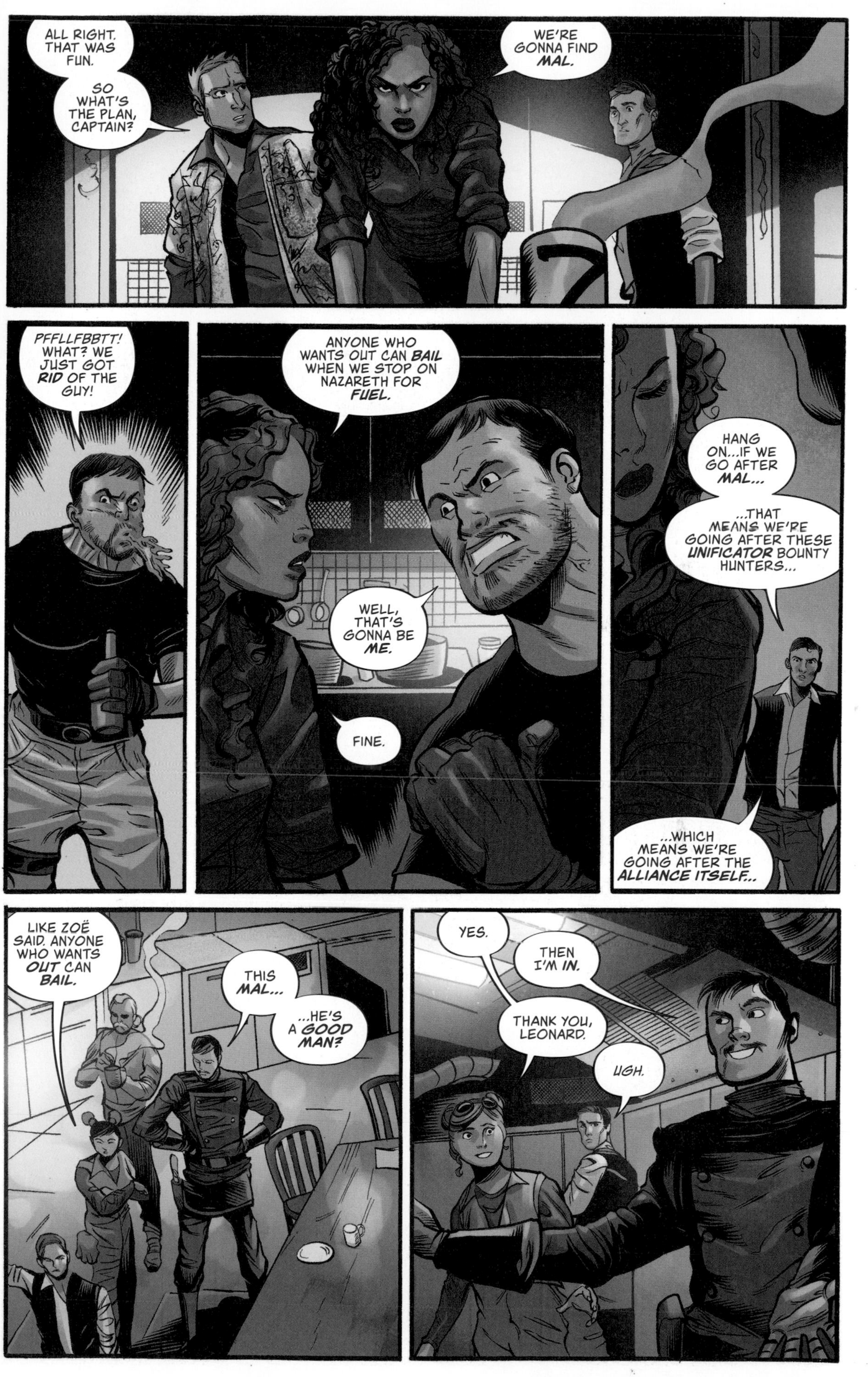
ALL RIGHT. THAT WAS FUN.
SO WHAT'S THE PLAN, CAPTAIN?
WE'RE GONNA FIND *MAL.*
PFFLLFBBTT! WHAT? WE JUST GOT *RID* OF THE GUY!
ANYONE WHO WANTS OUT CAN *BAIL* WHEN WE STOP ON NAZARETH FOR *FUEL.*
WELL, THAT'S GONNA BE *ME.*
FINE.
HANG ON...IF WE GO AFTER *MAL...*
...THAT MEANS WE'RE GOING AFTER THESE *UNIFICATOR* BOUNTY HUNTERS...
...WHICH MEANS WE'RE GOING AFTER THE *ALLIANCE ITSELF...*
LIKE ZOË SAID. ANYONE WHO WANTS *OUT* CAN *BAIL.*
THIS *MAL...*
...HE'S A *GOOD MAN?*
YES.
THEN I'M *IN.*
THANK YOU, LEONARD.
UGH.

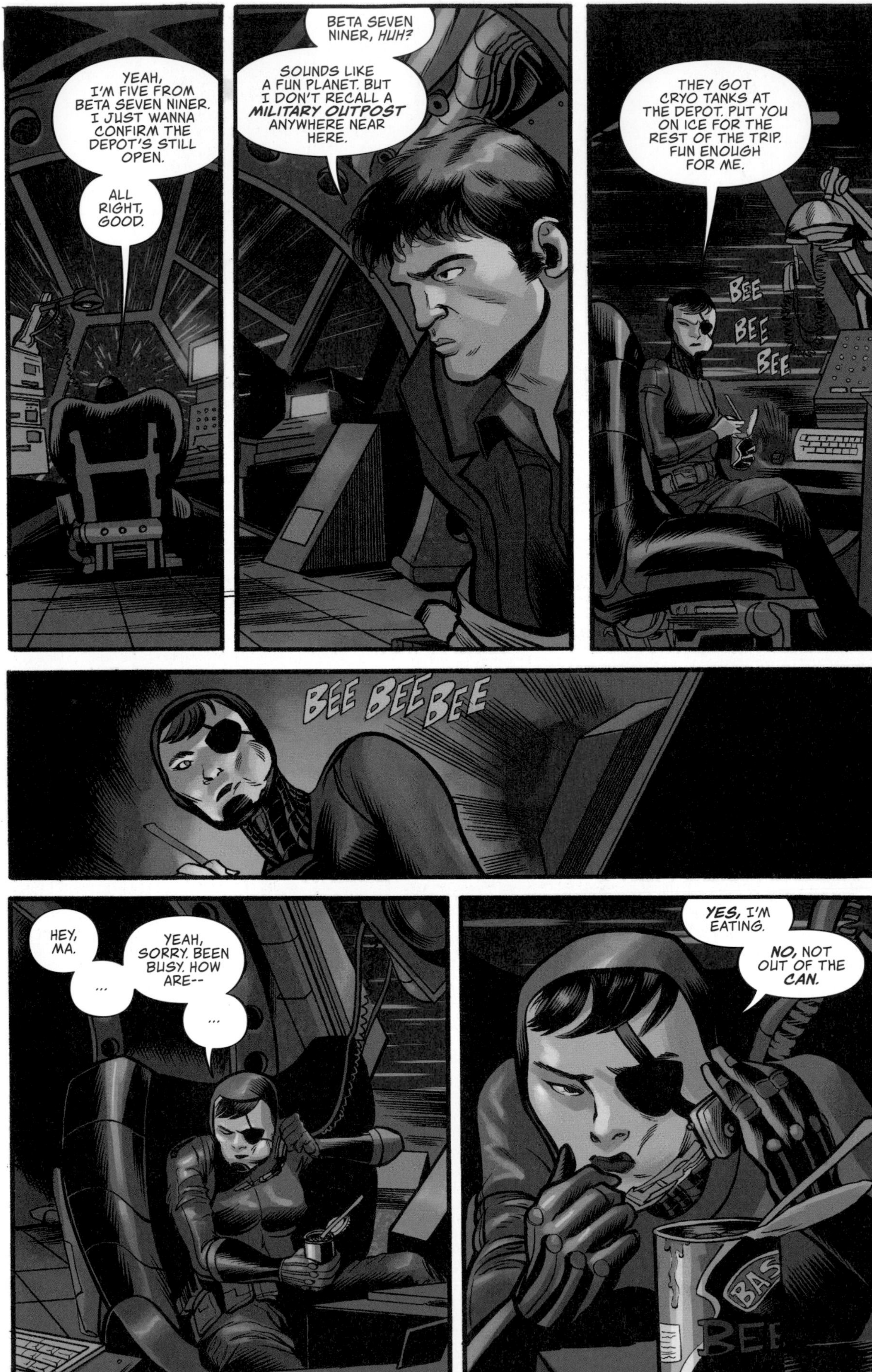
YEAH, I'M FIVE FROM BETA SEVEN NINER. I JUST WANNA CONFIRM THE DEPOT'S STILL OPEN.
ALL RIGHT, GOOD.
BETA SEVEN NINER, *HUH?*
SOUNDS LIKE A FUN PLANET. BUT I DON'T RECALL A ***MILITARY OUTPOST*** ANYWHERE NEAR HERE.
THEY GOT CRYO TANKS AT THE DEPOT. PUT YOU ON ICE FOR THE REST OF THE TRIP. FUN ENOUGH FOR ME.
BEE BEE BEE
BEE BEE BEE
HEY, MA.
...
YEAH, SORRY. BEEN BUSY. HOW ARE--
...
YES, I'M EATING.
NO, NOT OUT OF THE ***CAN.***

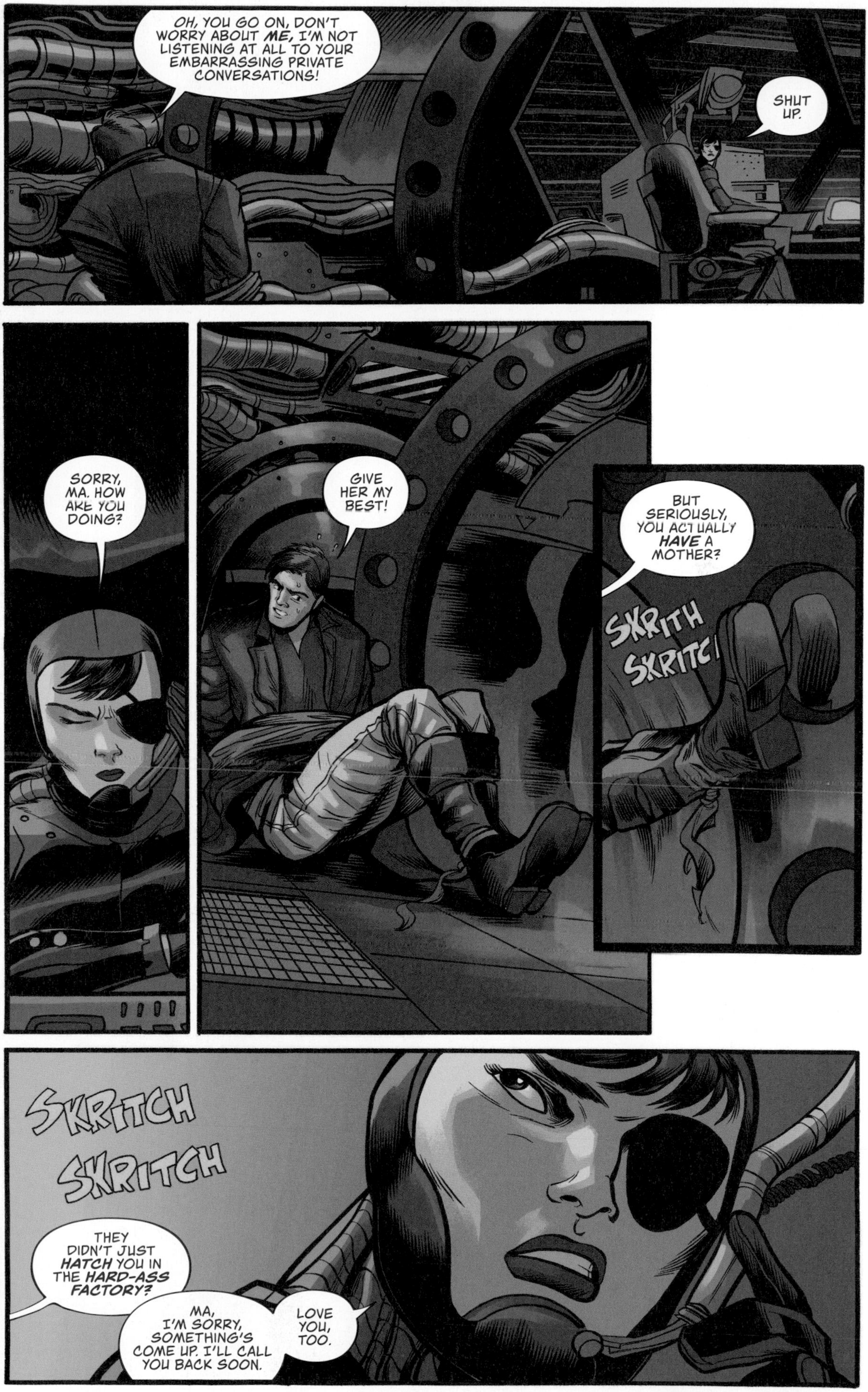
OH, YOU GO ON, DON'T WORRY ABOUT **ME,** I'M NOT LISTENING AT ALL TO YOUR EMBARRASSING PRIVATE CONVERSATIONS!
SHUT UP.
SORRY, MA. HOW ARE YOU DOING?
GIVE HER MY BEST!
BUT SERIOUSLY, YOU ACTUALLY **HAVE** A MOTHER?
SKRITH
SKRITCH
SKRITCH
SKRITCH
THEY DIDN'T JUST **HATCH** YOU IN THE **HARD-ASS FACTORY?**
MA, I'M SORRY, SOMETHING'S COME UP. I'LL CALL YOU BACK SOON.
LOVE YOU, TOO.

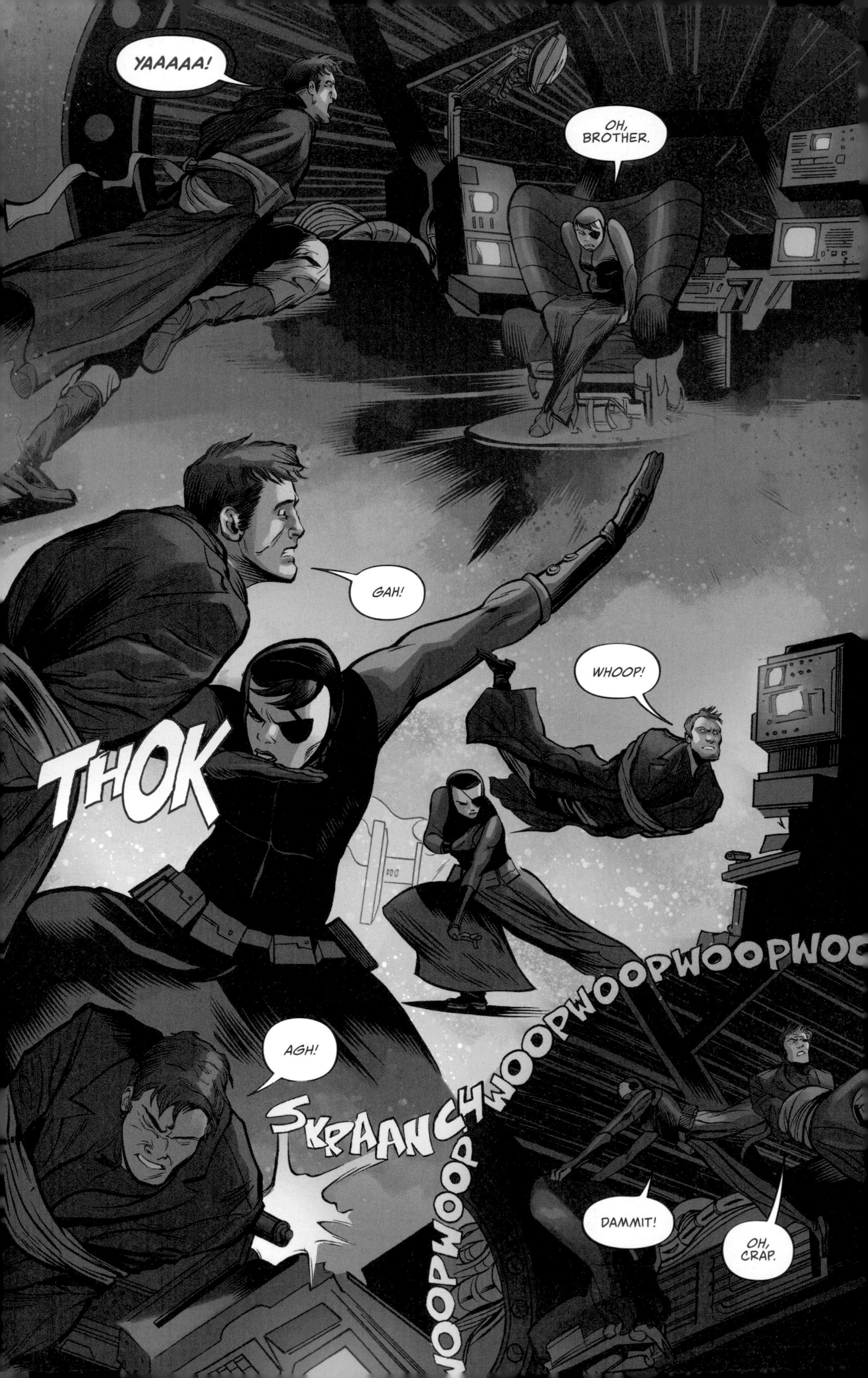
YAAAAA!
OH, BROTHER.
GAH!
THOK
WHOOP!
AGH!
SKRAANCH
WOOPWOOPWOOPWOOPWOOPWOO
DAMMIT!
OH, CRAP.

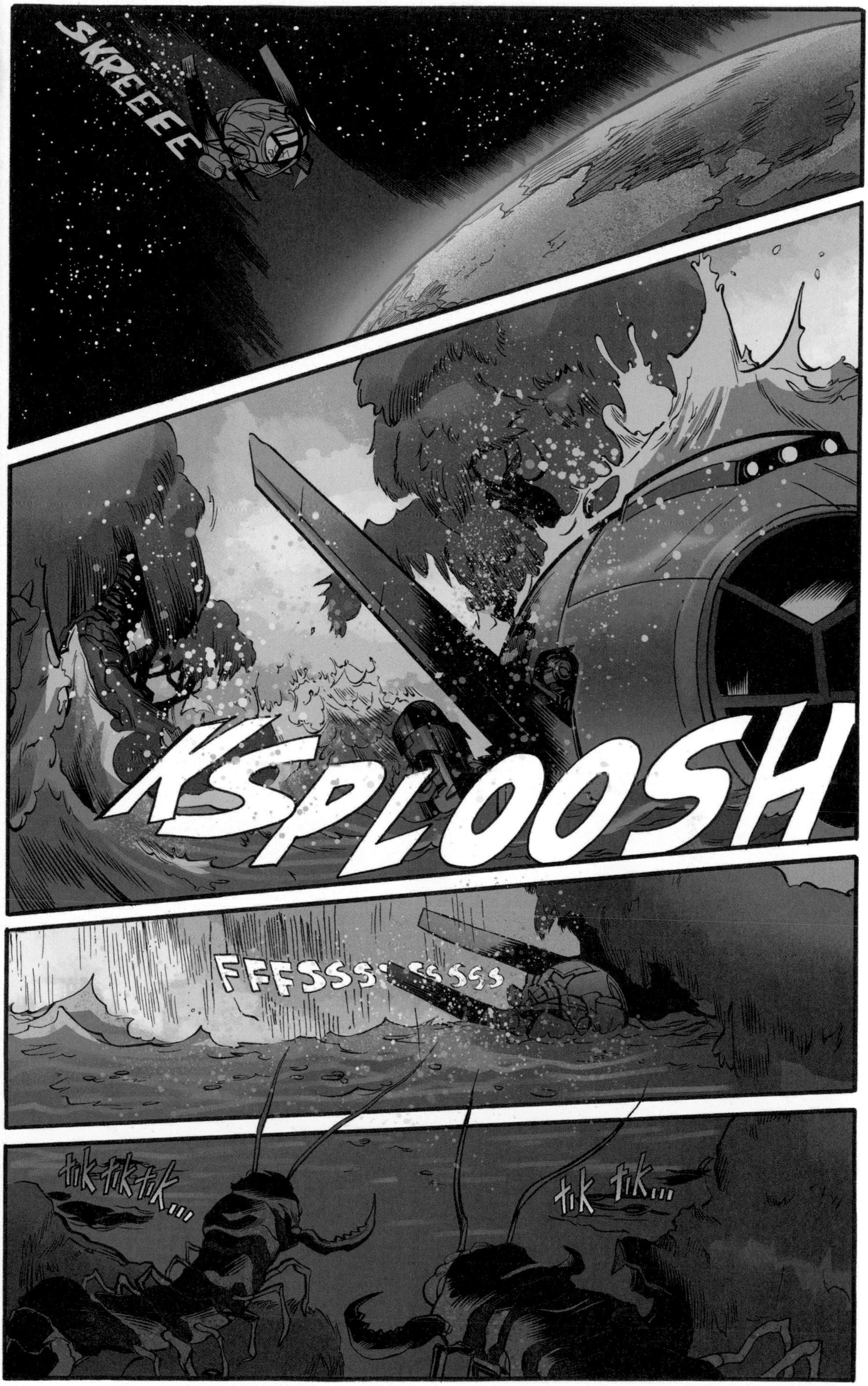
SKREEEEE
KSPLOOSH
FFFSSSS-SSSSS
tik tik tik...
tik tik...

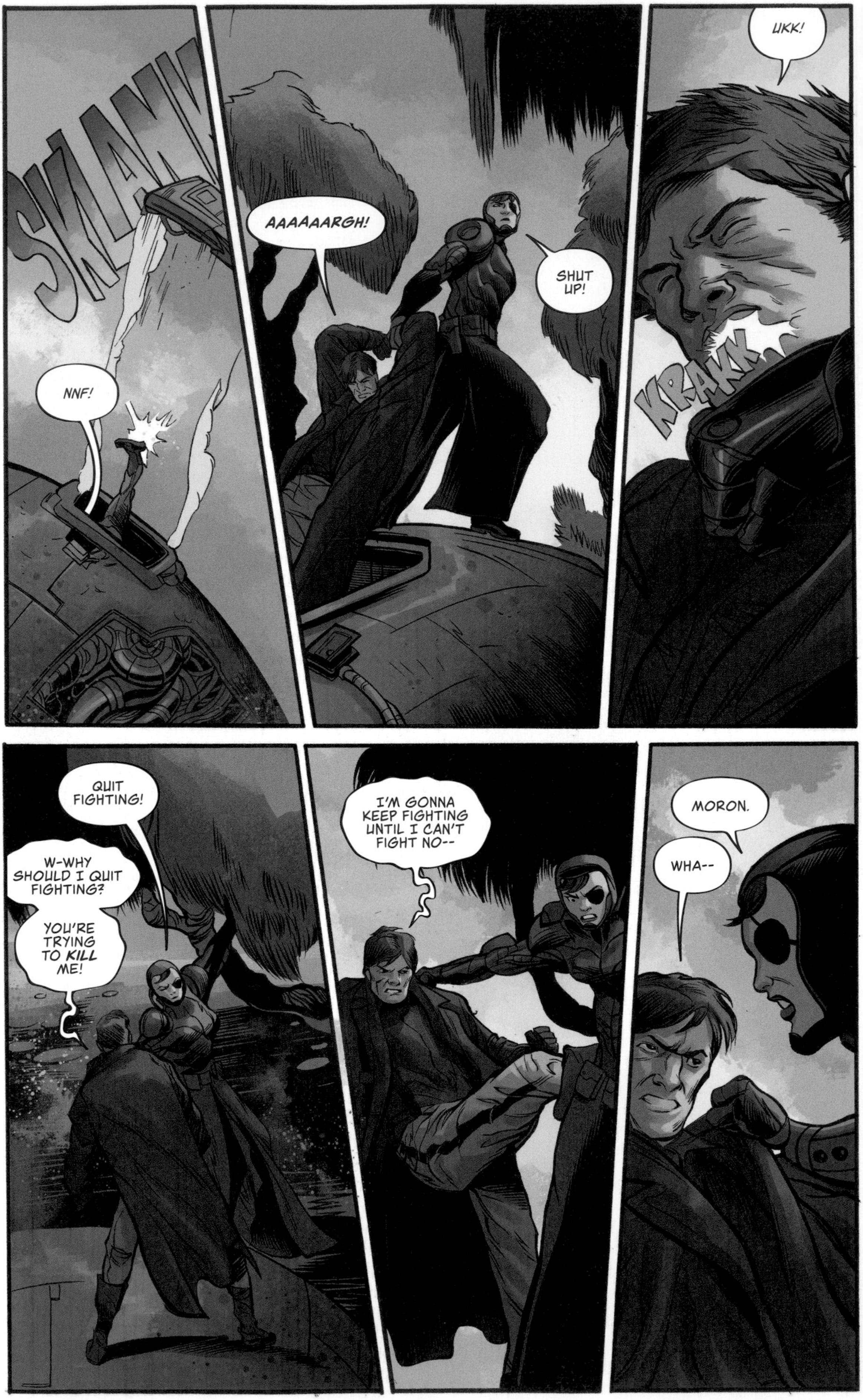
SKLANK
NNF!
AAAAAARGH!
SHUT UP!
UKK!
KRAKK
QUIT FIGHTING!
W-WHY SHOULD I QUIT FIGHTING?
YOU'RE TRYING TO **KILL** ME!
I'M GONNA KEEP FIGHTING UNTIL I CAN'T FIGHT NO--
MORON.
WHA--

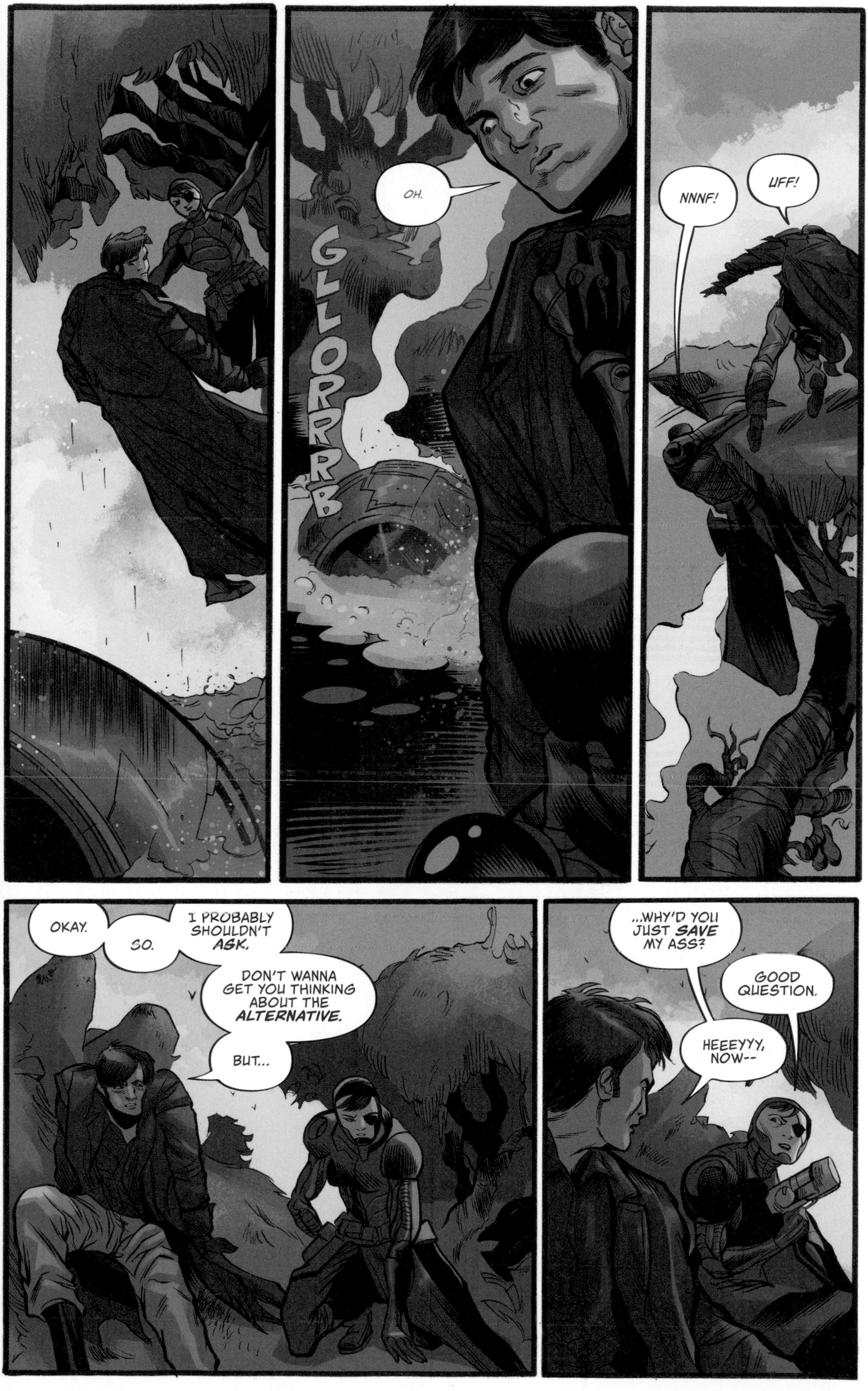
OH.
GLLORRRB
NNNF!
UFF!
OKAY.
SO.
I PROBABLY SHOULDN'T ASK.
DON'T WANNA GET YOU THINKING ABOUT THE ALTERNATIVE.
BUT...
...WHY'D YOU JUST SAVE MY ASS?
GOOD QUESTION.
HEEEYYY, NOW--

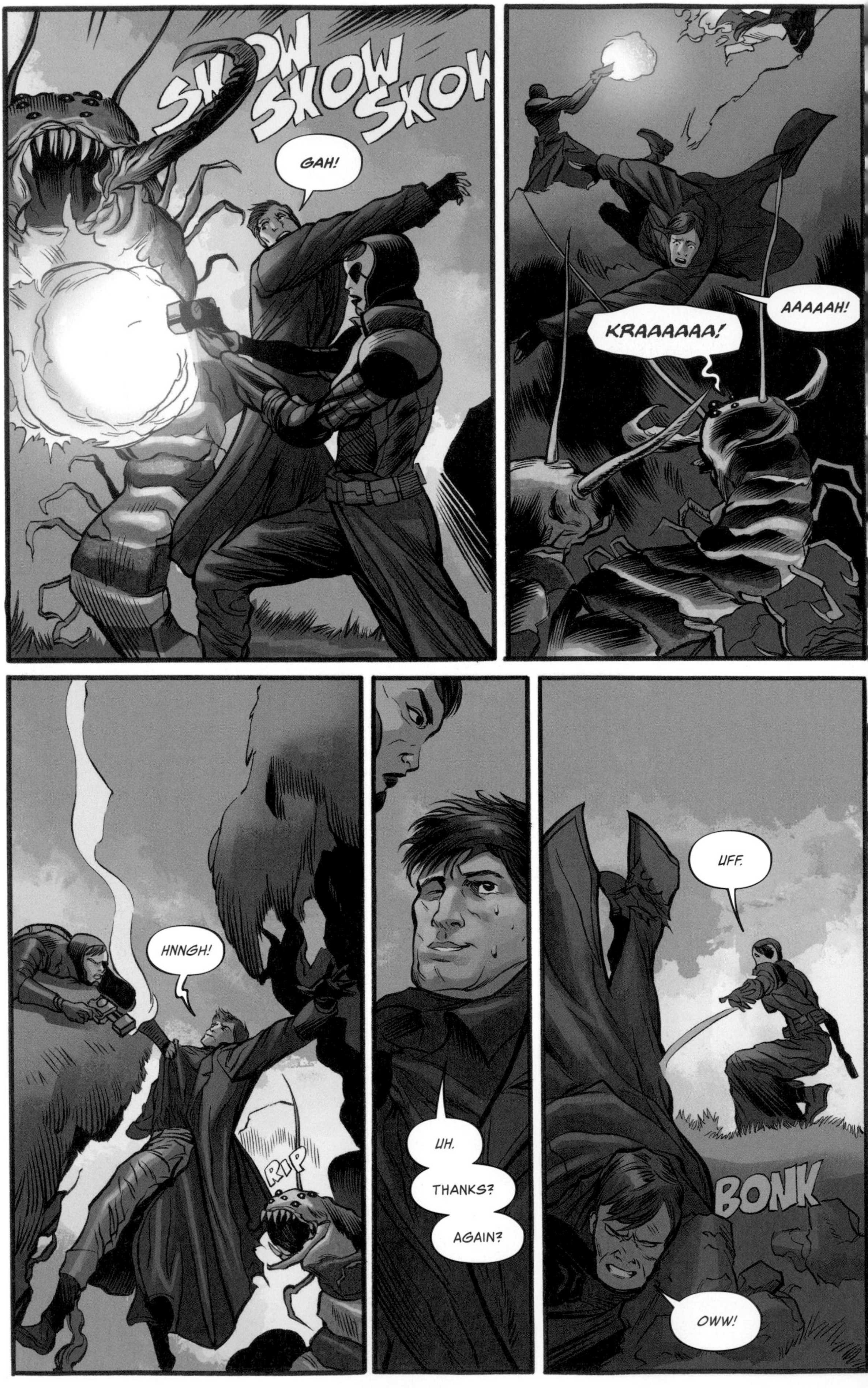
SKOW SKOW SKOW
GAH!
AAAAAH!
KRAAAAAA!
HNNGH!
RIP
UH.
THANKS?
AGAIN?
UFF.
BONK
OWW!

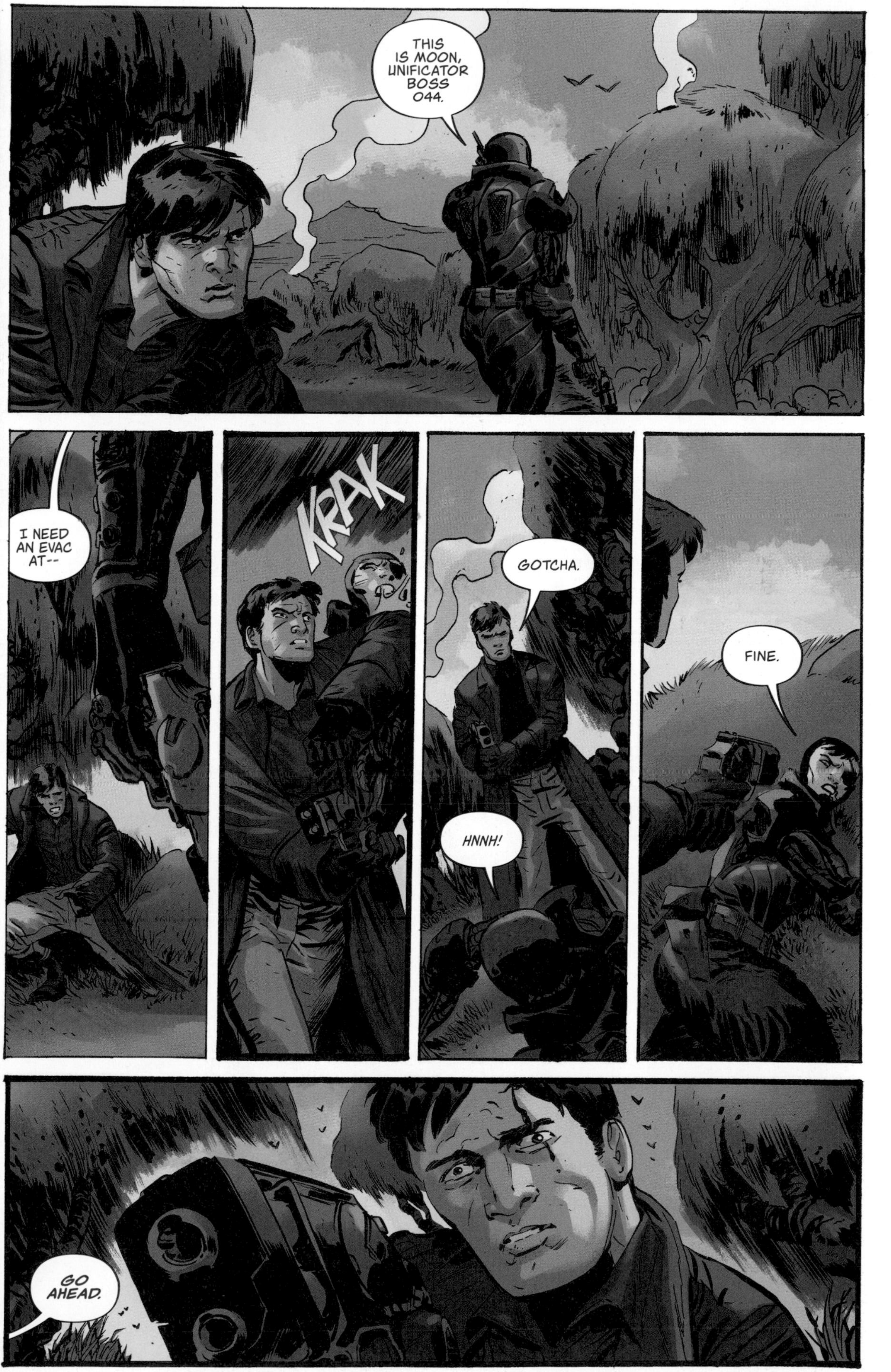
THIS IS MOON, UNIFICATOR BOSS 044.
I NEED AN EVAC AT--
KRAK
GOTCHA.
HNNH!
FINE.
GO AHEAD.

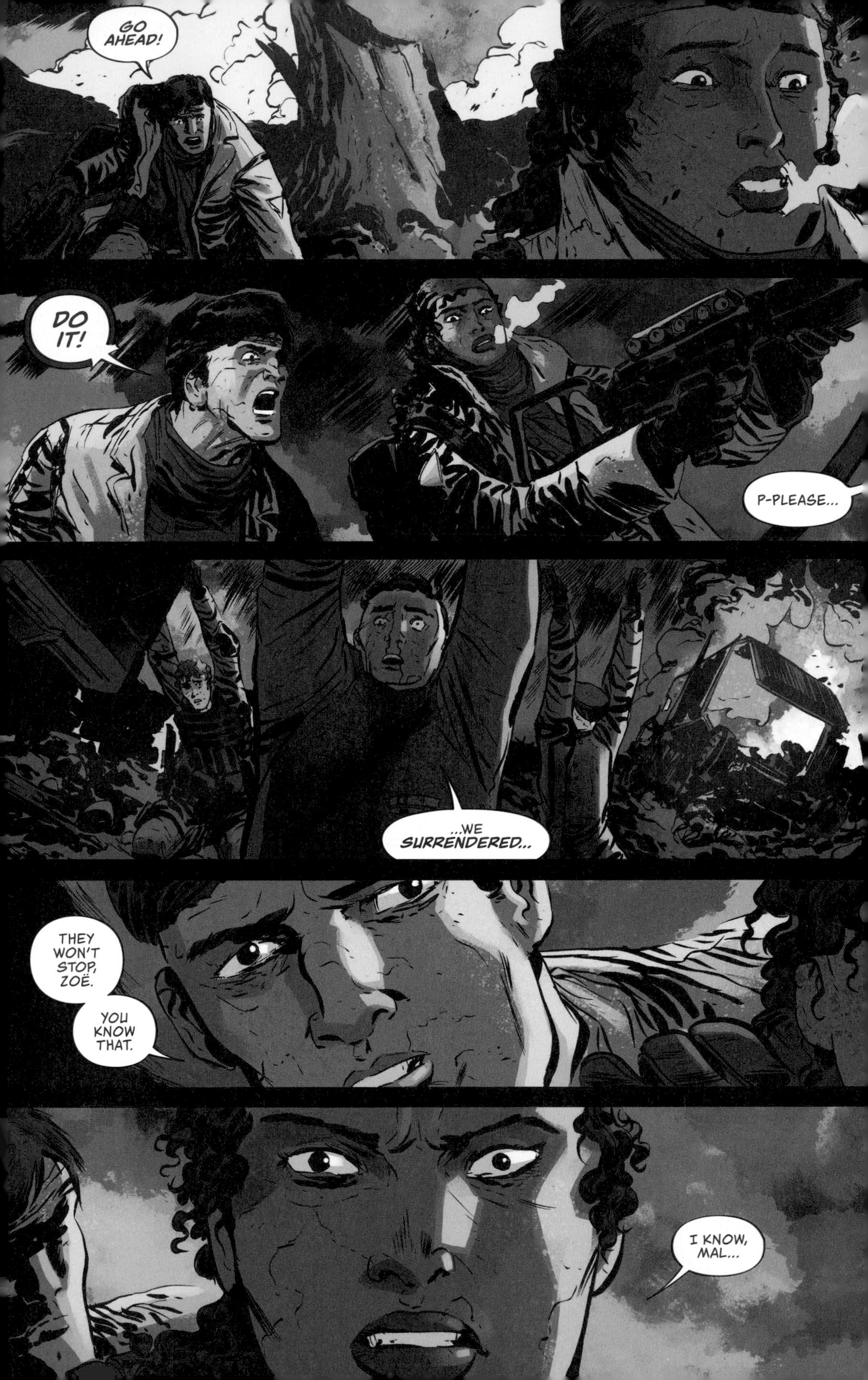
GO AHEAD!
DO IT!
P-PLEASE...
...WE SURRENDERED...
THEY WON'T STOP, ZOË.
YOU KNOW THAT.
I KNOW, MAL...

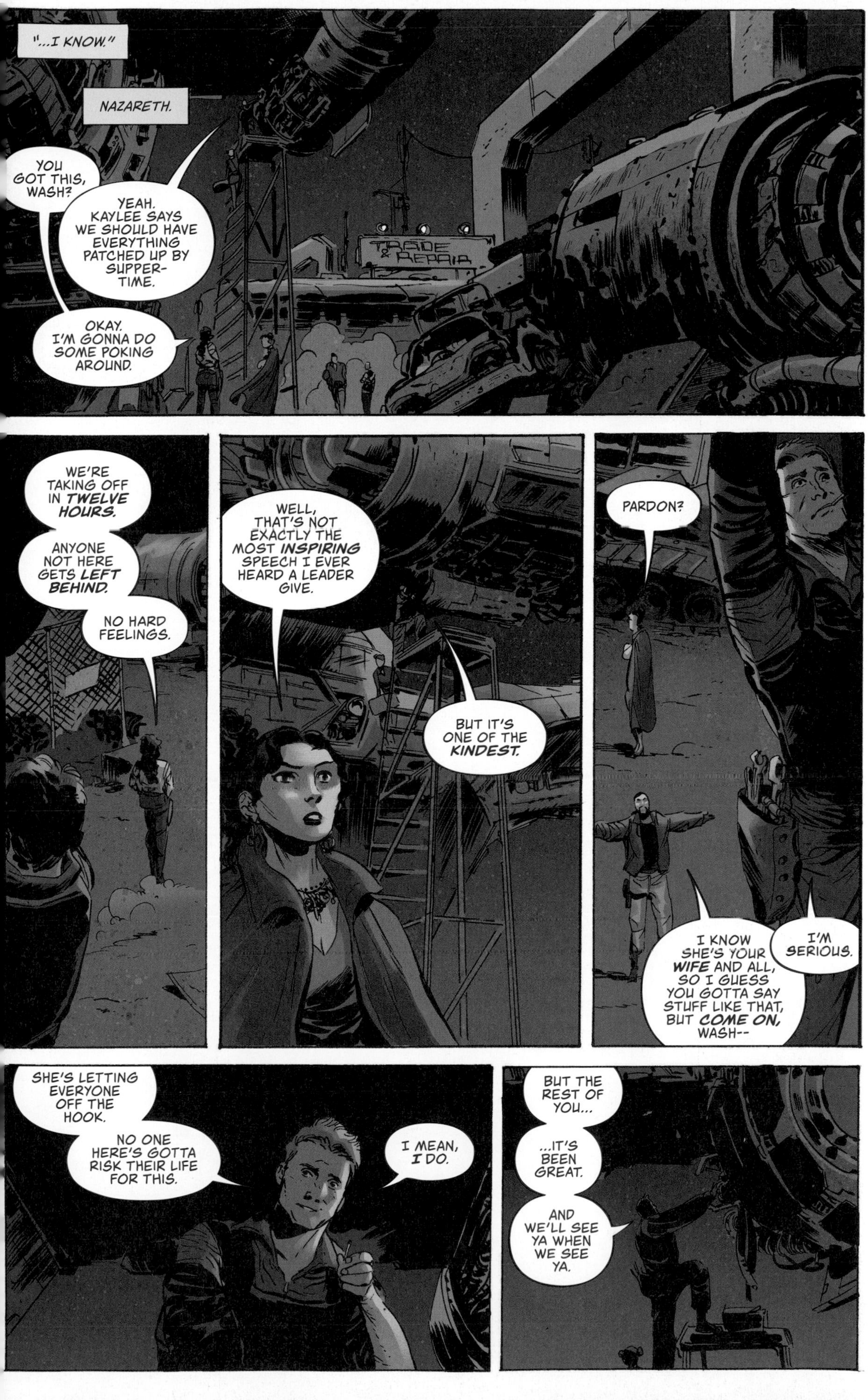
"...I KNOW."
NAZARETH.
YOU GOT THIS, WASH?
YEAH. KAYLEE SAYS WE SHOULD HAVE EVERYTHING PATCHED UP BY SUPPER-TIME.
OKAY. I'M GONNA DO SOME POKING AROUND.
TRADE & REPAIR
WE'RE TAKING OFF IN TWELVE HOURS.
ANYONE NOT HERE GETS LEFT BEHIND.
NO HARD FEELINGS.
WELL, THAT'S NOT EXACTLY THE MOST INSPIRING SPEECH I EVER HEARD A LEADER GIVE.
BUT IT'S ONE OF THE KINDEST.
PARDON?
I KNOW SHE'S YOUR WIFE AND ALL, SO I GUESS YOU GOTTA SAY STUFF LIKE THAT, BUT COME ON, WASH--
I'M SERIOUS.
SHE'S LETTING EVERYONE OFF THE HOOK.
NO ONE HERE'S GOTTA RISK THEIR LIFE FOR THIS.
I MEAN, I DO.
BUT THE REST OF YOU...
...IT'S BEEN GREAT.
AND WE'LL SEE YA WHEN WE SEE YA.

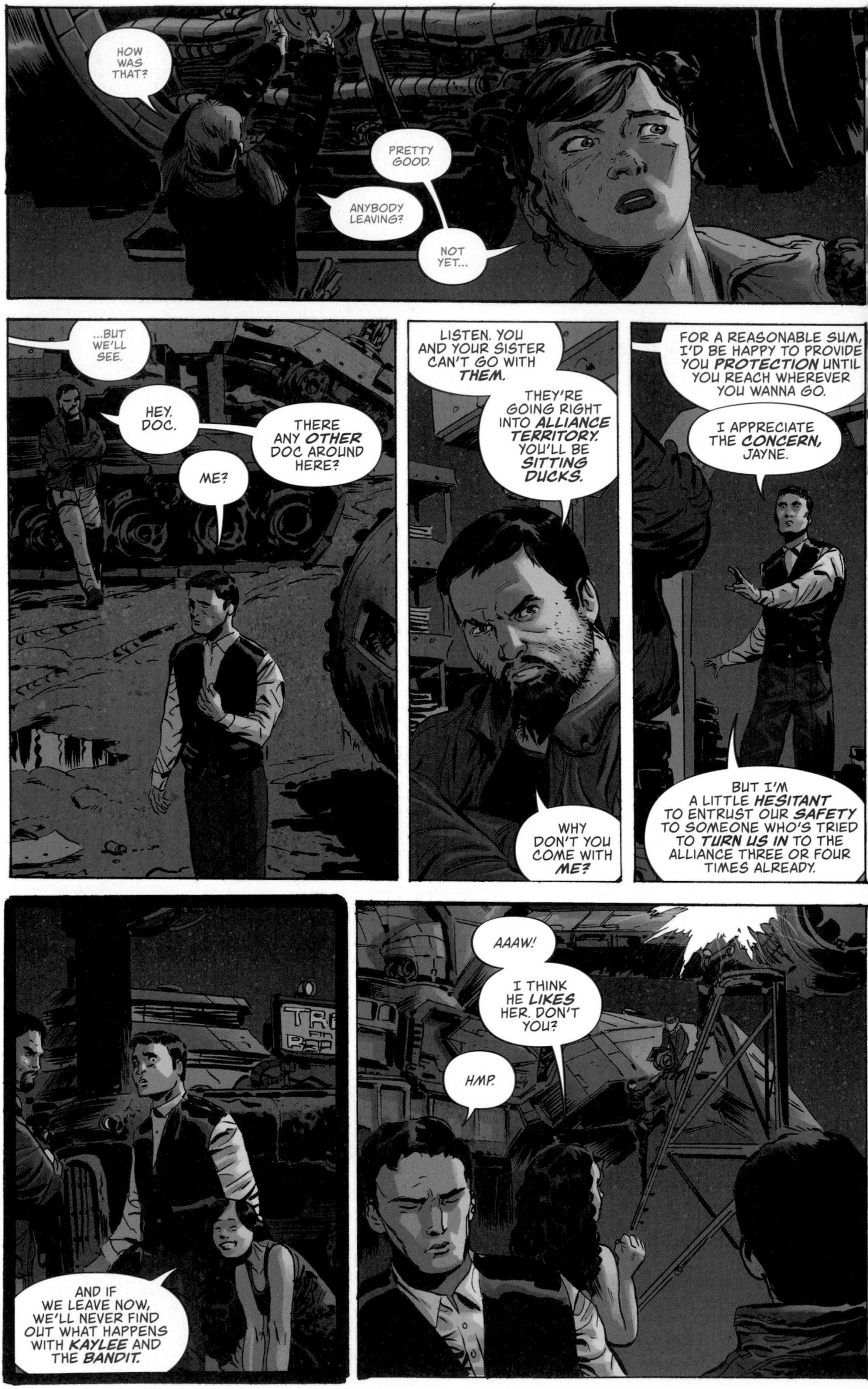
HOW WAS THAT?
PRETTY GOOD.
ANYBODY LEAVING?
NOT YET...
...BUT WE'LL SEE.
HEY. DOC.
ME?
THERE ANY OTHER DOC AROUND HERE?
LISTEN. YOU AND YOUR SISTER CAN'T GO WITH THEM.
THEY'RE GOING RIGHT INTO ALLIANCE TERRITORY. YOU'LL BE SITTING DUCKS.
WHY DON'T YOU COME WITH ME?
FOR A REASONABLE SUM, I'D BE HAPPY TO PROVIDE YOU PROTECTION UNTIL YOU REACH WHEREVER YOU WANNA GO.
I APPRECIATE THE CONCERN, JAYNE.
BUT I'M A LITTLE HESITANT TO ENTRUST OUR SAFETY TO SOMEONE WHO'S TRIED TO TURN US IN TO THE ALLIANCE THREE OR FOUR TIMES ALREADY.
AND IF WE LEAVE NOW, WE'LL NEVER FIND OUT WHAT HAPPENS WITH KAYLEE AND THE BANDIT.
AAAW!
I THINK HE LIKES HER. DON'T YOU?
HMP.

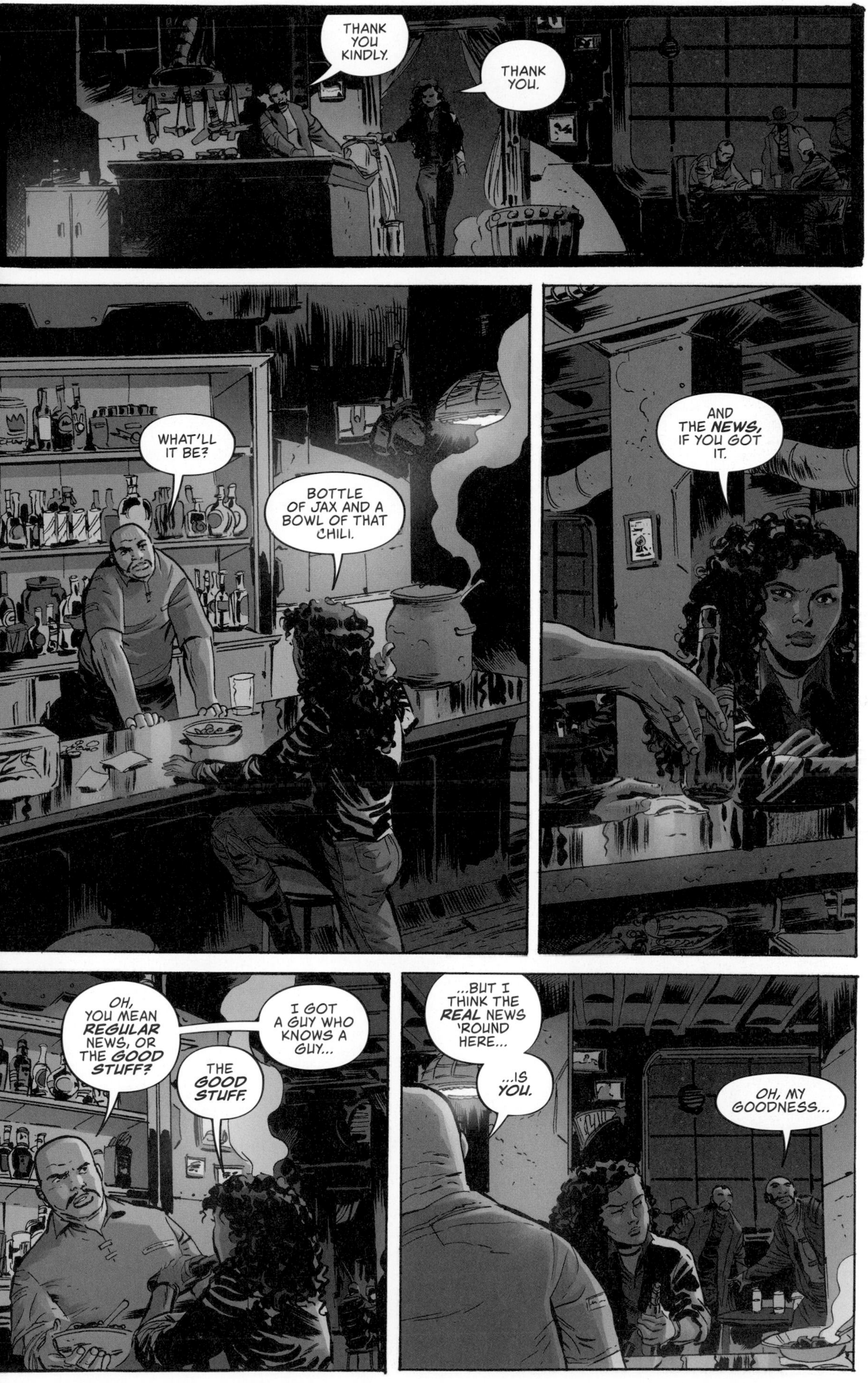
THANK YOU KINDLY.
THANK YOU.
WHAT'LL IT BE?
BOTTLE OF JAX AND A BOWL OF THAT CHILI.
AND THE NEWS, IF YOU GOT IT.
OH, YOU MEAN REGULAR NEWS, OR THE GOOD STUFF?
THE GOOD STUFF.
I GOT A GUY WHO KNOWS A GUY...
...BUT I THINK THE REAL NEWS 'ROUND HERE...
...IS YOU.
OH, MY GOODNESS...

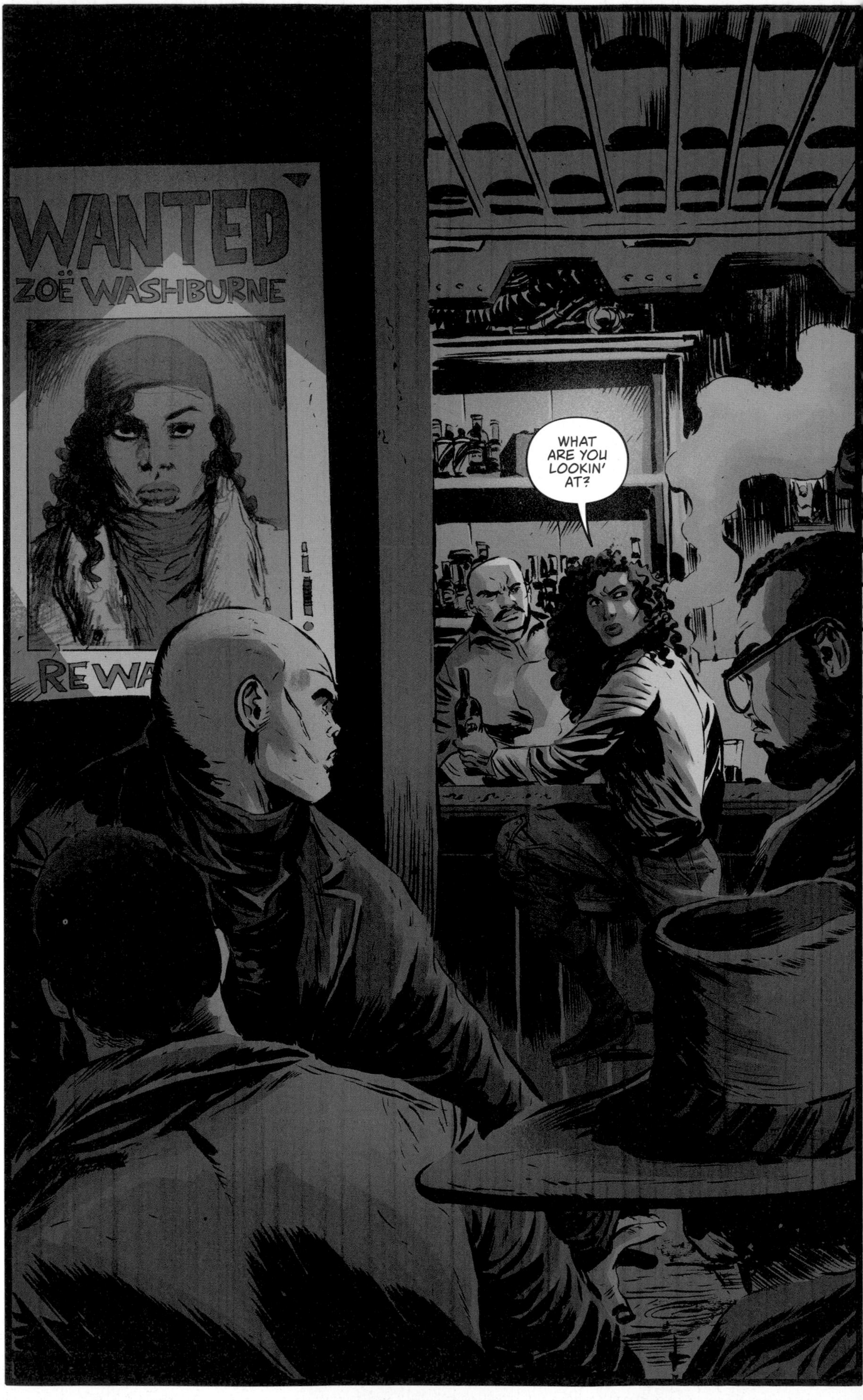
WANTED
ZOË WASHBURNE
REWA
WHAT ARE YOU LOOKIN' AT?

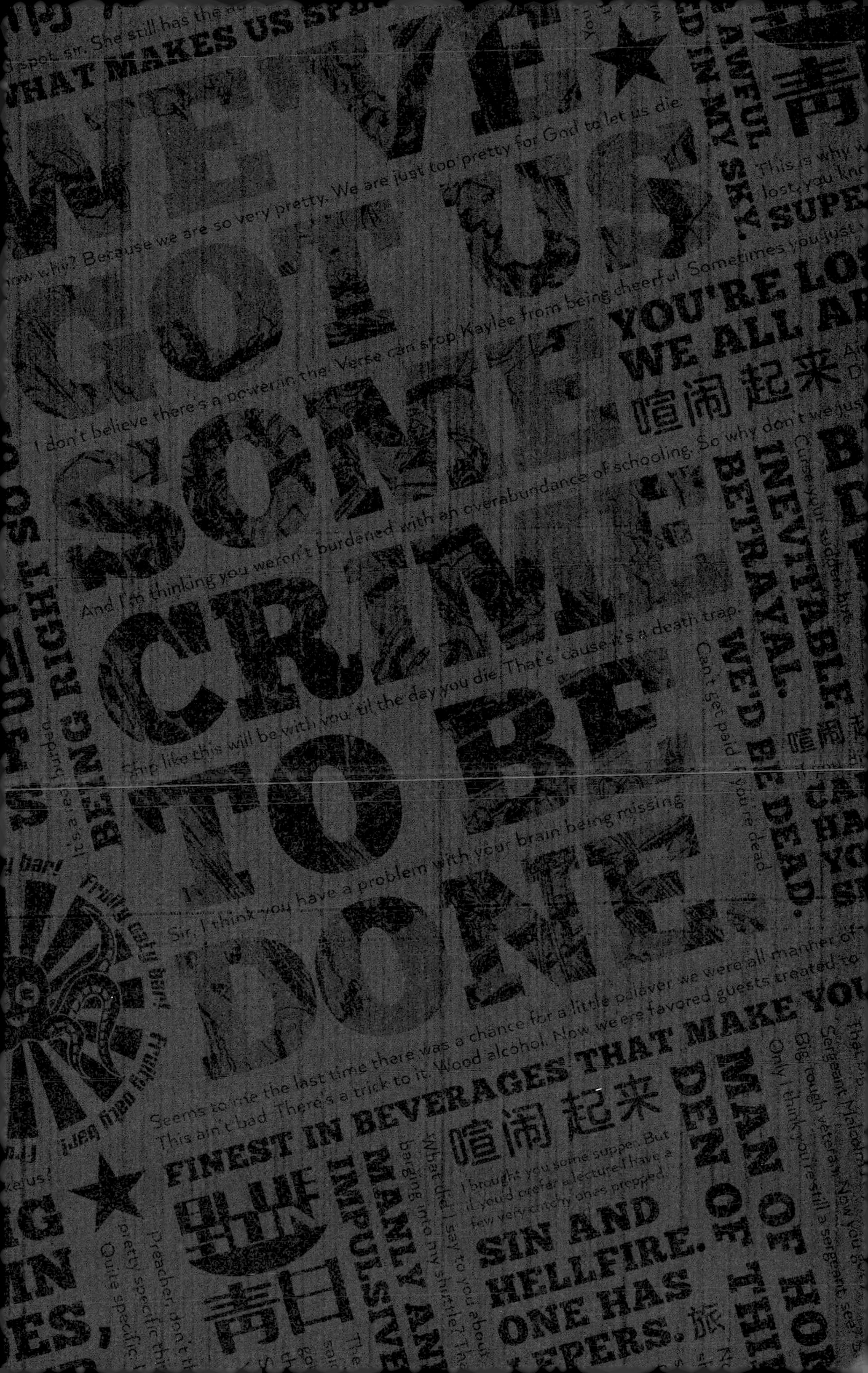

THAT MAKES US
despot, sir. She still has the
GOT US
SOME
CRIME
TO BE
DONE.
now why? Because we are so very pretty. We are just too pretty for God to let us die.
I don't believe there's a power in the 'Verse can stop Kaylee from being cheerful. Sometimes you just
And I'm thinking you weren't burdened with an overabundance of schooling. So why don't we just
Ship like this will be with you 'til the day you die. That's 'cause it's a death trap.
Sir, I think you have a problem with your brain being missing.
Seems to me the last time there was a chance for a little palaver we were all manner of
This ain't bad. There's a trick to it. Wood alcohol. Now we are favored guests treated to
FINEST IN BEVERAGES THAT MAKE YOU
YOU'RE LO
WE ALL A
喧闹起来
IN MY SKY.
INEVITABLE.
BETRAYAL.
WE'D BE DEAD.
BEING RIGHT
SIN AND HELLFIRE.
ONE HAS
DEN OF
MAN OF
IMPULSIVE
MANLY
喧闹起来

CHAPTER SIX

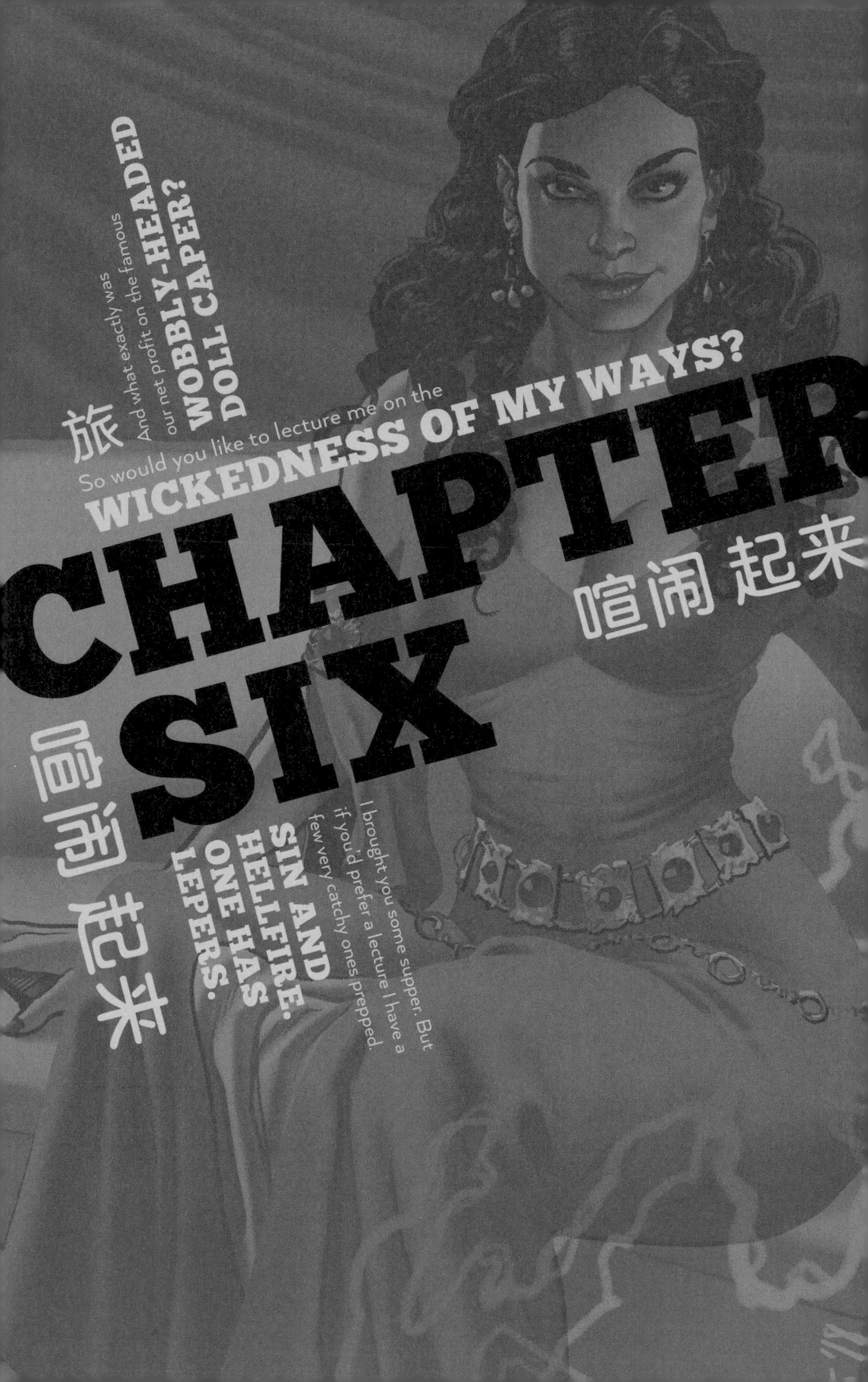
旅
And what exactly was our net profit on the famous WOBBLY-HEADED DOLL CAPER?
So would you like to lecture me on the WICKEDNESS OF MY WAYS?
喧闹起来
喧闹起来
I brought you some supper. But if you'd prefer a lecture I have a few very catchy ones prepped.
SIN AND HELLFIRE. ONE HAS LEPERS.

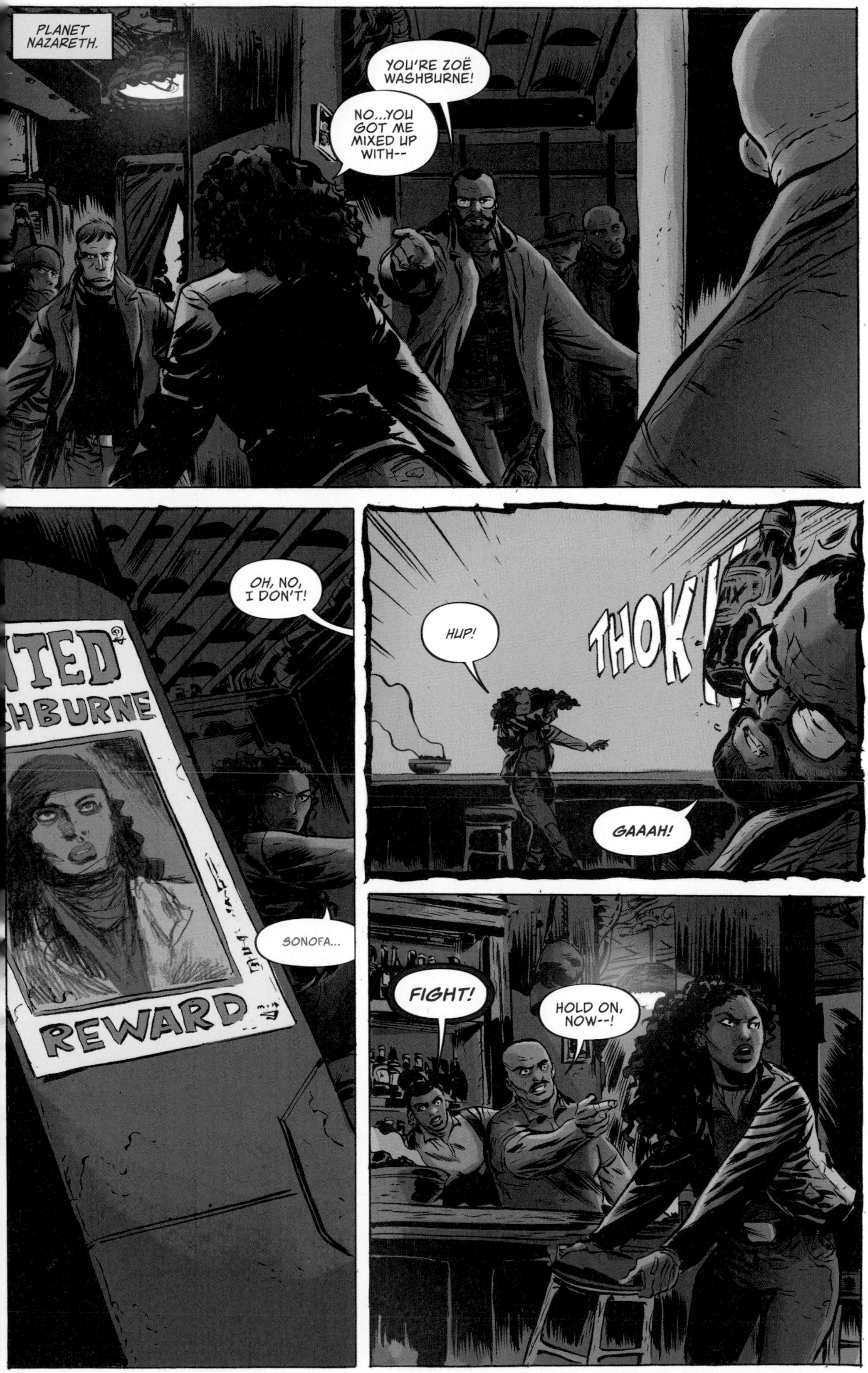

PLANET NAZARETH.
YOU'RE ZOË WASHBURNE!
NO...YOU GOT ME MIXED UP WITH--
OH, NO, I DON'T!
TED
SHBURNE
REWARD
SONOFA...
HUP!
THOK!
GAAAH!
FIGHT!
HOLD ON, NOW--!

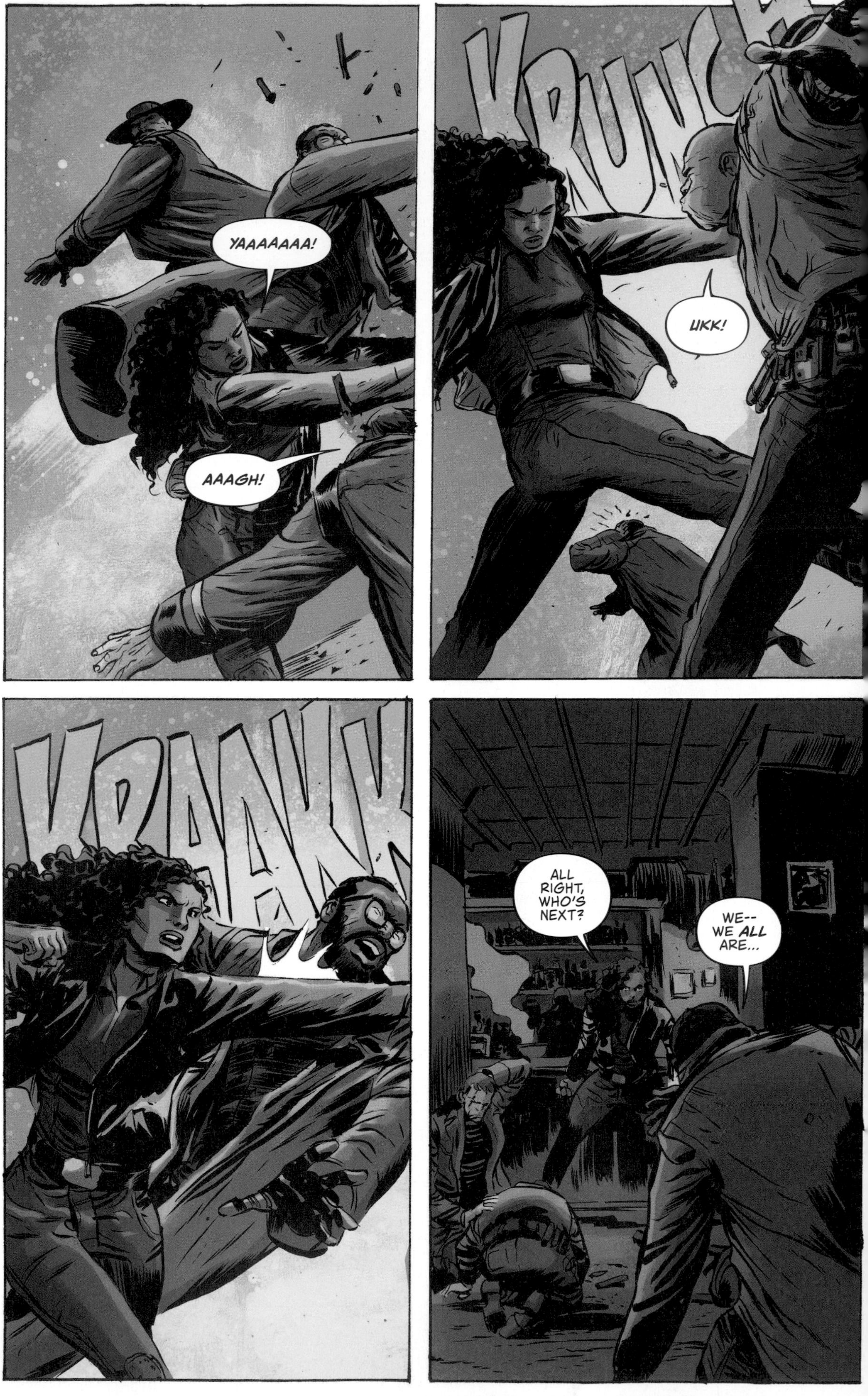
YAAAAAAA!
AAAGH!
KRUNCH
UKK!
KRANK
ALL RIGHT, WHO'S NEXT?
WE-- WE ALL ARE...

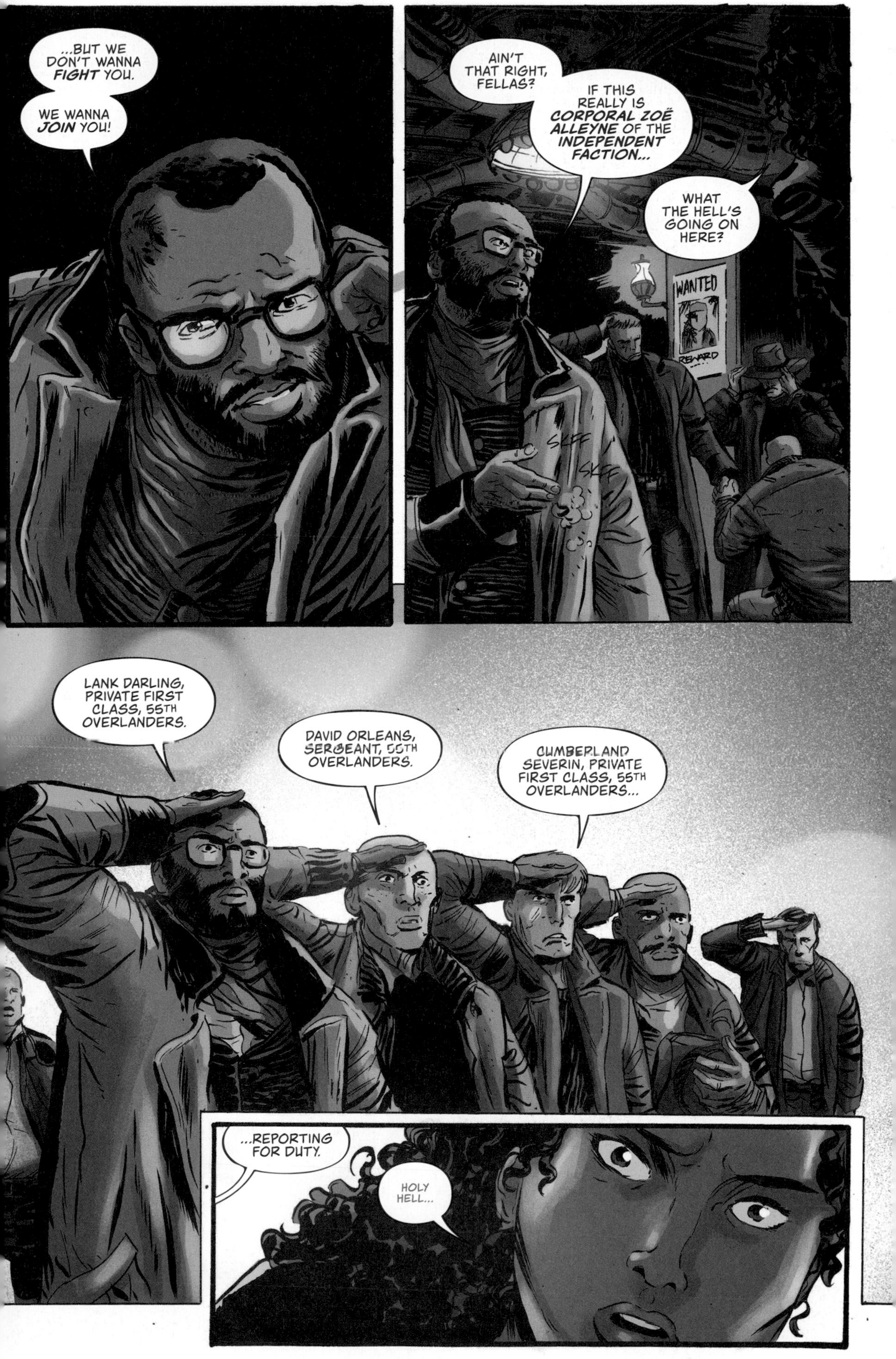
...BUT WE DON'T WANNA FIGHT YOU.
WE WANNA JOIN YOU!
AIN'T THAT RIGHT, FELLAS?
IF THIS REALLY IS CORPORAL ZOË ALLEYNE OF THE INDEPENDENT FACTION...
WHAT THE HELL'S GOING ON HERE?
WANTED
REWARD
SKFF
SKFF
LANK DARLING, PRIVATE FIRST CLASS, 55TH OVERLANDERS.
DAVID ORLEANS, SERGEANT, 55TH OVERLANDERS.
CUMBERLAND SEVERIN, PRIVATE FIRST CLASS, 55TH OVERLANDERS...
...REPORTING FOR DUTY.
HOLY HELL...

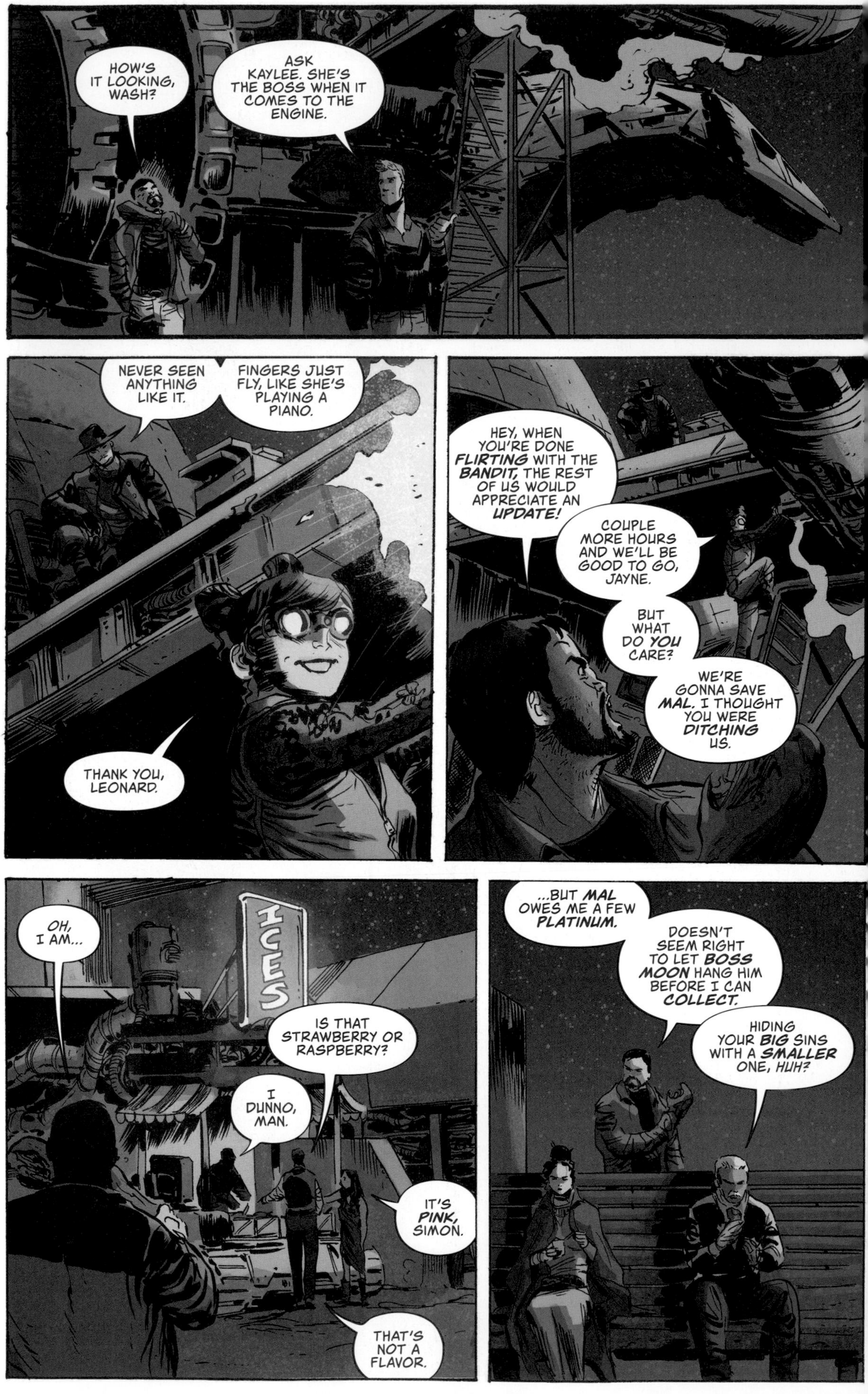
HOW'S IT LOOKING, WASH?
ASK KAYLEE. SHE'S THE BOSS WHEN IT COMES TO THE ENGINE.
NEVER SEEN ANYTHING LIKE IT.
FINGERS JUST FLY, LIKE SHE'S PLAYING A PIANO.
THANK YOU, LEONARD.
HEY, WHEN YOU'RE DONE FLIRTING WITH THE BANDIT, THE REST OF US WOULD APPRECIATE AN UPDATE!
COUPLE MORE HOURS AND WE'LL BE GOOD TO GO, JAYNE.
BUT WHAT DO YOU CARE?
WE'RE GONNA SAVE MAL. I THOUGHT YOU WERE DITCHING US.
OH, I AM...
ICES
IS THAT STRAWBERRY OR RASPBERRY?
I DUNNO, MAN.
IT'S PINK, SIMON.
THAT'S NOT A FLAVOR.
...BUT MAL OWES ME A FEW PLATINUM.
DOESN'T SEEM RIGHT TO LET BOSS MOON HANG HIM BEFORE I CAN COLLECT.
HIDING YOUR BIG SINS WITH A SMALLER ONE, HUH?

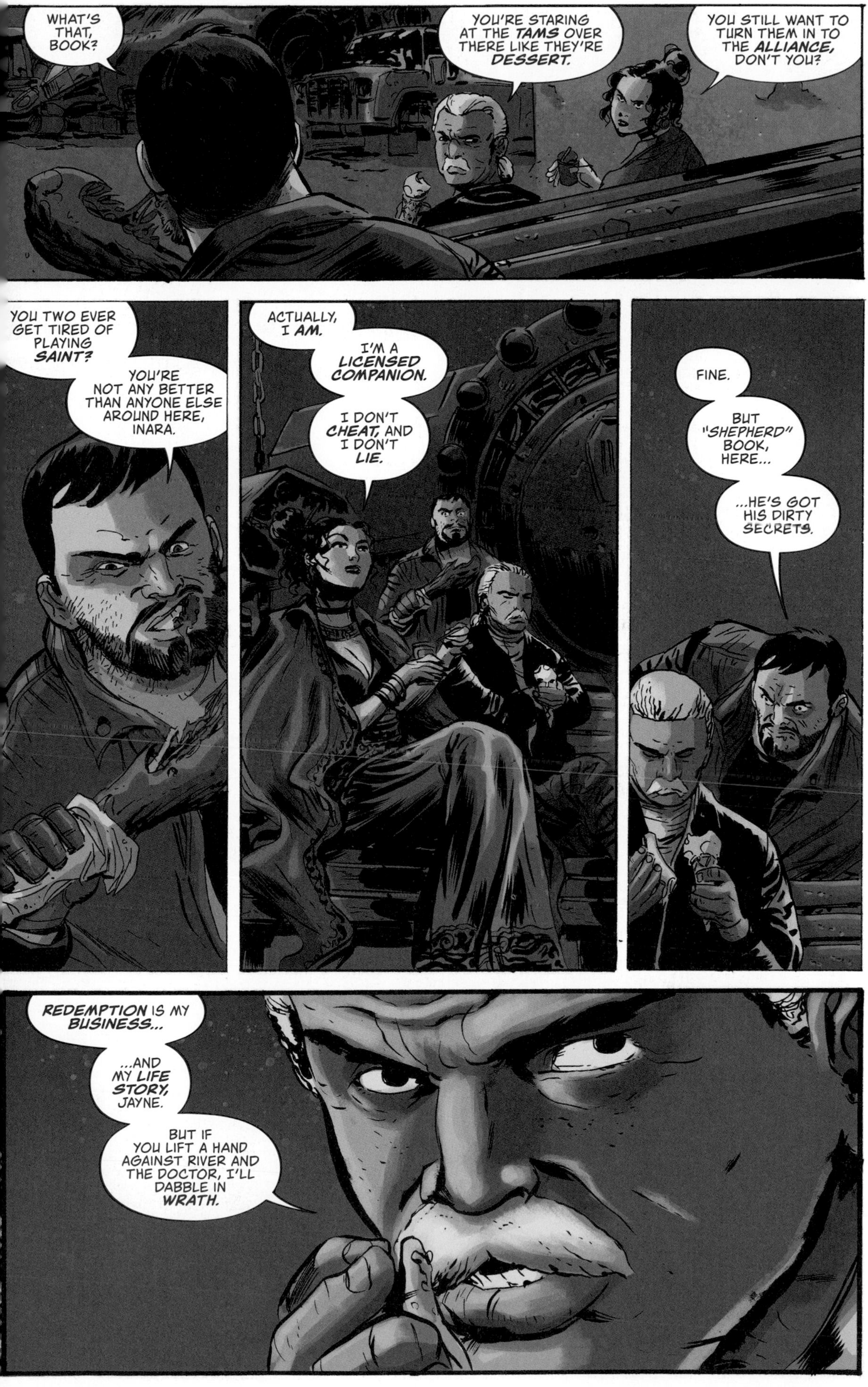
WHAT'S THAT, BOOK?
YOU'RE STARING AT THE TAMS OVER THERE LIKE THEY'RE DESSERT.
YOU STILL WANT TO TURN THEM IN TO THE ALLIANCE, DON'T YOU?
YOU TWO EVER GET TIRED OF PLAYING SAINT?
YOU'RE NOT ANY BETTER THAN ANYONE ELSE AROUND HERE, INARA.
ACTUALLY, I AM.
I'M A LICENSED COMPANION.
I DON'T CHEAT, AND I DON'T LIE.
FINE.
BUT "SHEPHERD" BOOK, HERE...
...HE'S GOT HIS DIRTY SECRETS.
REDEMPTION IS MY BUSINESS...
...AND MY LIFE STORY, JAYNE.
BUT IF YOU LIFT A HAND AGAINST RIVER AND THE DOCTOR, I'LL DABBLE IN WRATH.

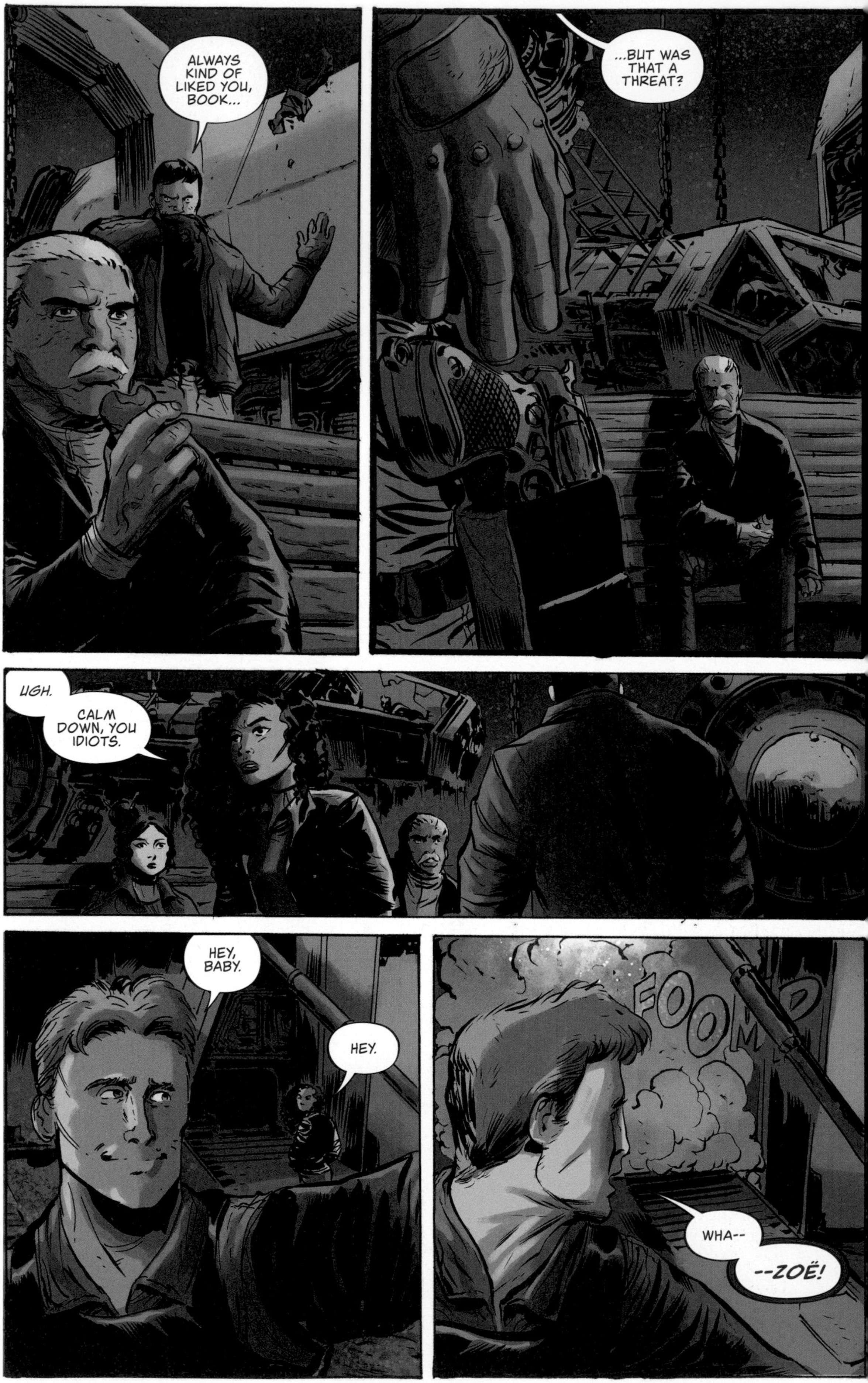
ALWAYS KIND OF LIKED YOU, BOOK...
...BUT WAS THAT A THREAT?
UGH.
CALM DOWN, YOU IDIOTS.
HEY, BABY.
HEY.
FOOMP
WHA--
--ZOË!

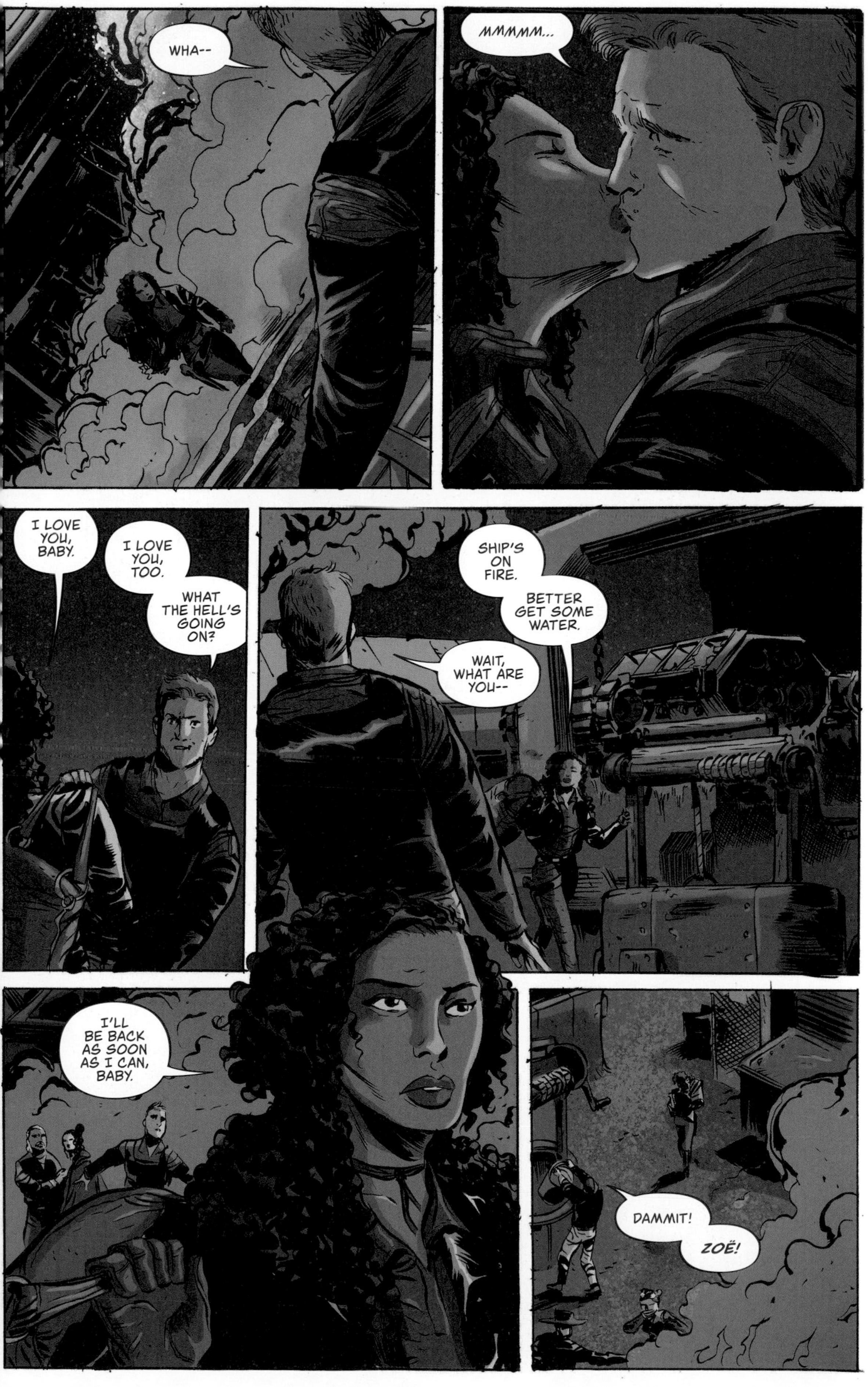
WHA--
MMMMM...
I LOVE YOU, BABY.
I LOVE YOU, TOO.
WHAT THE HELL'S GOING ON?
SHIP'S ON FIRE.
BETTER GET SOME WATER.
WAIT, WHAT ARE YOU--
I'LL BE BACK AS SOON AS I CAN, BABY.
DAMMIT!
ZOË!

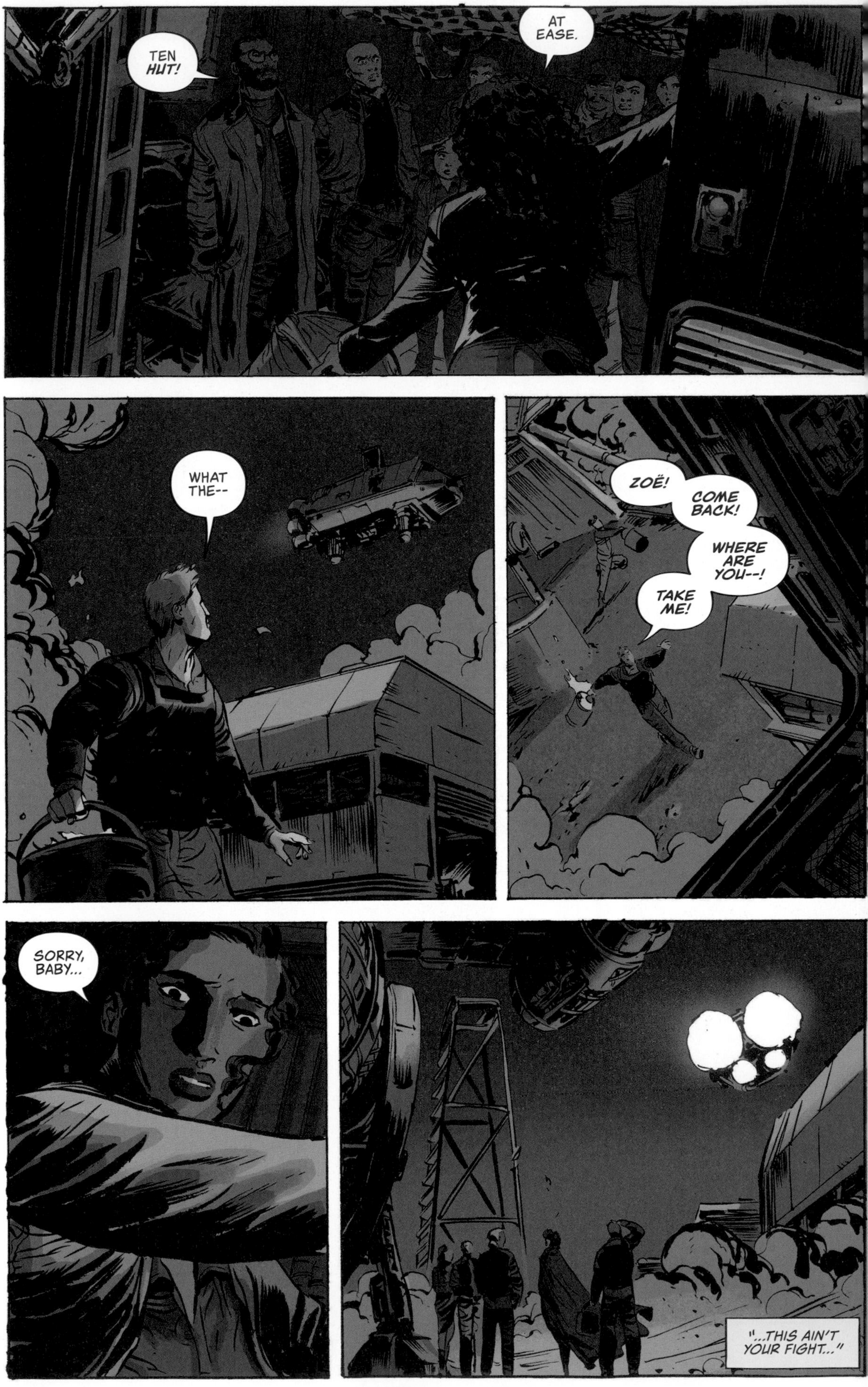

TEN HUT!
AT EASE.
WHAT THE--
ZOË!
COME BACK!
WHERE ARE YOU--!
TAKE ME!
SORRY, BABY...
"...THIS AIN'T YOUR FIGHT..."

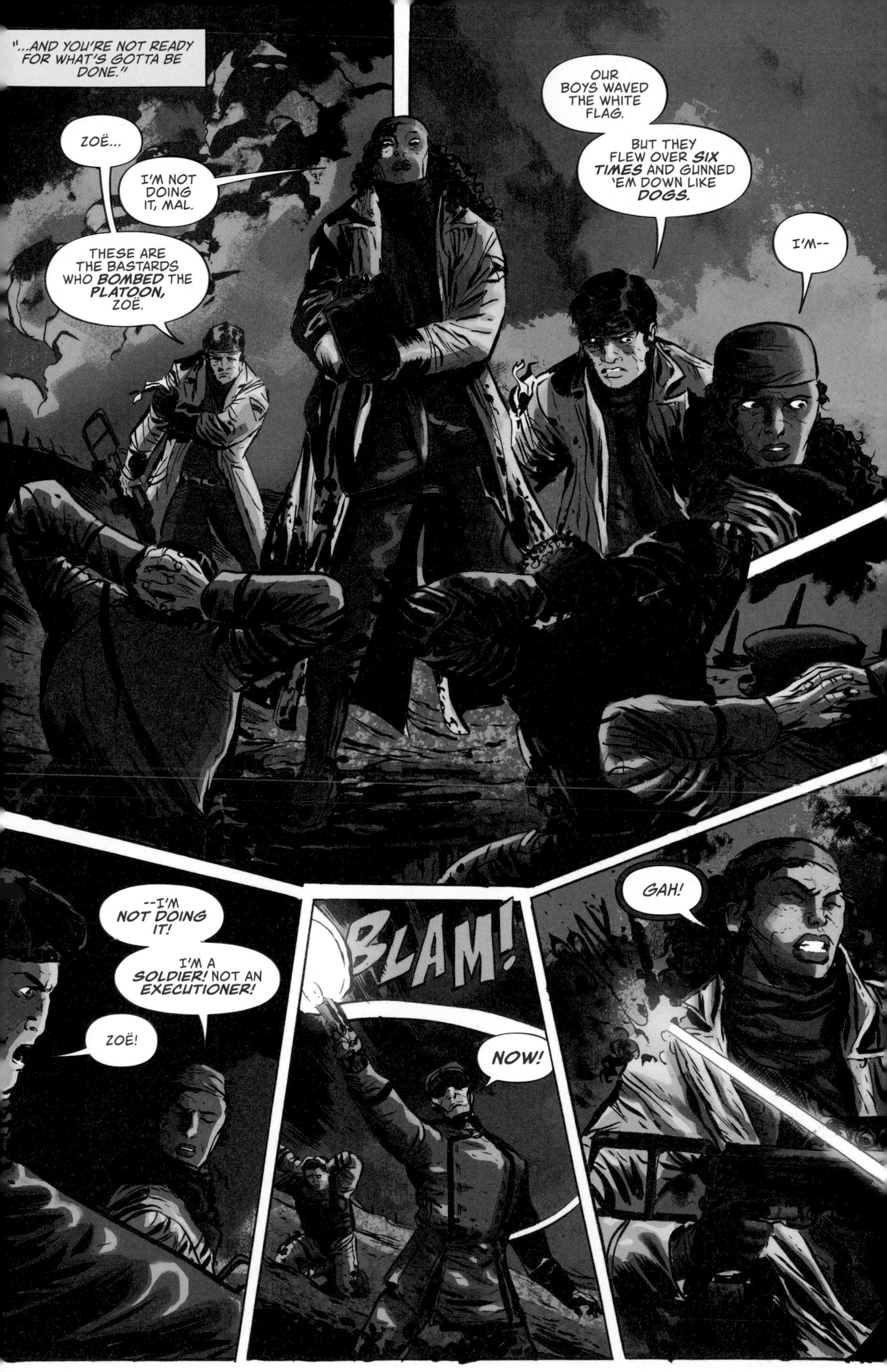
"...AND YOU'RE NOT READY FOR WHAT'S GOTTA BE DONE."
ZOË...
I'M NOT DOING IT, MAL.
THESE ARE THE BASTARDS WHO BOMBED THE PLATOON, ZOË.
OUR BOYS WAVED THE WHITE FLAG.
BUT THEY FLEW OVER SIX TIMES AND GUNNED 'EM DOWN LIKE DOGS.
I'M--
--I'M NOT DOING IT!
I'M A SOLDIER! NOT AN EXECUTIONER!
ZOË!
BLAM!
NOW!
GAH!

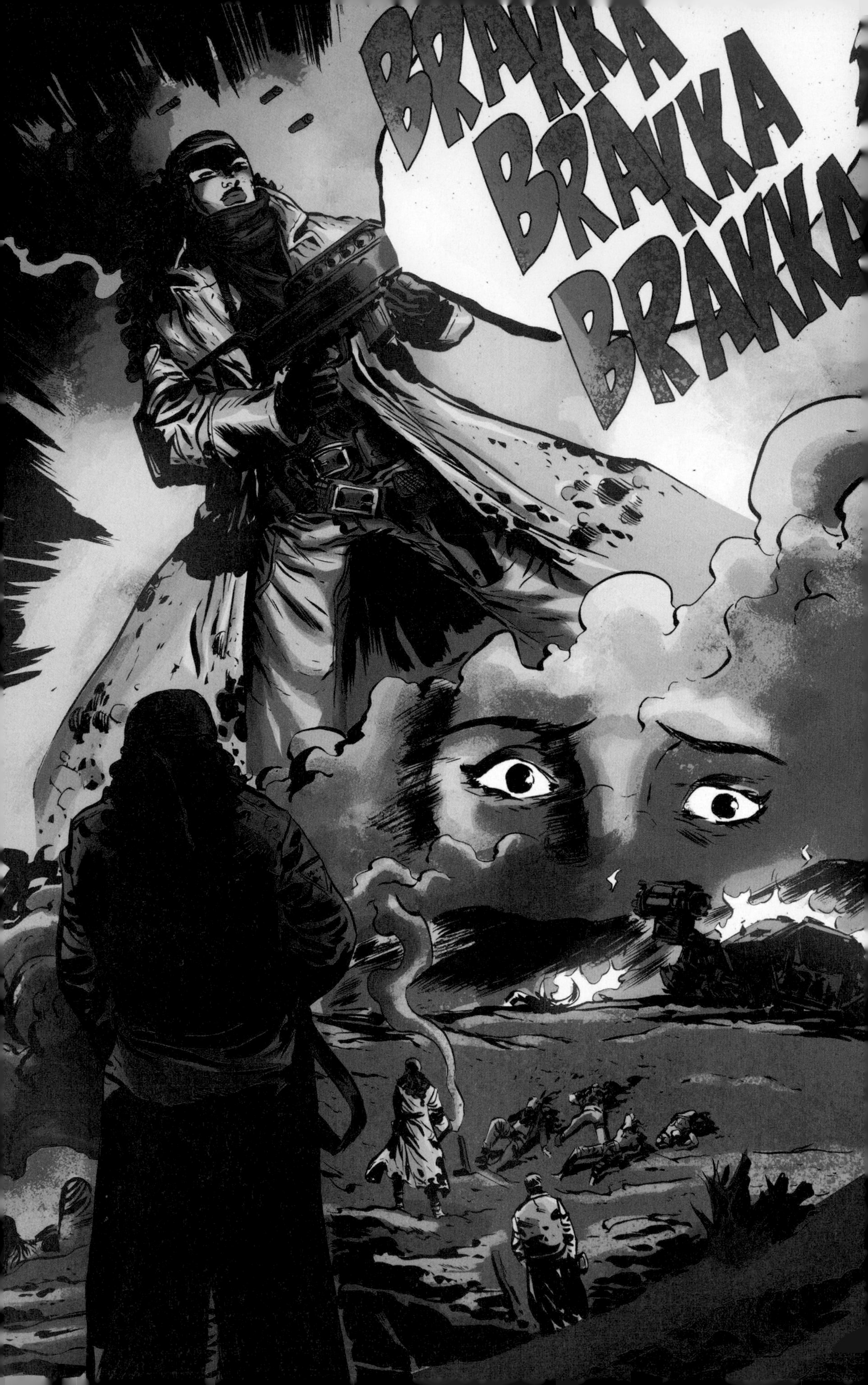
BRAKKA
BRAKKA
BRAKKA

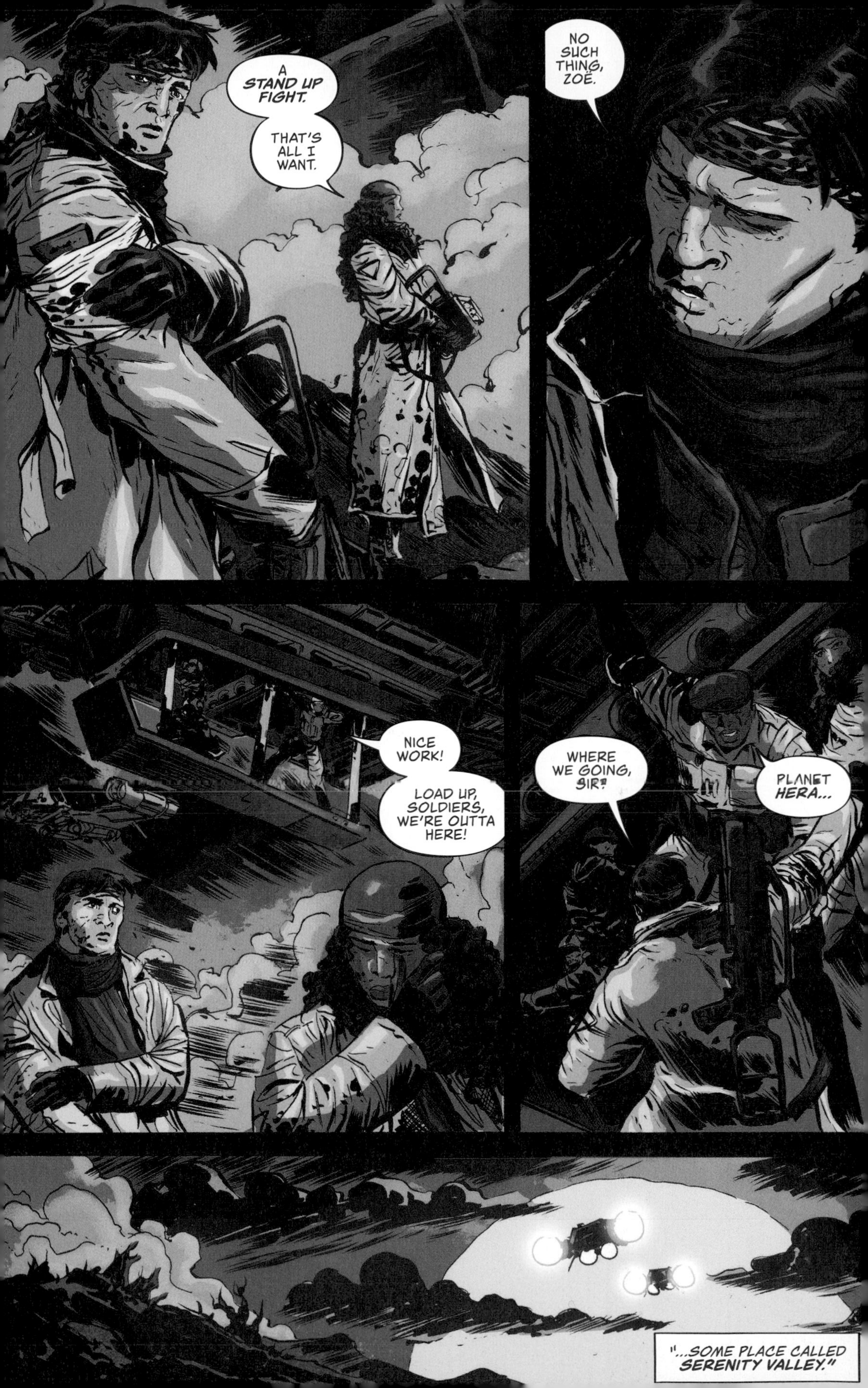
A STAND UP FIGHT.
THAT'S ALL I WANT.
NO SUCH THING, ZOË.
NICE WORK!
LOAD UP, SOLDIERS, WE'RE OUTTA HERE!
WHERE WE GOING, SIR?
PLANET HERA...
"...SOME PLACE CALLED SERENITY VALLEY."

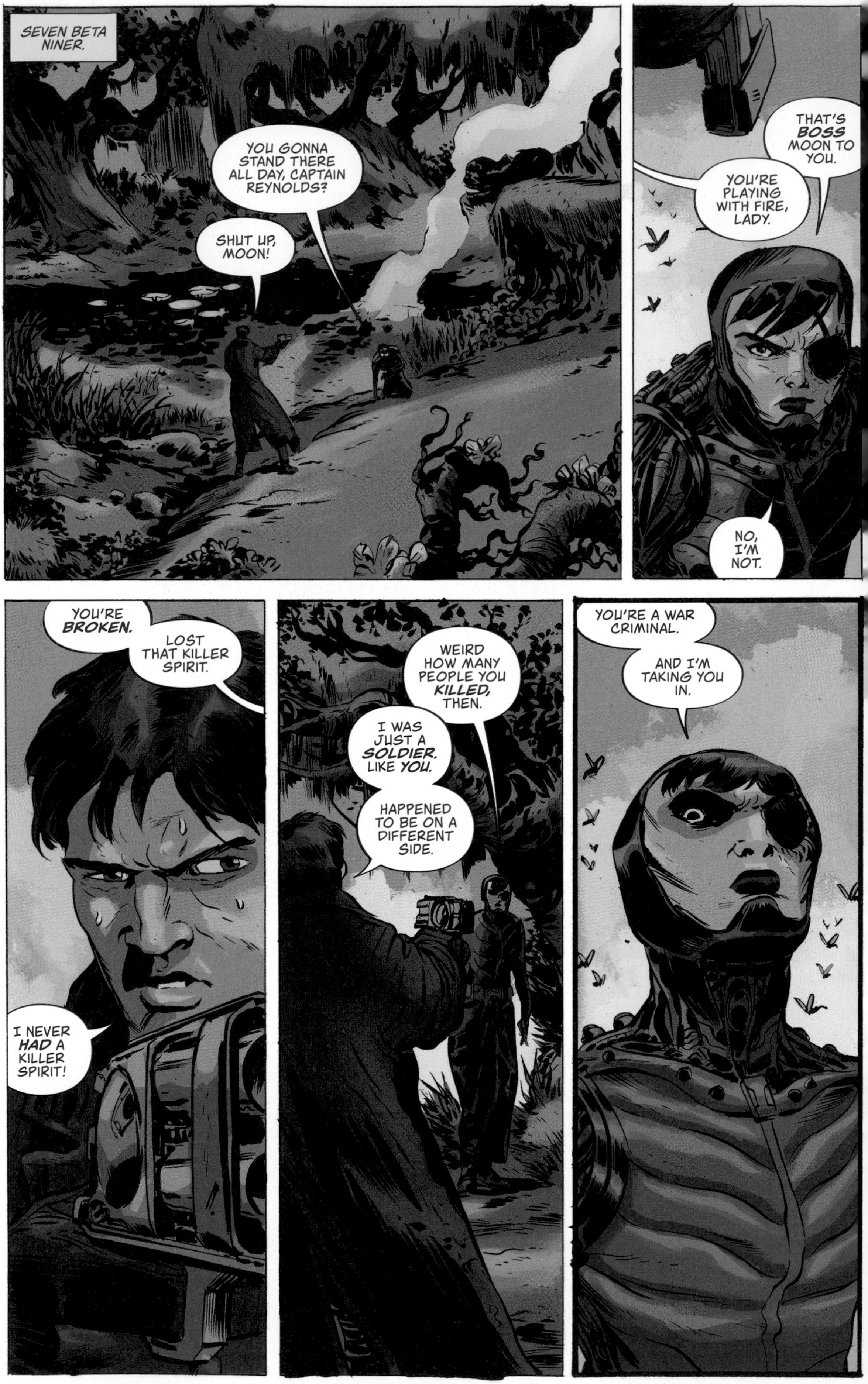
SEVEN BETA NINER.
YOU GONNA STAND THERE ALL DAY, CAPTAIN REYNOLDS?
SHUT UP, MOON!
THAT'S **BOSS** MOON TO YOU.
YOU'RE PLAYING WITH FIRE, LADY.
NO, I'M NOT.
YOU'RE **BROKEN.**
LOST THAT KILLER SPIRIT.
I NEVER **HAD** A KILLER SPIRIT!
WEIRD HOW MANY PEOPLE YOU **KILLED,** THEN.
I WAS JUST A **SOLDIER.** LIKE **YOU.**
HAPPENED TO BE ON A DIFFERENT SIDE.
YOU'RE A WAR CRIMINAL.
AND I'M TAKING YOU IN.

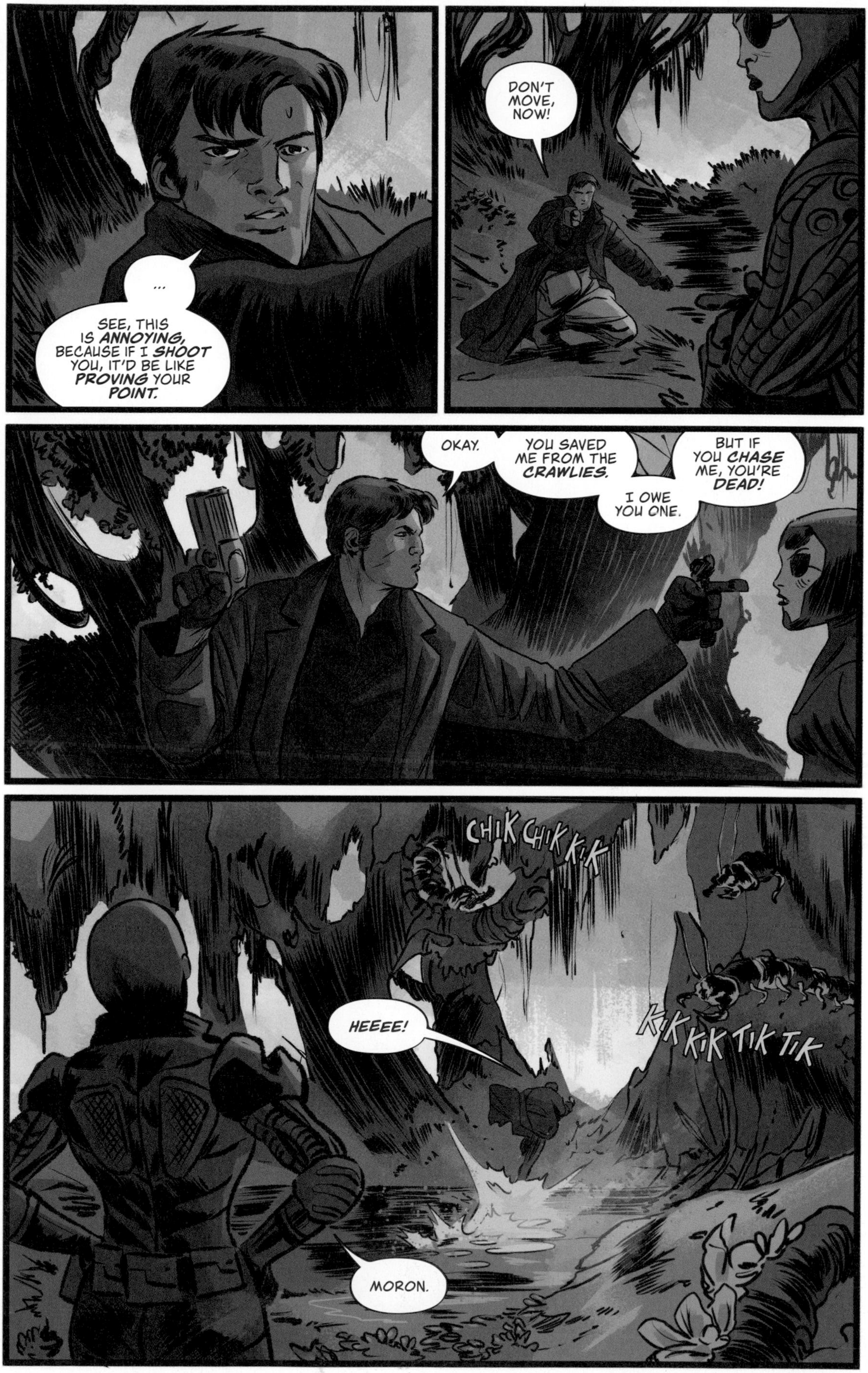
...
SEE, THIS IS ANNOYING, BECAUSE IF I SHOOT YOU, IT'D BE LIKE PROVING YOUR POINT.
DON'T MOVE, NOW!
OKAY.
YOU SAVED ME FROM THE CRAWLIES.
I OWE YOU ONE.
BUT IF YOU CHASE ME, YOU'RE DEAD!
CHIK CHIK KIK
KIK KIK TIK TIK
HEEEE!
MORON.

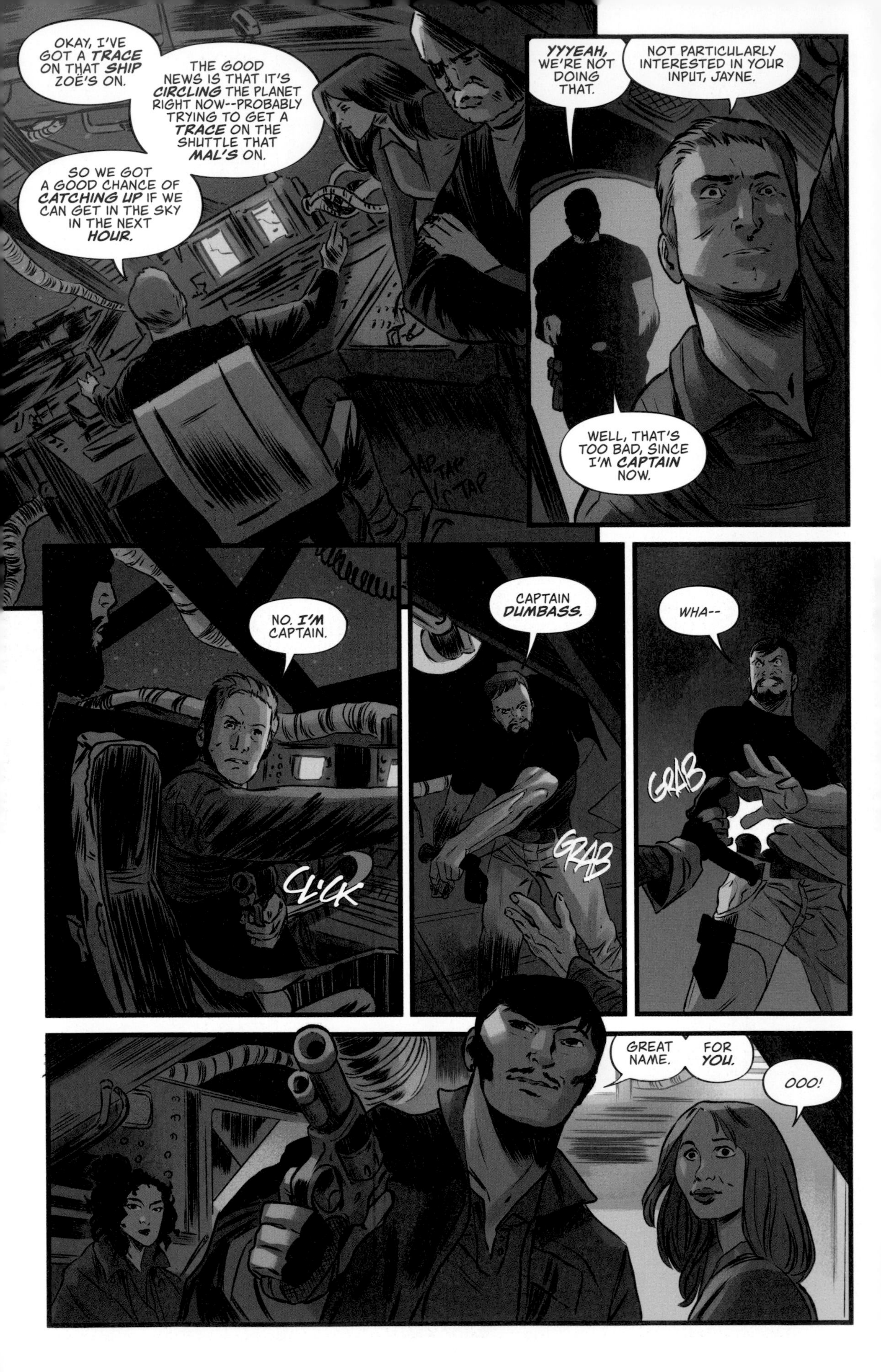
OKAY, I'VE GOT A TRACE ON THAT SHIP ZOË'S ON.
THE GOOD NEWS IS THAT IT'S CIRCLING THE PLANET RIGHT NOW--PROBABLY TRYING TO GET A TRACE ON THE SHUTTLE THAT MAL'S ON.
SO WE GOT A GOOD CHANCE OF CATCHING UP IF WE CAN GET IN THE SKY IN THE NEXT HOUR.
TAP TAP TAP
YYYEAH, WE'RE NOT DOING THAT.
NOT PARTICULARLY INTERESTED IN YOUR INPUT, JAYNE.
WELL, THAT'S TOO BAD, SINCE I'M CAPTAIN NOW.
NO. I'M CAPTAIN.
CLICK
CAPTAIN DUMBASS.
GRAB
WHA--
GRAB
GREAT NAME.
FOR YOU.
OOO!

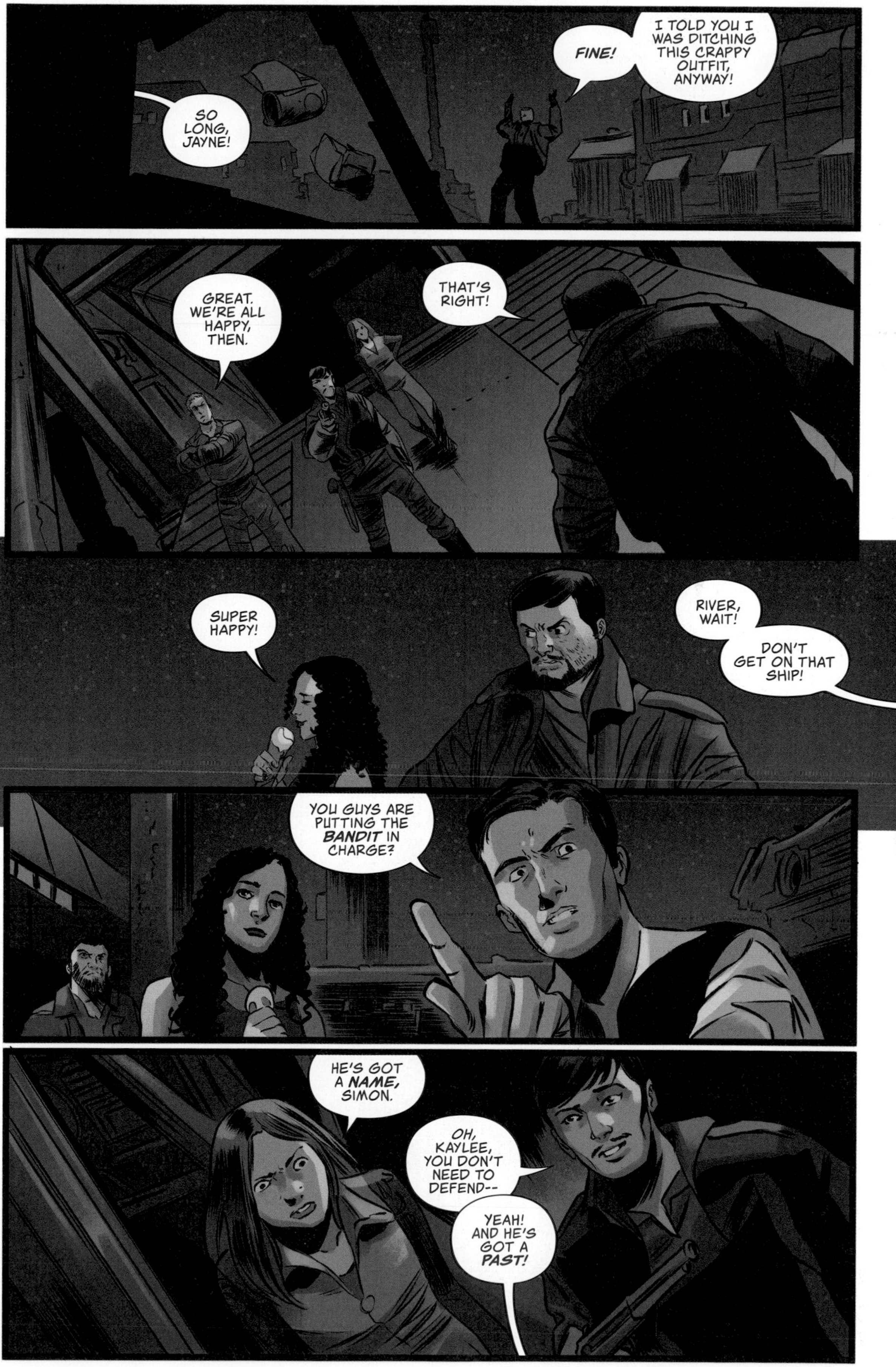
SO LONG, JAYNE!
FINE!
I TOLD YOU I WAS DITCHING THIS CRAPPY OUTFIT, ANYWAY!
GREAT. WE'RE ALL HAPPY, THEN.
THAT'S RIGHT!
SUPER HAPPY!
RIVER, WAIT!
DON'T GET ON THAT SHIP!
YOU GUYS ARE PUTTING THE BANDIT IN CHARGE?
HE'S GOT A NAME, SIMON.
OH, KAYLEE, YOU DON'T NEED TO DEFEND--
YEAH! AND HE'S GOT A PAST!

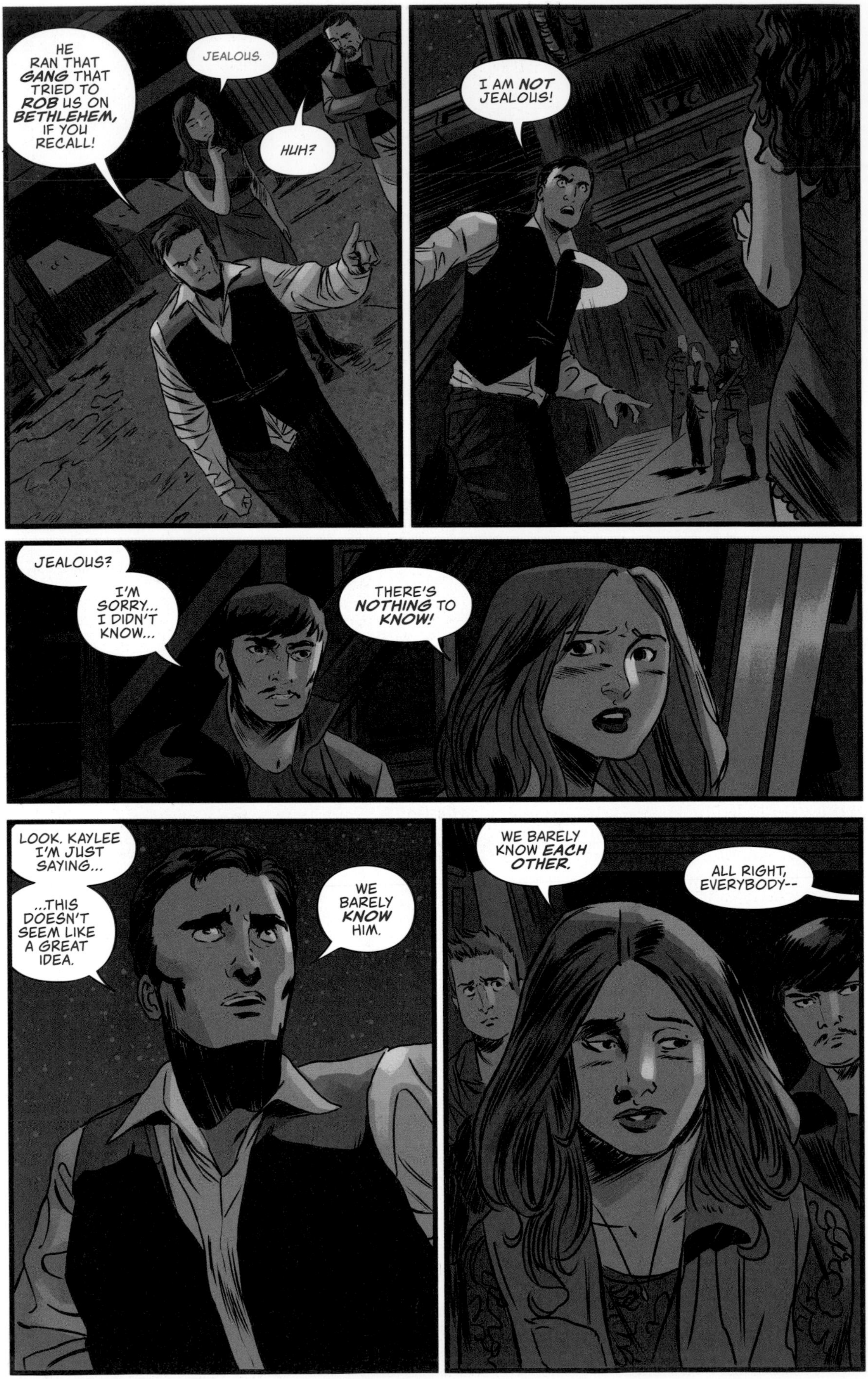
HE RAN THAT GANG THAT TRIED TO ROB US ON BETHLEHEM, IF YOU RECALL!
JEALOUS.
HUH?
I AM NOT JEALOUS!
JEALOUS?
I'M SORRY... I DIDN'T KNOW...
THERE'S NOTHING TO KNOW!
LOOK. KAYLEE I'M JUST SAYING...
...THIS DOESN'T SEEM LIKE A GREAT IDEA.
WE BARELY KNOW HIM.
WE BARELY KNOW EACH OTHER.
ALL RIGHT, EVERYBODY--

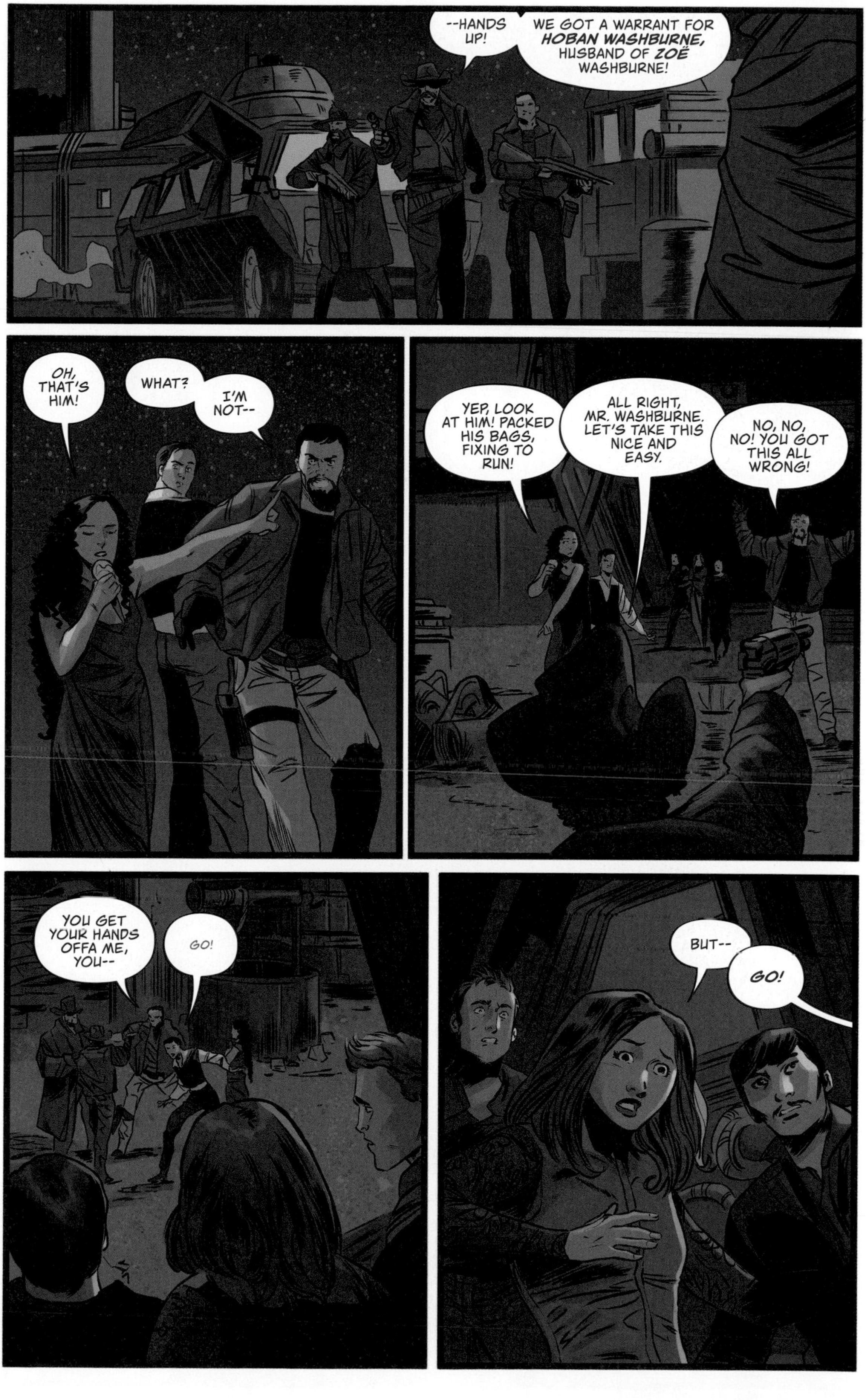
--HANDS UP!
WE GOT A WARRANT FOR HOBAN WASHBURNE, HUSBAND OF ZOË WASHBURNE!
OH, THAT'S HIM!
WHAT?
I'M NOT--
YEP, LOOK AT HIM! PACKED HIS BAGS, FIXING TO RUN!
ALL RIGHT, MR. WASHBURNE. LET'S TAKE THIS NICE AND EASY.
NO, NO, NO! YOU GOT THIS ALL WRONG!
YOU GET YOUR HANDS OFFA ME, YOU--
GO!
BUT--
GO!

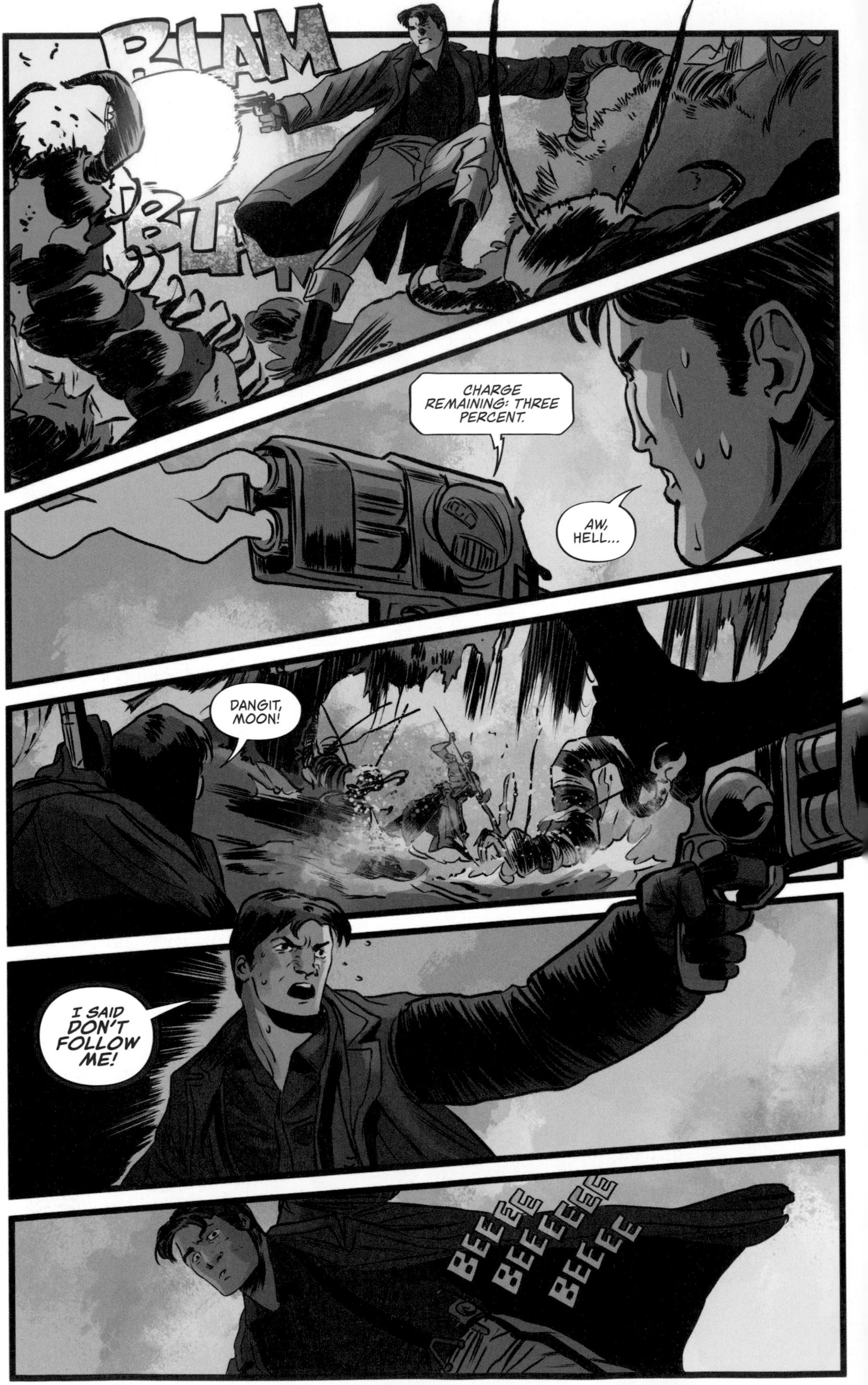
BLAM
BLAM
CHARGE REMAINING: THREE PERCENT.
AW, HELL...
DANGIT, MOON!
I SAID DON'T FOLLOW ME!
BEEEE
BEEEEEE
BEEEE

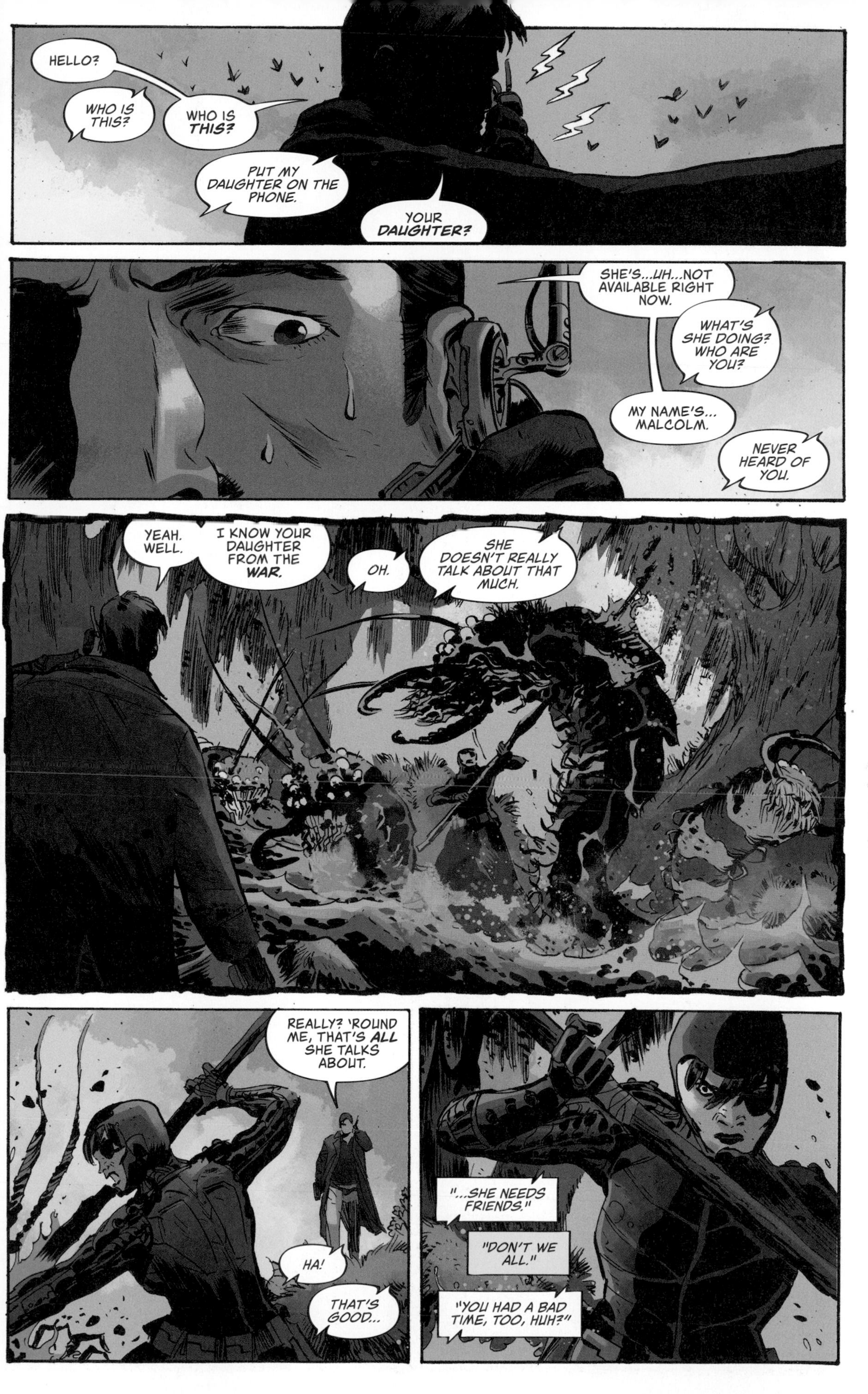
HELLO?
WHO IS THIS?
WHO IS THIS?
PUT MY DAUGHTER ON THE PHONE.
YOUR DAUGHTER?
SHE'S...UH...NOT AVAILABLE RIGHT NOW.
WHAT'S SHE DOING? WHO ARE YOU?
MY NAME'S... MALCOLM.
NEVER HEARD OF YOU.
YEAH. WELL.
I KNOW YOUR DAUGHTER FROM THE WAR.
OH.
SHE DOESN'T REALLY TALK ABOUT THAT MUCH.
REALLY? 'ROUND ME, THAT'S ALL SHE TALKS ABOUT.
HA!
THAT'S GOOD...
"...SHE NEEDS FRIENDS."
"DON'T WE ALL."
"YOU HAD A BAD TIME, TOO, HUH?"

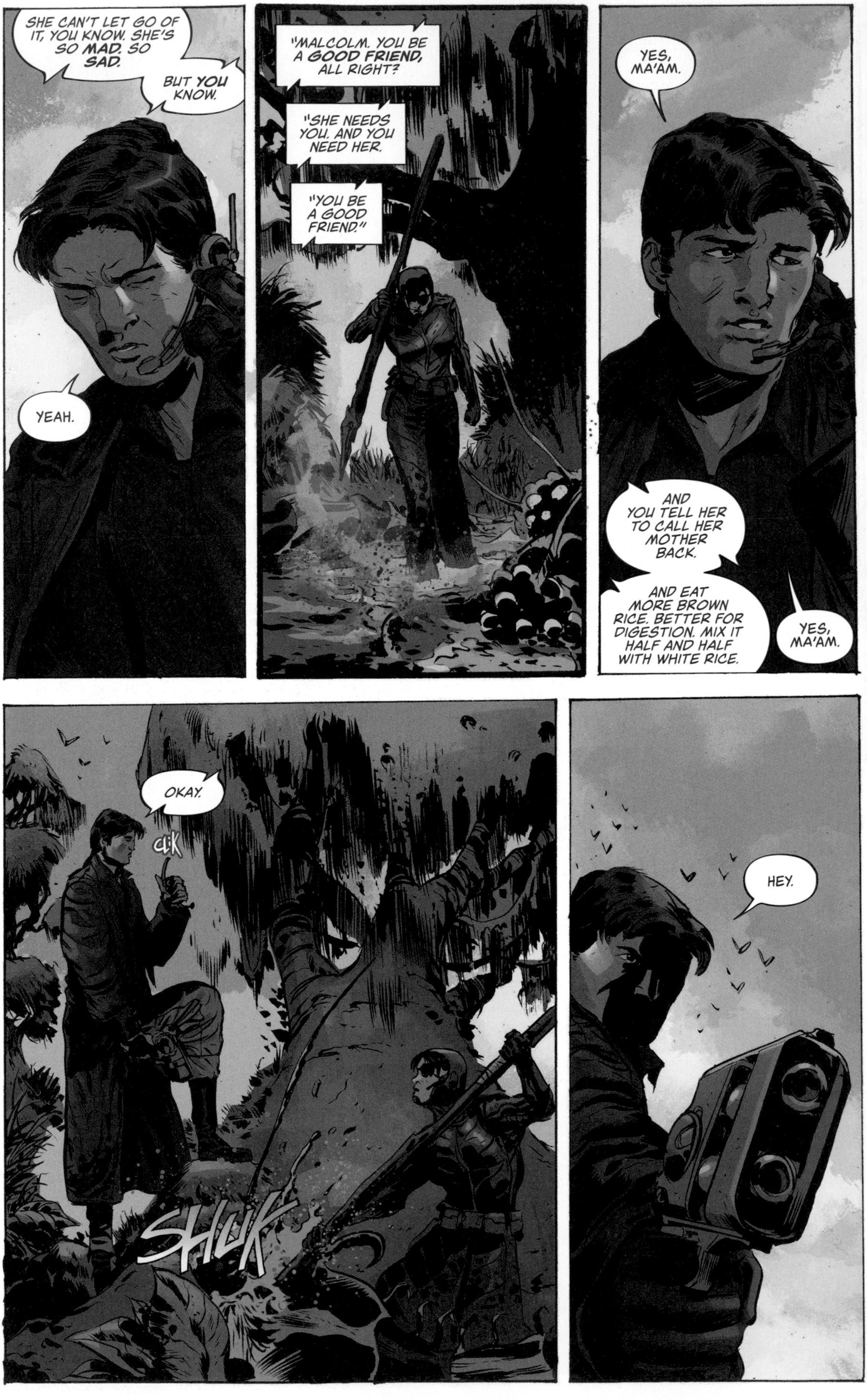
SHE CAN'T LET GO OF IT, YOU KNOW. SHE'S SO MAD. SO SAD.
BUT YOU KNOW.
YEAH.
"MALCOLM. YOU BE A GOOD FRIEND, ALL RIGHT?
"SHE NEEDS YOU. AND YOU NEED HER.
"YOU BE A GOOD FRIEND."
YES, MA'AM.
AND YOU TELL HER TO CALL HER MOTHER BACK.
AND EAT MORE BROWN RICE. BETTER FOR DIGESTION. MIX IT HALF AND HALF WITH WHITE RICE.
YES, MA'AM.
OKAY.
CLIK
SHUK
HEY.

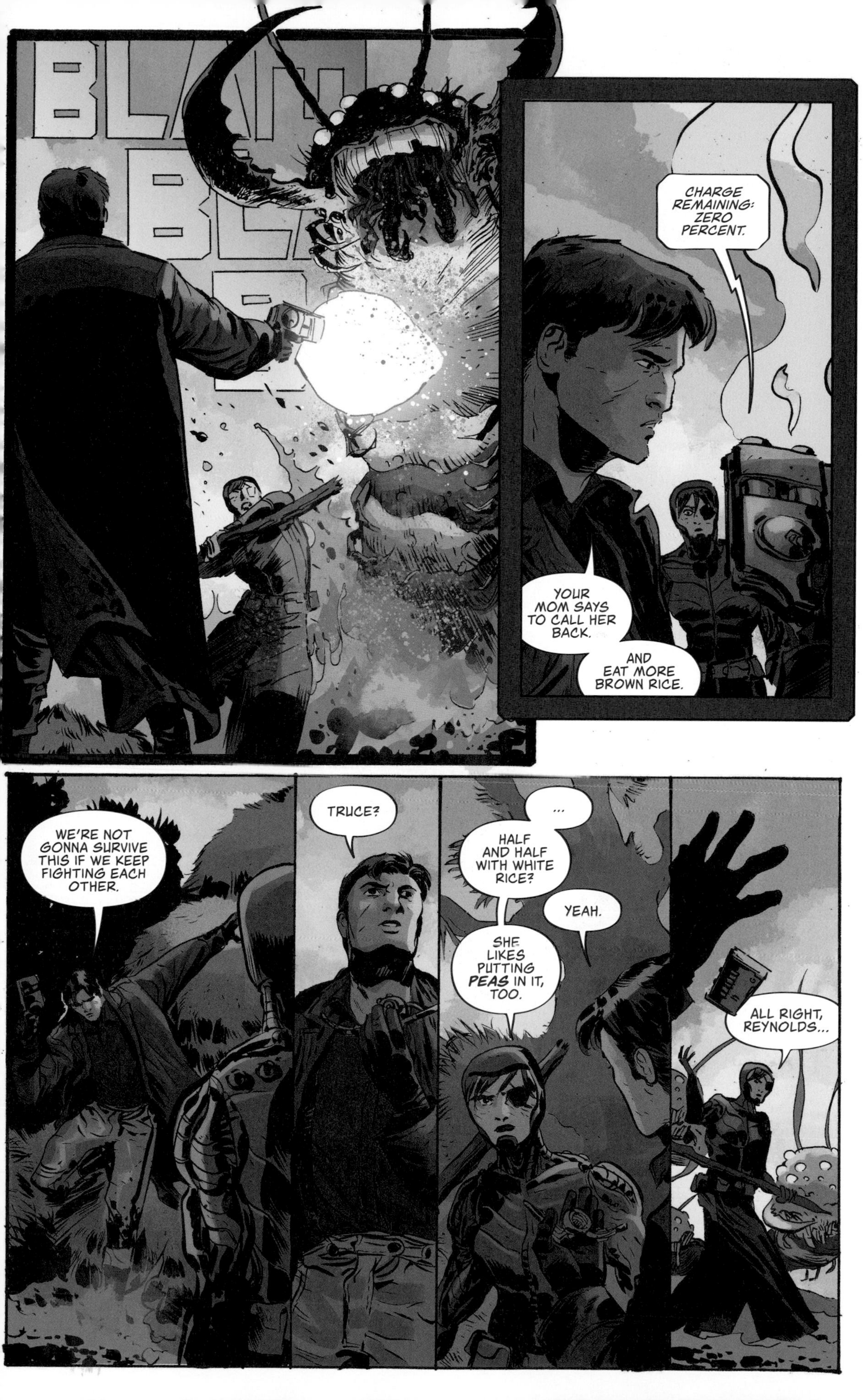
CHARGE REMAINING: ZERO PERCENT.
YOUR MOM SAYS TO CALL HER BACK.
AND EAT MORE BROWN RICE.
WE'RE NOT GONNA SURVIVE THIS IF WE KEEP FIGHTING EACH OTHER.
TRUCE?
...
HALF AND HALF WITH WHITE RICE?
YEAH.
SHE LIKES PUTTING PEAS IN IT, TOO.
ALL RIGHT, REYNOLDS...

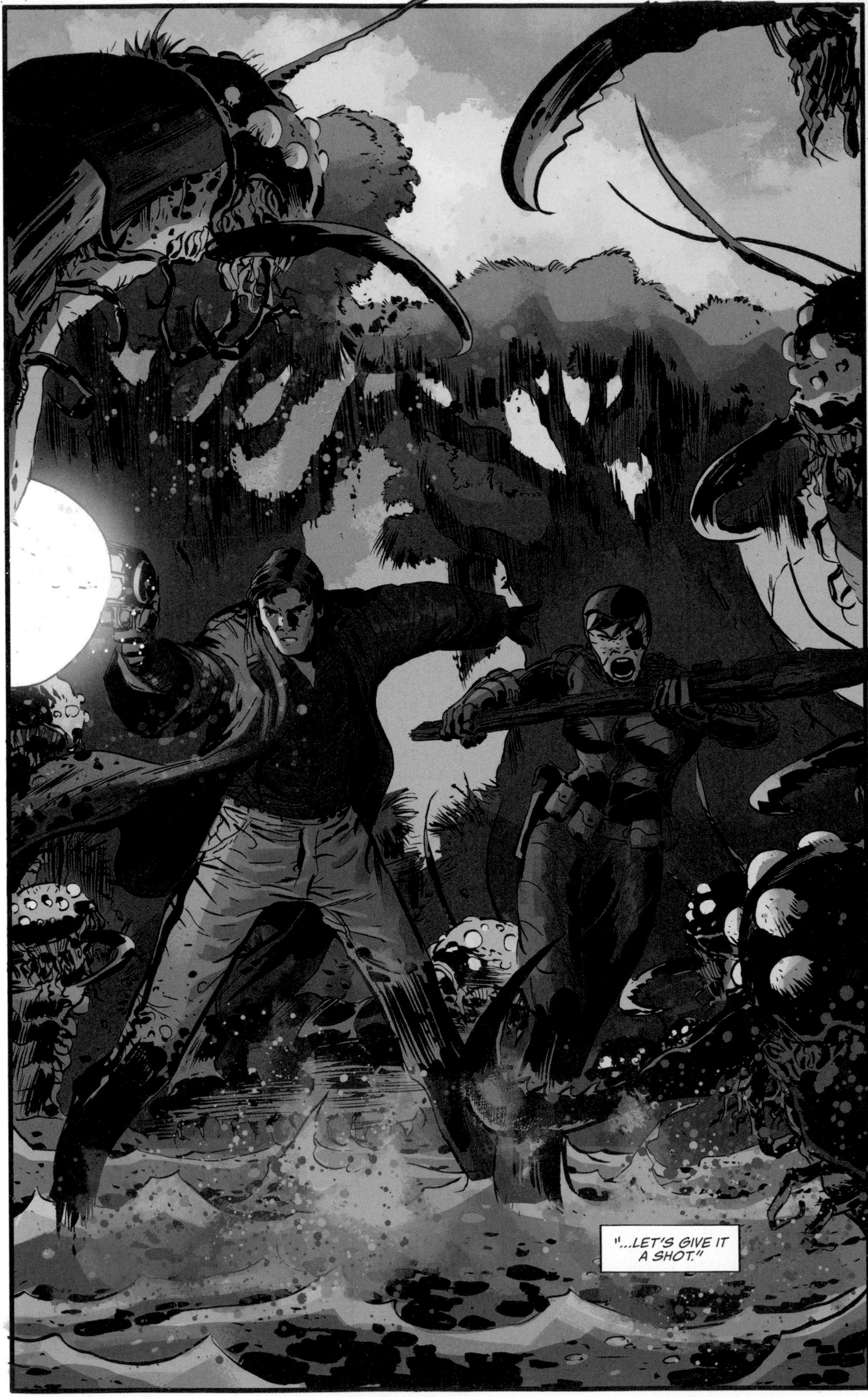
"...LET'S GIVE IT A SHOT."

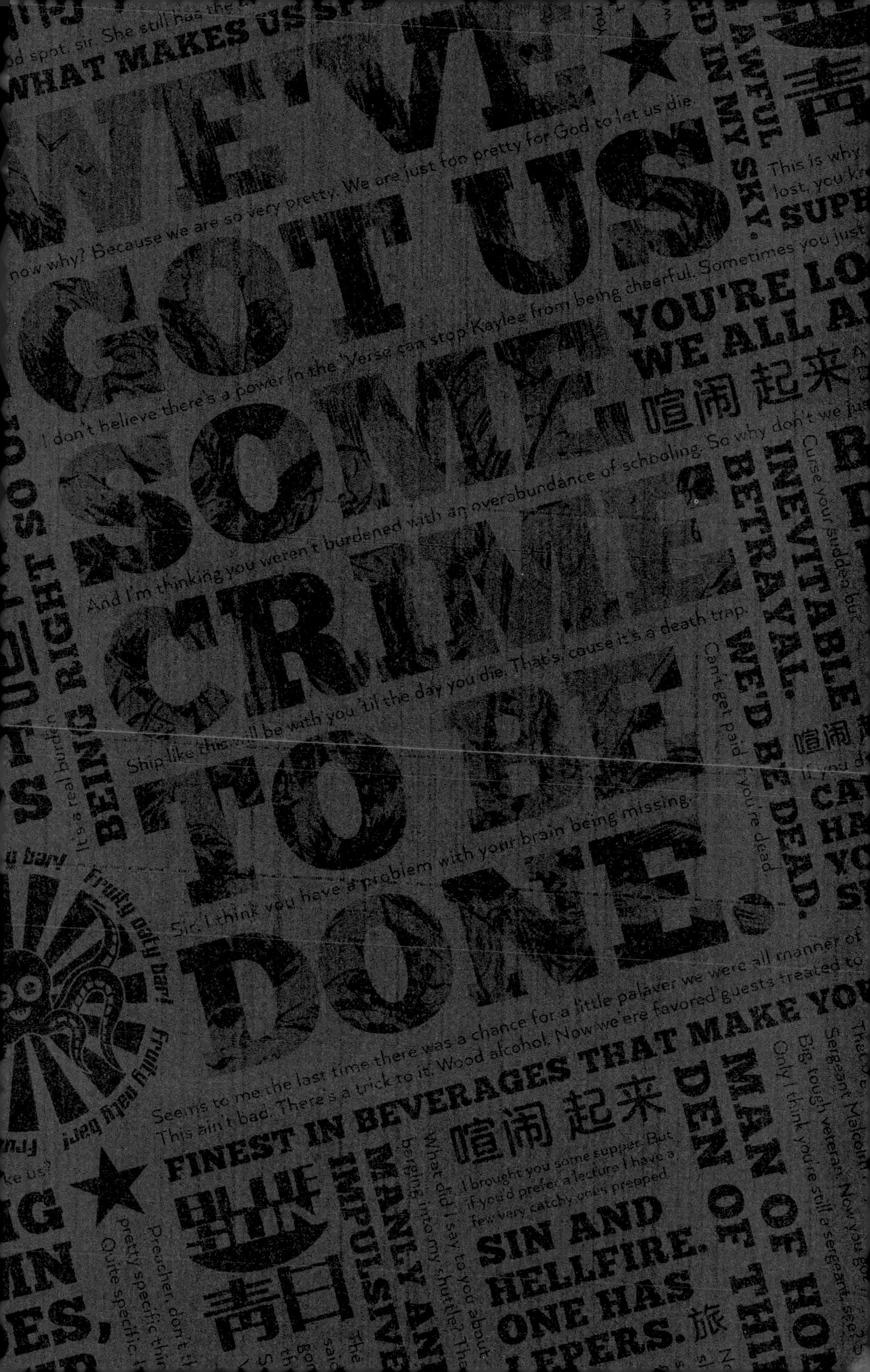
WE'VE GOT US SOME CRIME TO BE DONE.
WHAT MAKES US
AWFUL IN MY SKY.
You know why? Because we are so very pretty. We are just too pretty for God to let us die.
I don't believe there's a power in the 'Verse can stop Kaylee from being cheerful. Sometimes you just
And I'm thinking you weren't burdened with an overabundance of schooling. So why don't we just
Ship like this, it'll be with you 'til the day you die. That's 'cause it's a death trap.
Sir, I think you have a problem with your brain being missing.
YOU'RE LO
WE ALL A
喧闹起来
INEVITABLE BETRAYAL.
WE'D BE DEAD.
Can't get paid if you're dead.
BEING RIGHT SO
It's a real burden
Fruity oaty bar!
Seems to me the last time there was a chance for a little palaver we were all manner of
This ain't bad. There's a trick to it. Wood alcohol. Now we're favored guests treated to
FINEST IN BEVERAGES THAT MAKE YOU
喧闹起来
I brought you some supper. But if you'd prefer a lecture I have a few very catchy ones prepped.
What did I say to you about bringing into my shuttle?
MANY AN IMPULSIVE
SIN AND HELLFIRE. ONE HAS LEPERS.
DEN OF
MAN OF THE HO
Big tough veteran. Now you go
Only I think you're still a sergeant
Sergeant Malcolm
Preacher, don't
pretty specific
Quite specific
青日

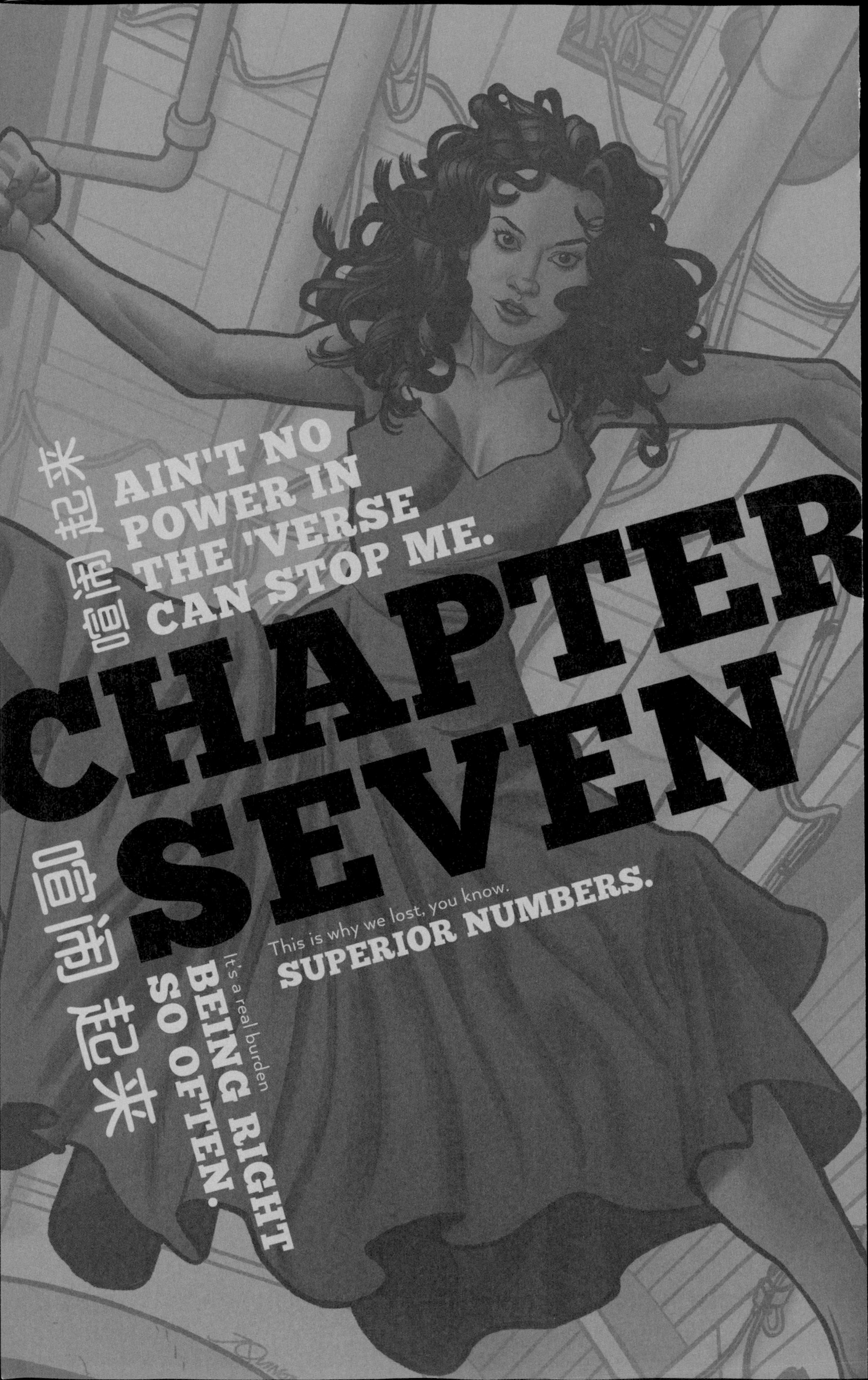
AIN'T NO POWER IN THE 'VERSE CAN STOP ME.
CHAPTER SEVEN
This is why we lost, you know. SUPERIOR NUMBERS.
It's a real burden BEING RIGHT SO OFTEN.

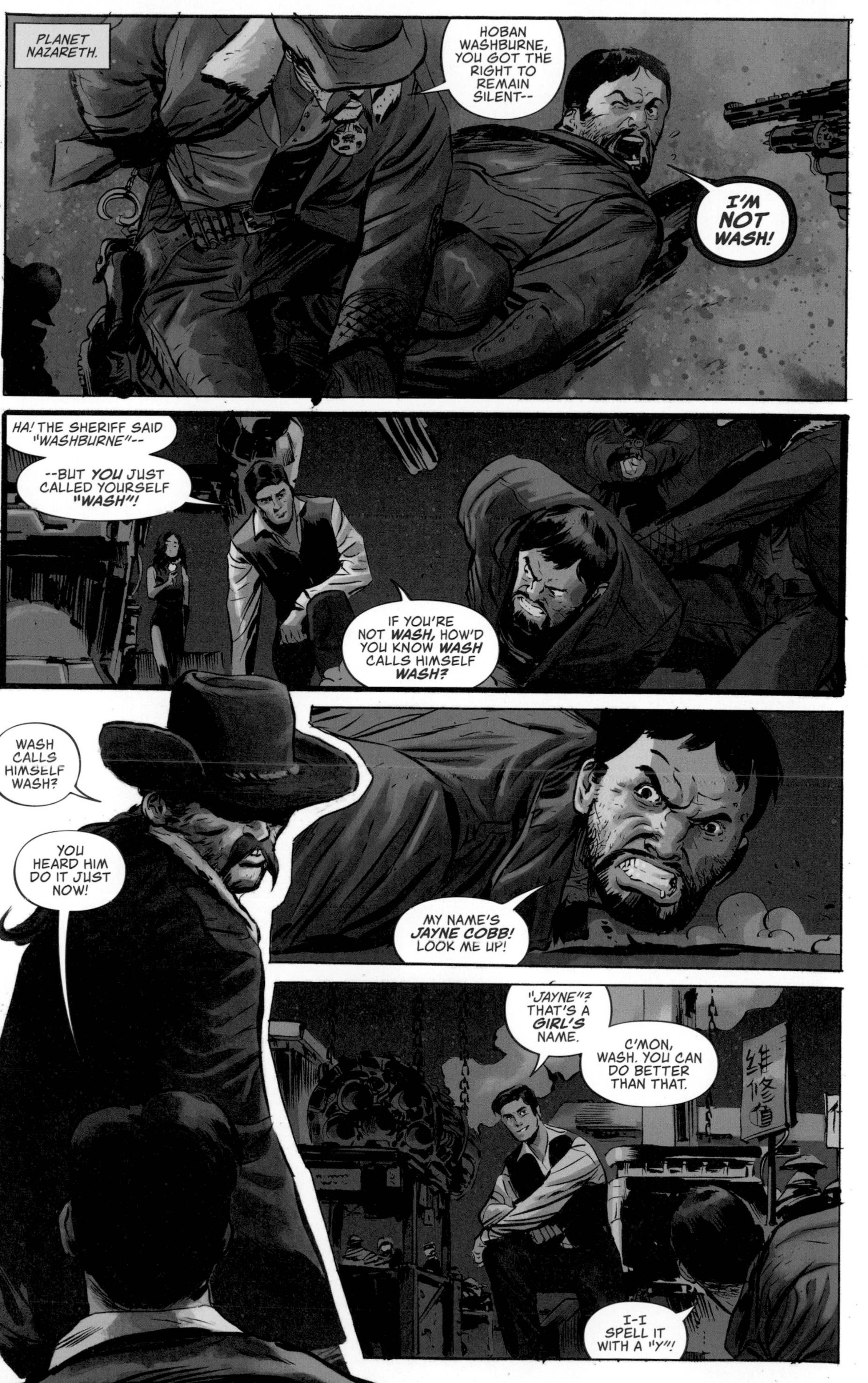
PLANET NAZARETH.
HOBAN WASHBURNE, YOU GOT THE RIGHT TO REMAIN SILENT--
I'M NOT WASH!
HA! THE SHERIFF SAID "WASHBURNE"--
--BUT YOU JUST CALLED YOURSELF "WASH"!
IF YOU'RE NOT WASH, HOW'D YOU KNOW WASH CALLS HIMSELF WASH?
WASH CALLS HIMSELF WASH?
YOU HEARD HIM DO IT JUST NOW!
MY NAME'S JAYNE COBB! LOOK ME UP!
"JAYNE"? THAT'S A GIRL'S NAME.
C'MON, WASH. YOU CAN DO BETTER THAN THAT.
I-I SPELL IT WITH A "Y"!

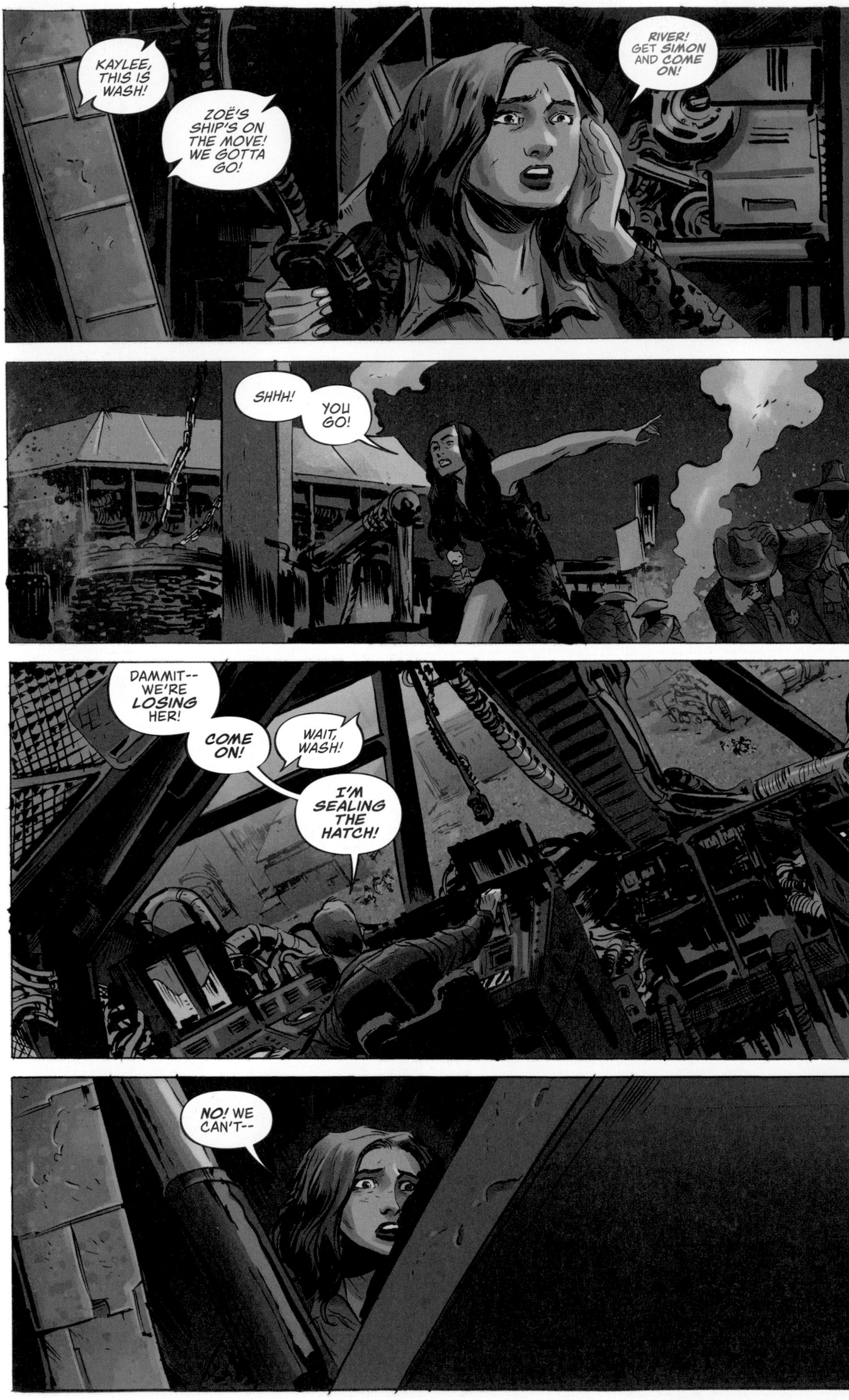
KAYLEE, THIS IS WASH!
ZOË'S SHIP'S ON THE MOVE! WE GOTTA GO!
RIVER! GET SIMON AND COME ON!
SHHH!
YOU GO!
DAMMIT-- WE'RE LOSING HER!
COME ON!
WAIT, WASH!
I'M SEALING THE HATCH!
NO! WE CAN'T--

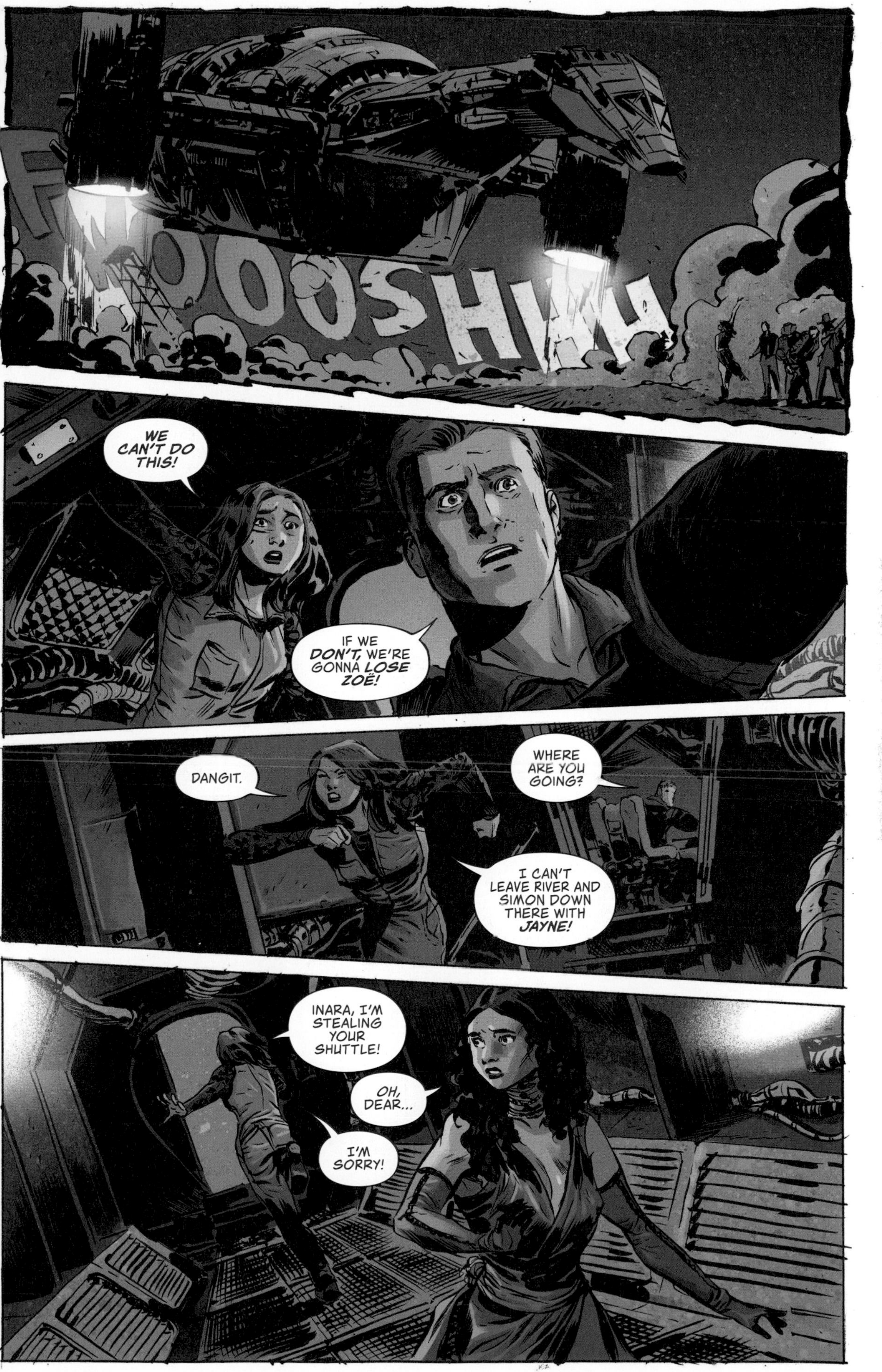
FWOOOOSHHH
WE CAN'T DO THIS!
IF WE DON'T, WE'RE GONNA LOSE ZOË!
DANGIT.
WHERE ARE YOU GOING?
I CAN'T LEAVE RIVER AND SIMON DOWN THERE WITH JAYNE!
INARA, I'M STEALING YOUR SHUTTLE!
OH, DEAR...
I'M SORRY!

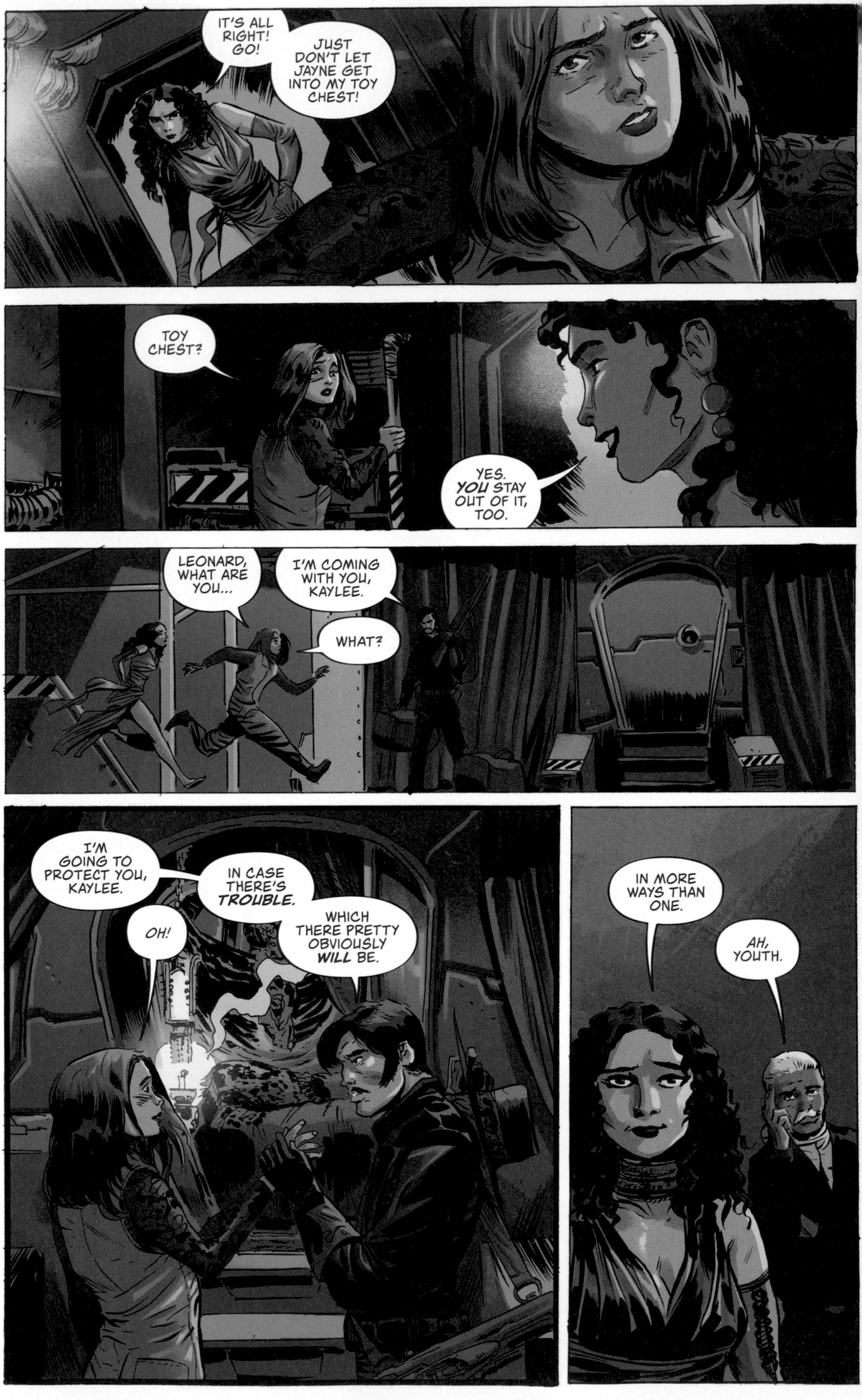
IT'S ALL RIGHT! GO!
JUST DON'T LET JAYNE GET INTO MY TOY CHEST!
TOY CHEST?
YES. ***YOU*** STAY OUT OF IT, TOO.
LEONARD, WHAT ARE YOU...
I'M COMING WITH YOU, KAYLEE.
WHAT?
I'M GOING TO PROTECT YOU, KAYLEE.
IN CASE THERE'S ***TROUBLE***.
OH!
WHICH THERE PRETTY OBVIOUSLY ***WILL*** BE.
IN MORE WAYS THAN ONE.
AH, YOUTH.

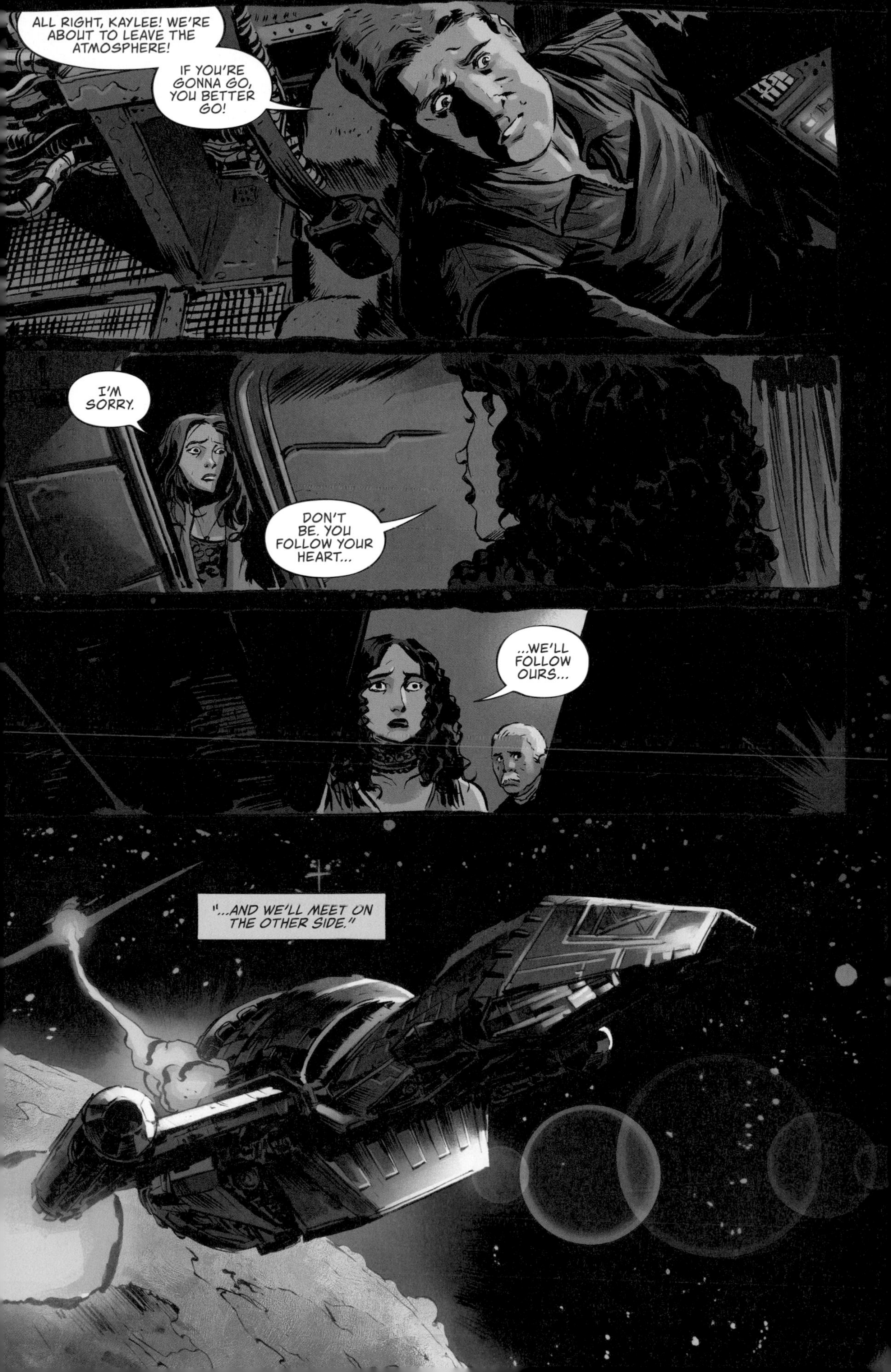
ALL RIGHT, KAYLEE! WE'RE ABOUT TO LEAVE THE ATMOSPHERE!
IF YOU'RE GONNA GO, YOU BETTER GO!
I'M SORRY.
DON'T BE. YOU FOLLOW YOUR HEART...
...WE'LL FOLLOW OURS...
"...AND WE'LL MEET ON THE OTHER SIDE."

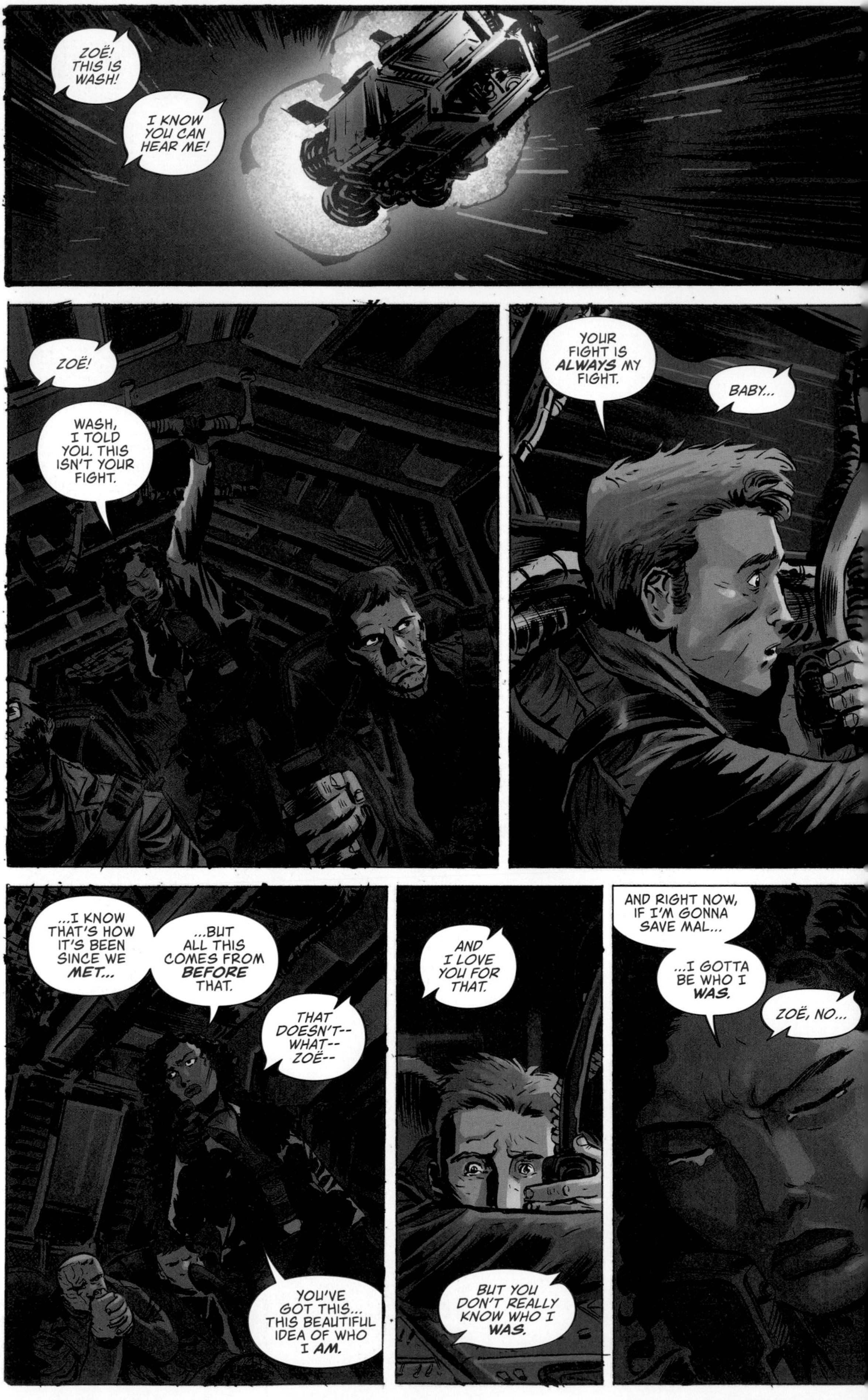
ZOË! THIS IS WASH!
I KNOW YOU CAN HEAR ME!
ZOË!
WASH, I TOLD YOU. THIS ISN'T YOUR FIGHT.
YOUR FIGHT IS ALWAYS MY FIGHT.
BABY...
...I KNOW THAT'S HOW IT'S BEEN SINCE WE MET...
...BUT ALL THIS COMES FROM BEFORE THAT.
THAT DOESN'T-- WHAT-- ZOË--
YOU'VE GOT THIS... THIS BEAUTIFUL IDEA OF WHO I AM.
AND I LOVE YOU FOR THAT.
BUT YOU DON'T REALLY KNOW WHO I WAS.
AND RIGHT NOW, IF I'M GONNA SAVE MAL...
...I GOTTA BE WHO I WAS.
ZOË, NO...

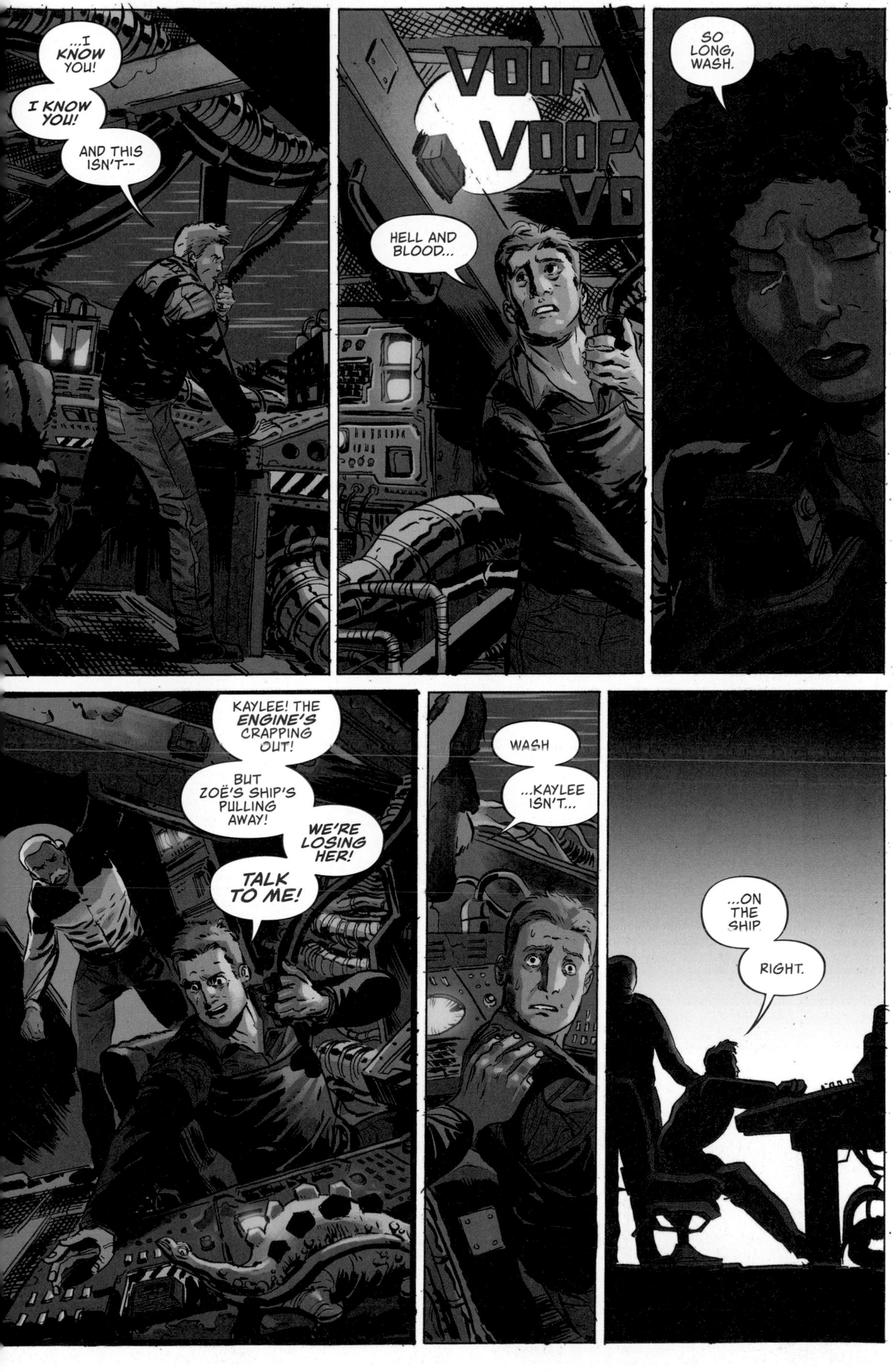
...I KNOW YOU!
I KNOW YOU!
AND THIS ISN'T--
VOOP VOOP VO
HELL AND BLOOD...
SO LONG, WASH.
KAYLEE! THE ENGINE'S CRAPPING OUT!
BUT ZOË'S SHIP'S PULLING AWAY!
WE'RE LOSING HER!
TALK TO ME!
WASH
...KAYLEE ISN'T...
...ON THE SHIP.
RIGHT.

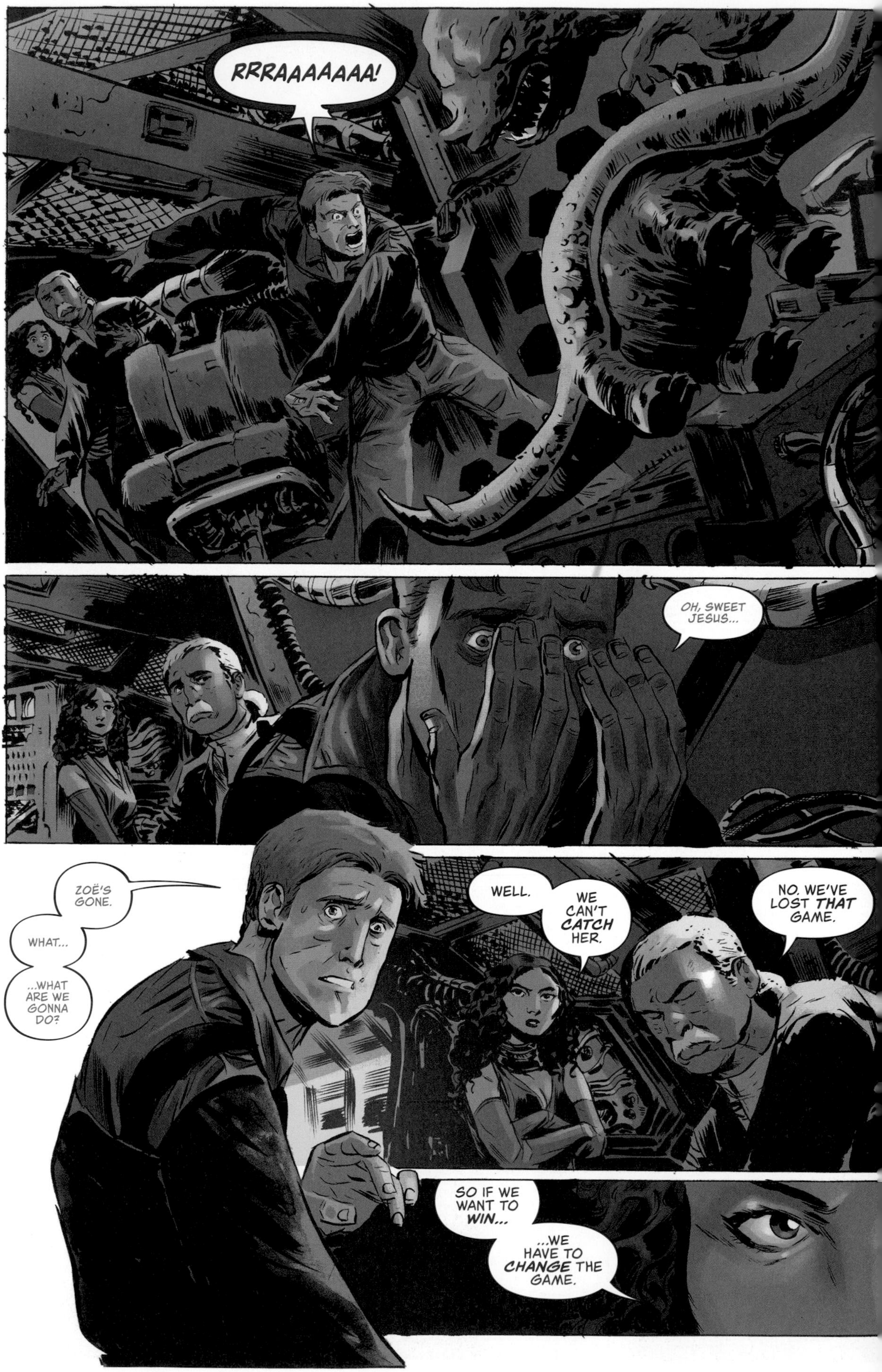
RRRAAAAAAA!
OH, SWEET JESUS...
ZOË'S GONE.
WHAT...
...WHAT ARE WE GONNA DO?
WELL.
WE CAN'T CATCH HER.
NO. WE'VE LOST THAT GAME.
SO IF WE WANT TO WIN...
...WE HAVE TO CHANGE THE GAME.

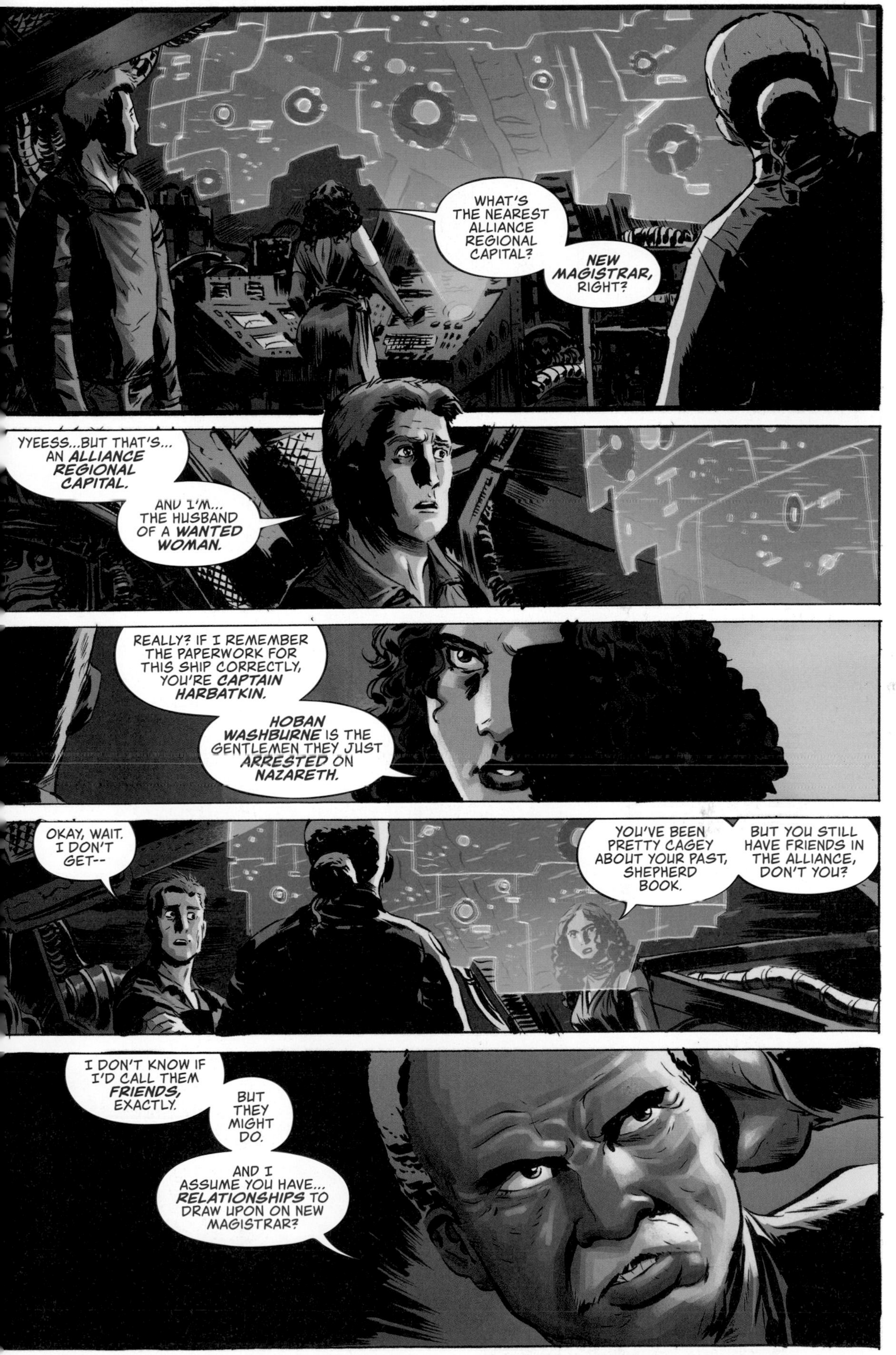
WHAT'S THE NEAREST ALLIANCE REGIONAL CAPITAL?
NEW MAGISTRAR, RIGHT?
YYEESS...BUT THAT'S... AN ALLIANCE REGIONAL CAPITAL.
AND I'M... THE HUSBAND OF A WANTED WOMAN.
REALLY? IF I REMEMBER THE PAPERWORK FOR THIS SHIP CORRECTLY, YOU'RE CAPTAIN HARBATKIN.
HOBAN WASHBURNE IS THE GENTLEMEN THEY JUST ARRESTED ON NAZARETH.
OKAY, WAIT. I DON'T GET--
YOU'VE BEEN PRETTY CAGEY ABOUT YOUR PAST, SHEPHERD BOOK.
BUT YOU STILL HAVE FRIENDS IN THE ALLIANCE, DON'T YOU?
I DON'T KNOW IF I'D CALL THEM FRIENDS, EXACTLY.
BUT THEY MIGHT DO.
AND I ASSUME YOU HAVE... RELATIONSHIPS TO DRAW UPON ON NEW MAGISTRAR?

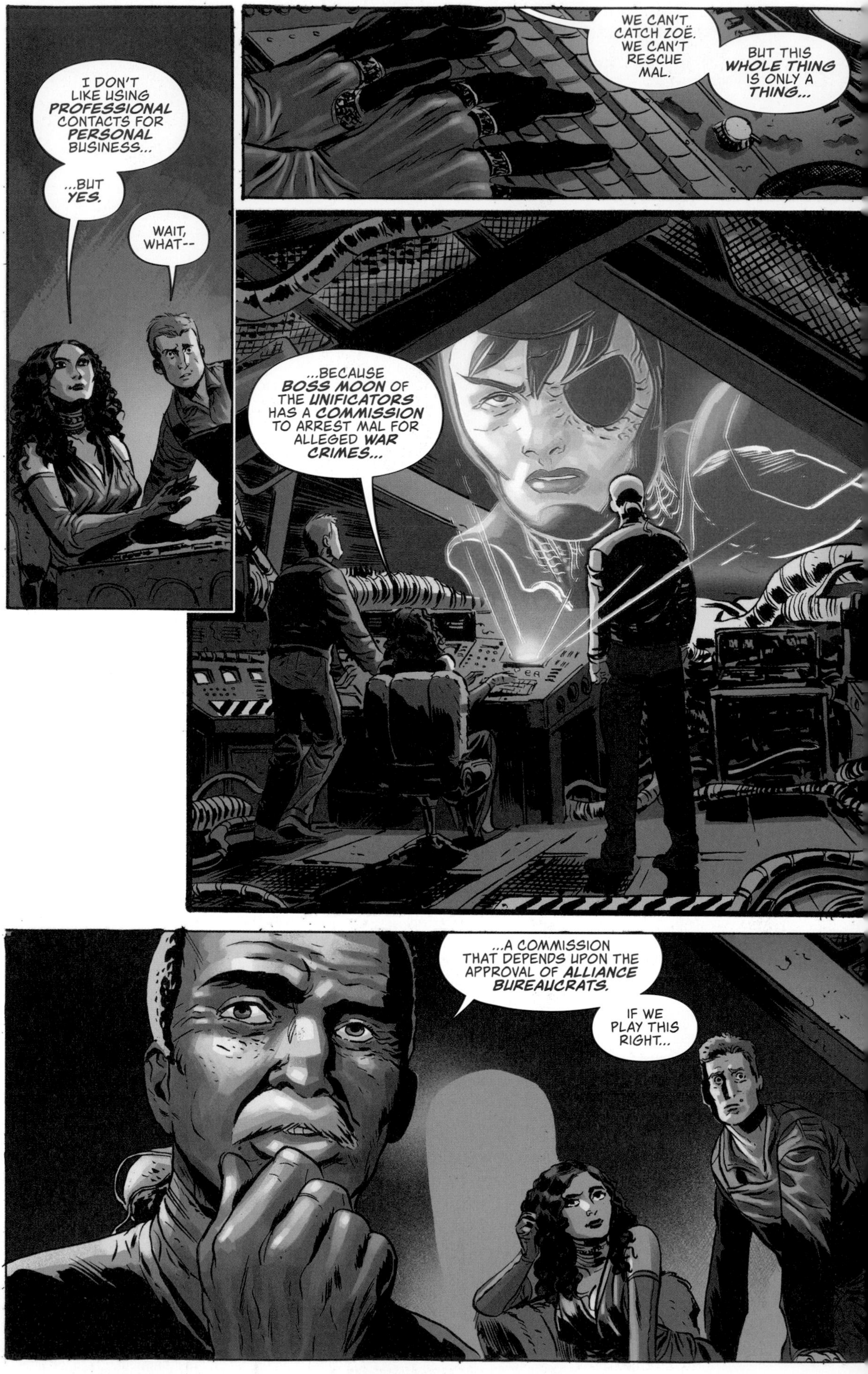
I DON'T LIKE USING PROFESSIONAL CONTACTS FOR PERSONAL BUSINESS...
...BUT YES.
WAIT, WHAT--
WE CAN'T CATCH ZOË. WE CAN'T RESCUE MAL.
BUT THIS WHOLE THING IS ONLY A THING...
...BECAUSE BOSS MOON OF THE UNIFICATORS HAS A COMMISSION TO ARREST MAL FOR ALLEGED WAR CRIMES...
...A COMMISSION THAT DEPENDS UPON THE APPROVAL OF ALLIANCE BUREAUCRATS.
IF WE PLAY THIS RIGHT...

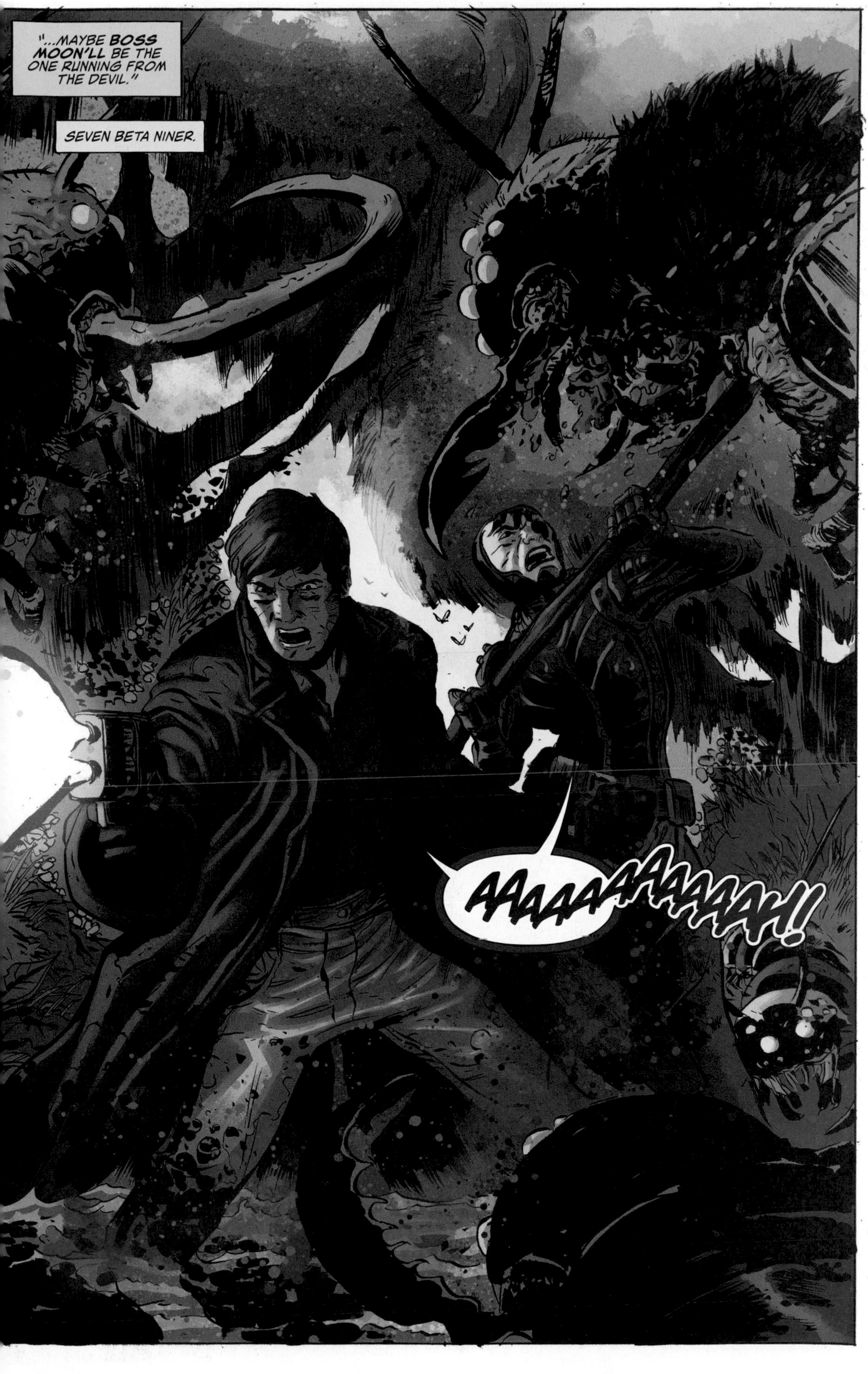
"...MAYBE BOSS MOON'LL BE THE ONE RUNNING FROM THE DEVIL."
SEVEN BETA NINER.
AAAAAAAAAAAAH!

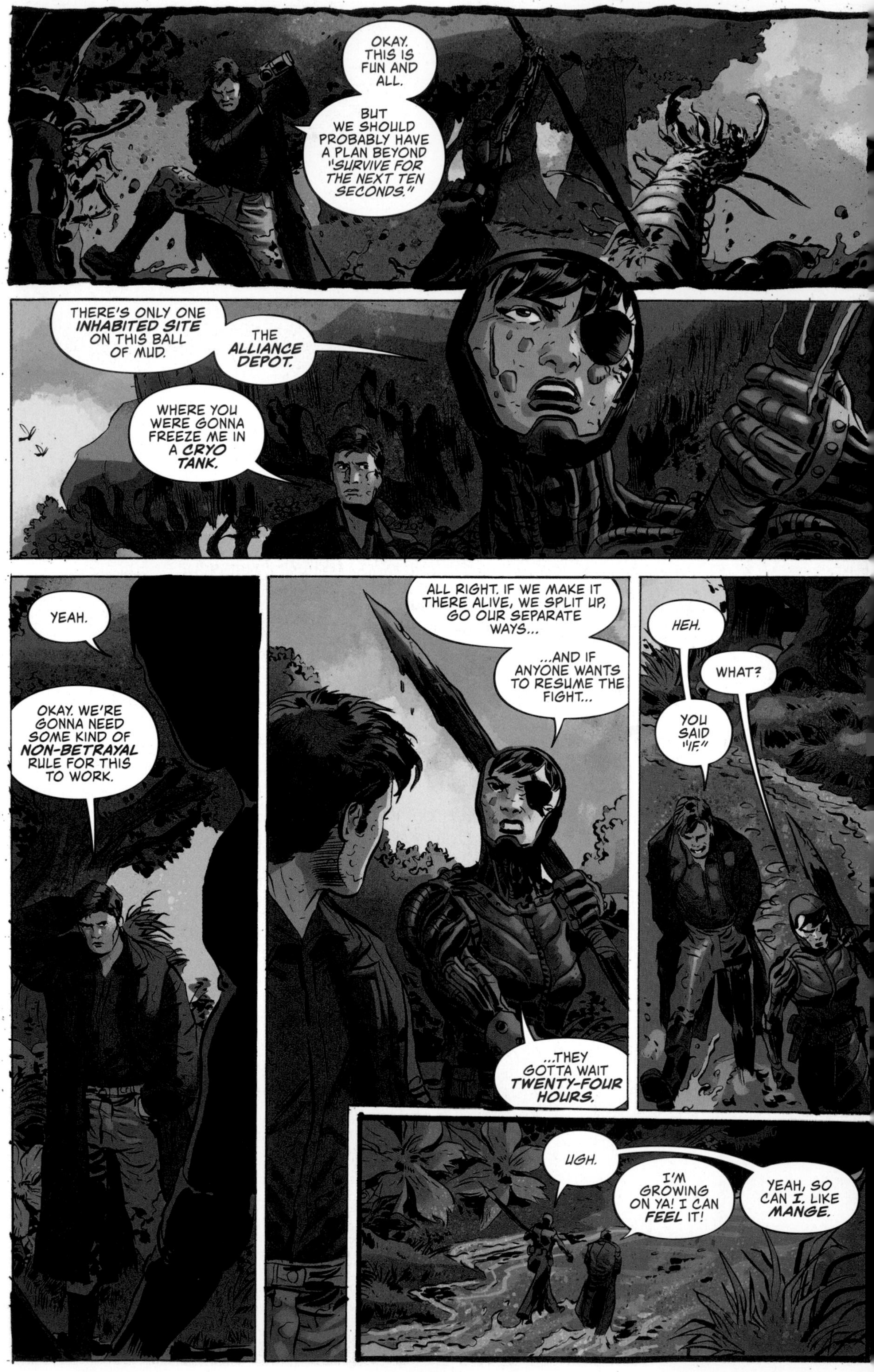
OKAY. THIS IS FUN AND ALL.
BUT WE SHOULD PROBABLY HAVE A PLAN BEYOND "SURVIVE FOR THE NEXT TEN SECONDS."
THERE'S ONLY ONE INHABITED SITE ON THIS BALL OF MUD.
THE ALLIANCE DEPOT.
WHERE YOU WERE GONNA FREEZE ME IN A CRYO TANK.
YEAH.
OKAY. WE'RE GONNA NEED SOME KIND OF NON-BETRAYAL RULE FOR THIS TO WORK.
ALL RIGHT. IF WE MAKE IT THERE ALIVE, WE SPLIT UP, GO OUR SEPARATE WAYS...
...AND IF ANYONE WANTS TO RESUME THE FIGHT...
...THEY GOTTA WAIT TWENTY-FOUR HOURS.
HEH.
WHAT?
YOU SAID "IF."
UGH.
I'M GROWING ON YA! I CAN FEEL IT!
YEAH, SO CAN I, LIKE MANGE.

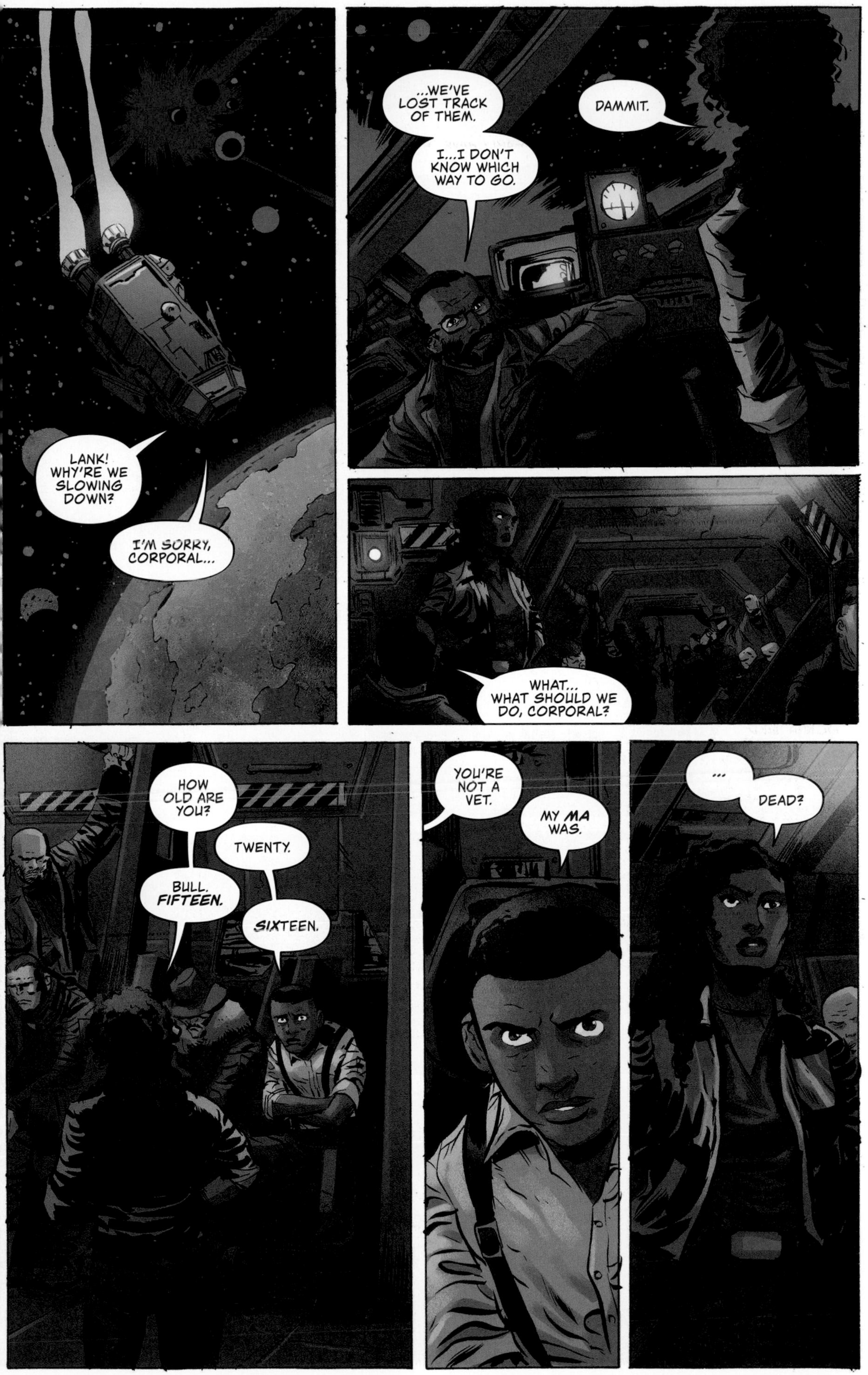
LANK! WHY'RE WE SLOWING DOWN?
I'M SORRY, CORPORAL...
...WE'VE LOST TRACK OF THEM.
I...I DON'T KNOW WHICH WAY TO GO.
DAMMIT.
WHAT... WHAT SHOULD WE DO, CORPORAL?
HOW OLD ARE YOU?
TWENTY.
BULL. FIFTEEN.
SIXTEEN.
YOU'RE NOT A VET.
MY MA WAS.
...
DEAD?

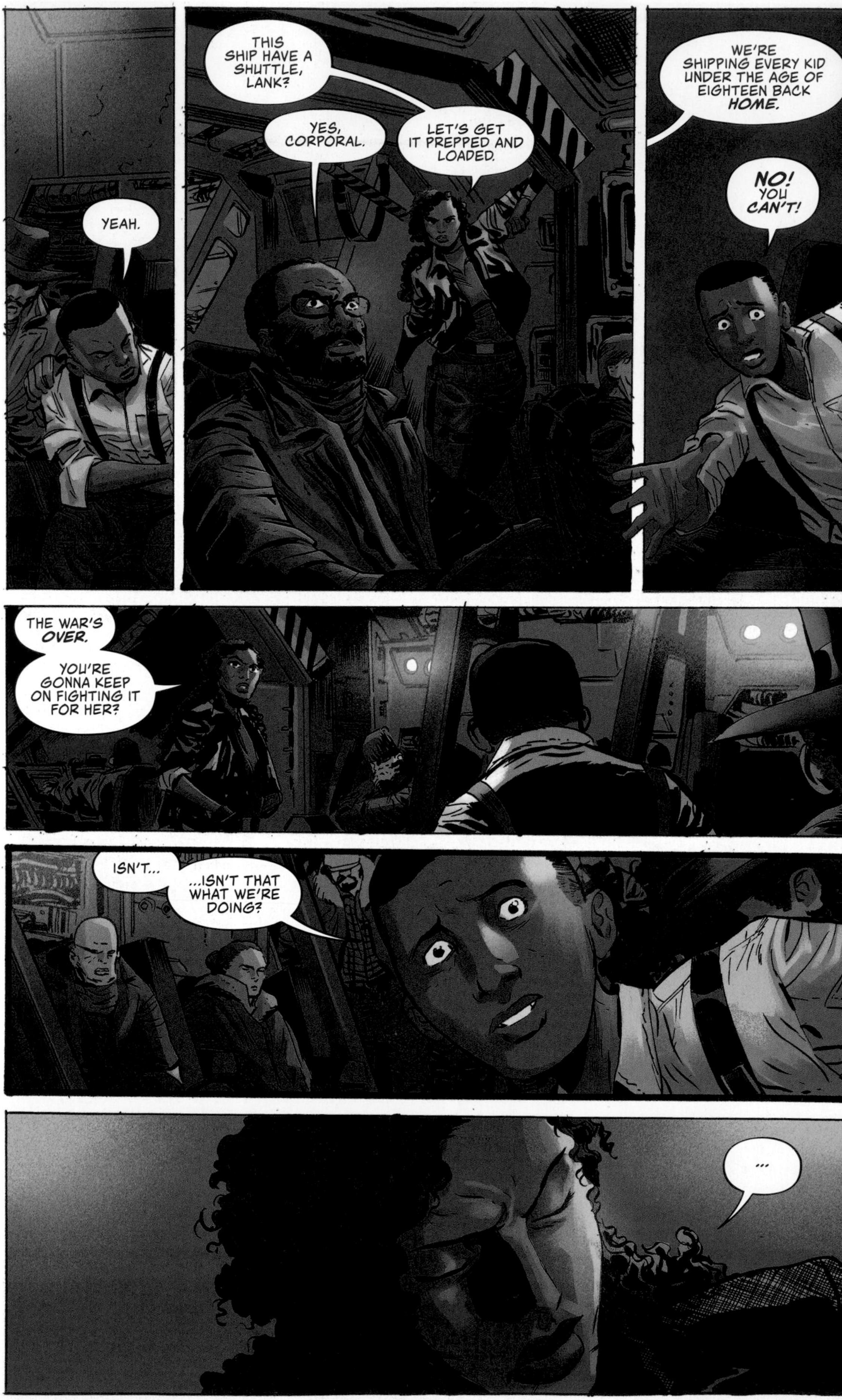
YEAH.
THIS SHIP HAVE A SHUTTLE, LANK?
YES, CORPORAL.
LET'S GET IT PREPPED AND LOADED.
WE'RE SHIPPING EVERY KID UNDER THE AGE OF EIGHTEEN BACK HOME.
NO! YOU CAN'T!
THE WAR'S OVER.
YOU'RE GONNA KEEP ON FIGHTING IT FOR HER?
ISN'T...
...ISN'T THAT WHAT WE'RE DOING?
...

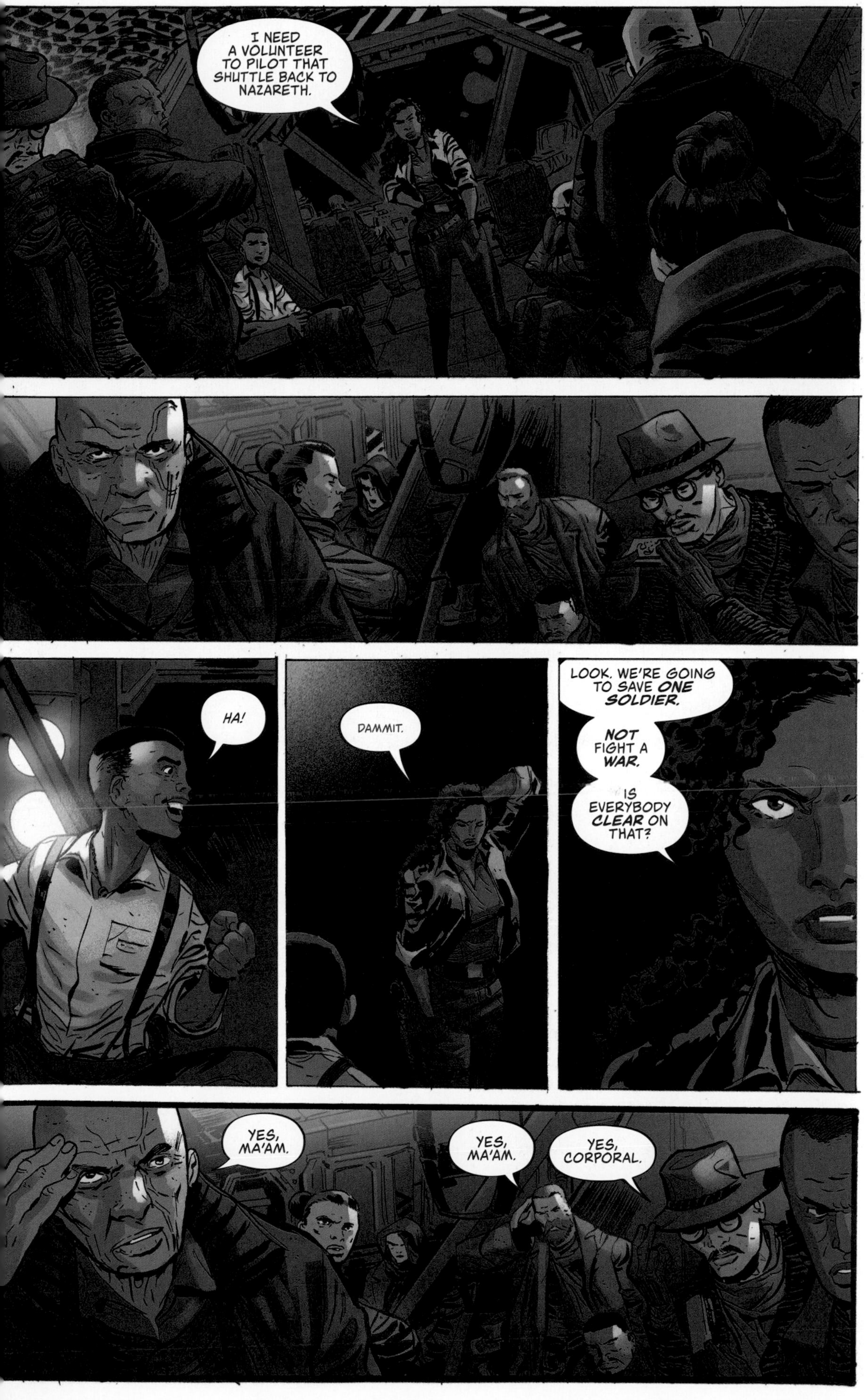
I NEED A VOLUNTEER TO PILOT THAT SHUTTLE BACK TO NAZARETH.
HA!
DAMMIT.
LOOK. WE'RE GOING TO SAVE ONE SOLDIER.
NOT FIGHT A WAR.
IS EVERYBODY CLEAR ON THAT?
YES, MA'AM.
YES, MA'AM.
YES, CORPORAL.

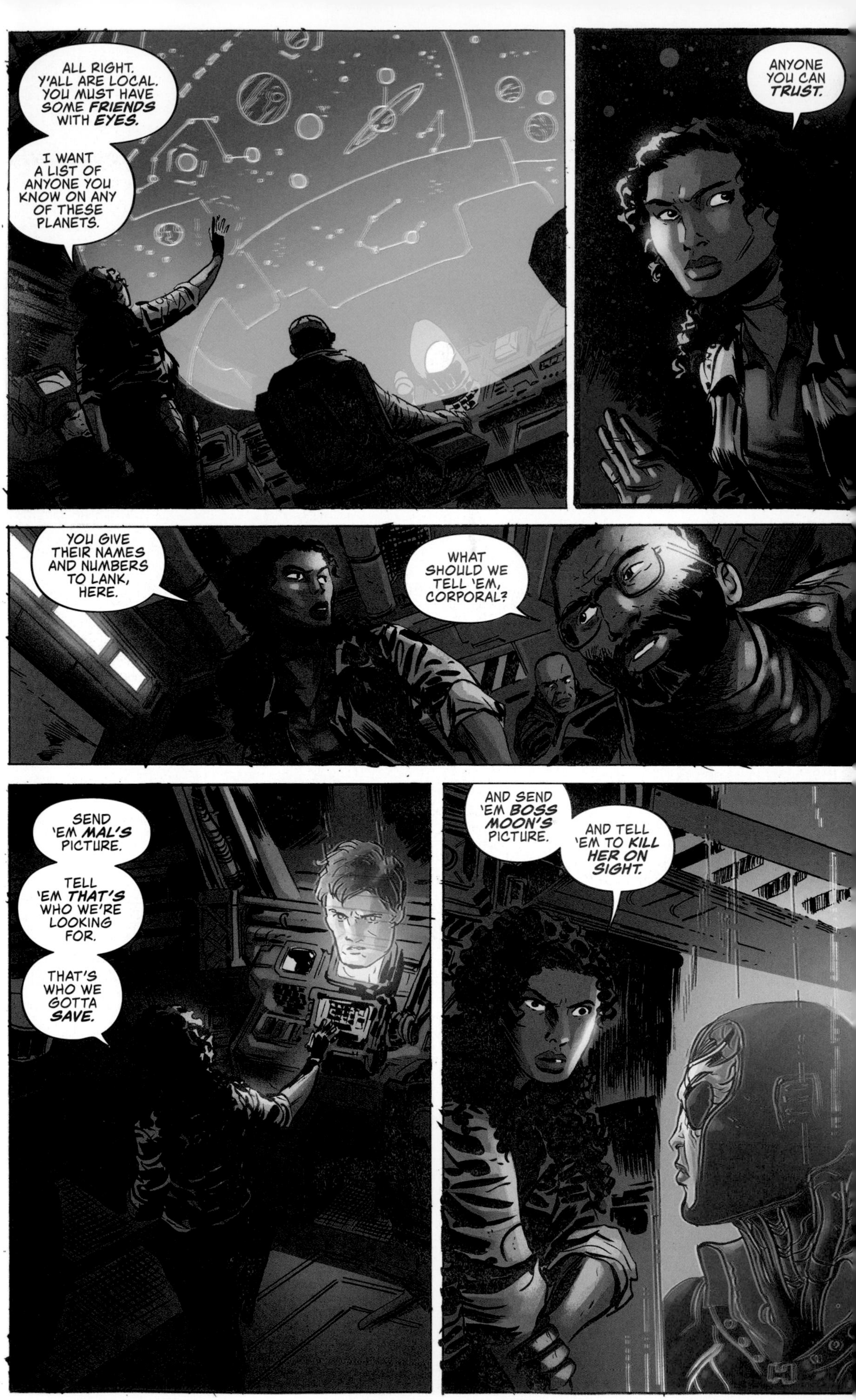
ALL RIGHT. Y'ALL ARE LOCAL. YOU MUST HAVE SOME FRIENDS WITH EYES.
I WANT A LIST OF ANYONE YOU KNOW ON ANY OF THESE PLANETS.
ANYONE YOU CAN TRUST.
YOU GIVE THEIR NAMES AND NUMBERS TO LANK, HERE.
WHAT SHOULD WE TELL 'EM, CORPORAL?
SEND 'EM MAL'S PICTURE.
TELL 'EM THAT'S WHO WE'RE LOOKING FOR.
THAT'S WHO WE GOTTA SAVE.
AND SEND 'EM BOSS MOON'S PICTURE.
AND TELL 'EM TO KILL HER ON SIGHT.

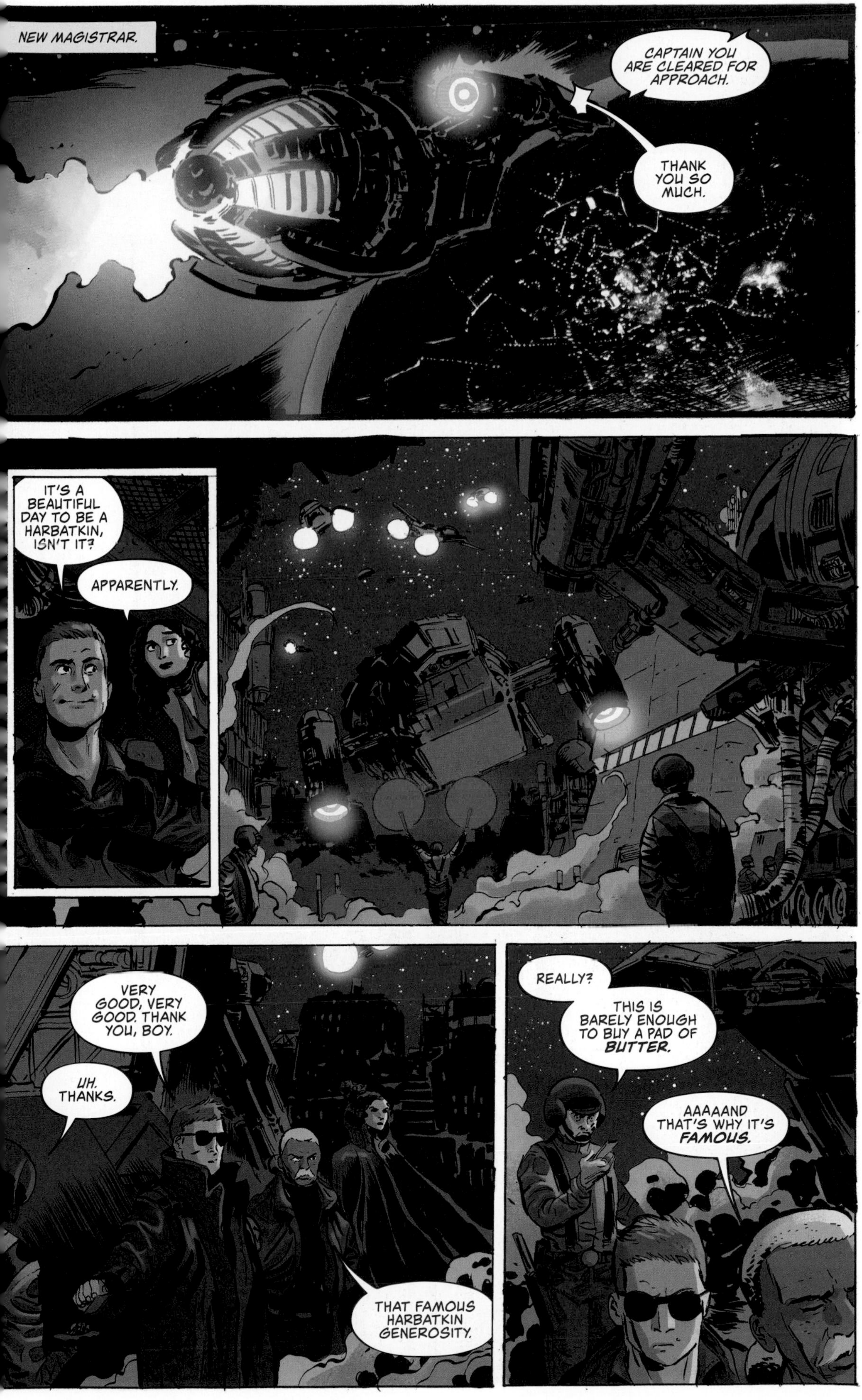
NEW MAGISTRAR.
CAPTAIN YOU ARE CLEARED FOR APPROACH.
THANK YOU SO MUCH.
IT'S A BEAUTIFUL DAY TO BE A HARBATKIN, ISN'T IT?
APPARENTLY.
VERY GOOD, VERY GOOD. THANK YOU, BOY.
UH. THANKS.
THAT FAMOUS HARBATKIN GENEROSITY.
REALLY?
THIS IS BARELY ENOUGH TO BUY A PAD OF BUTTER.
AAAAAND THAT'S WHY IT'S FAMOUS.

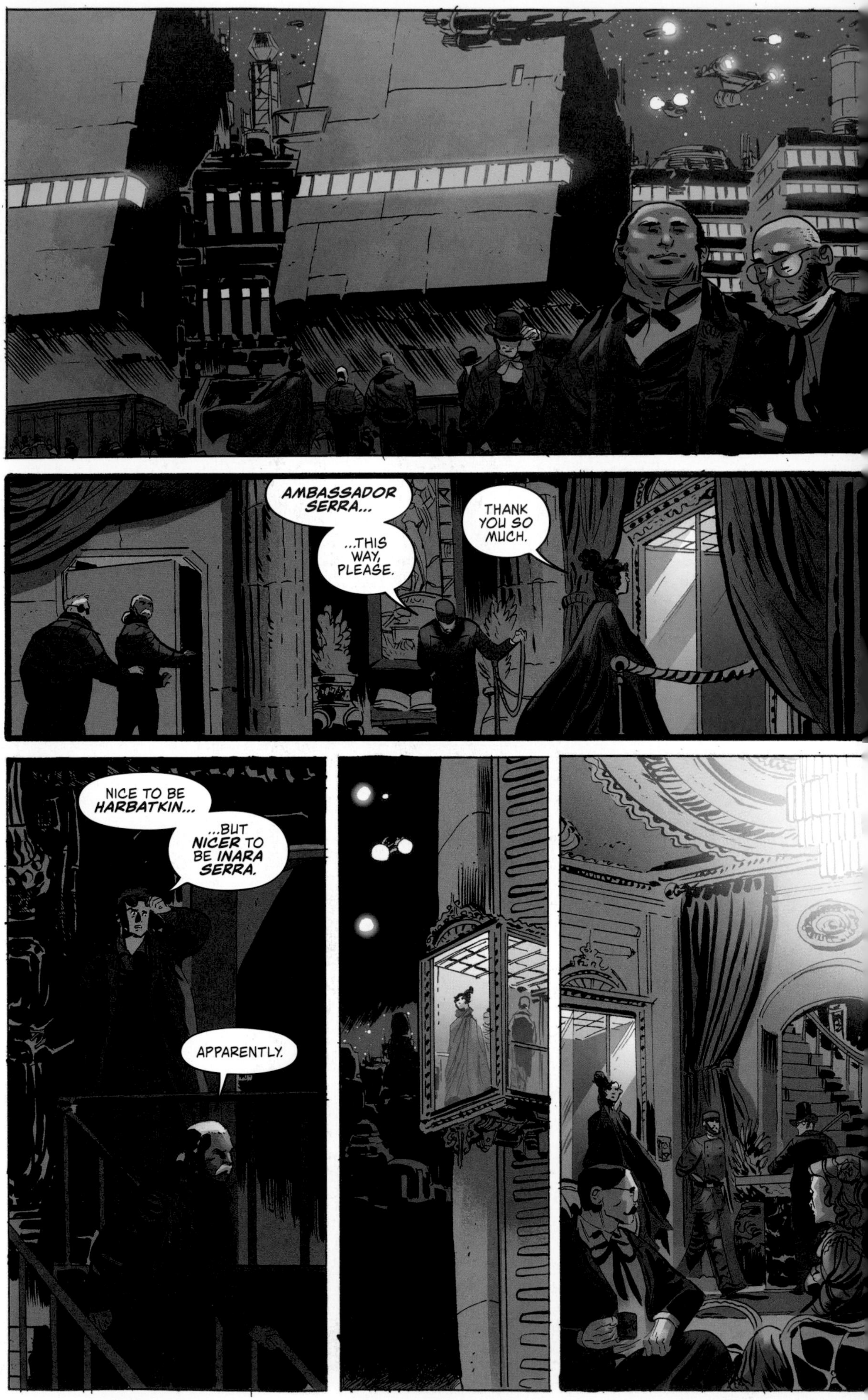
AMBASSADOR SERRA...
...THIS WAY, PLEASE.
THANK YOU SO MUCH.
NICE TO BE HARBATKIN...
...BUT NICER TO BE INARA SERRA.
APPARENTLY.

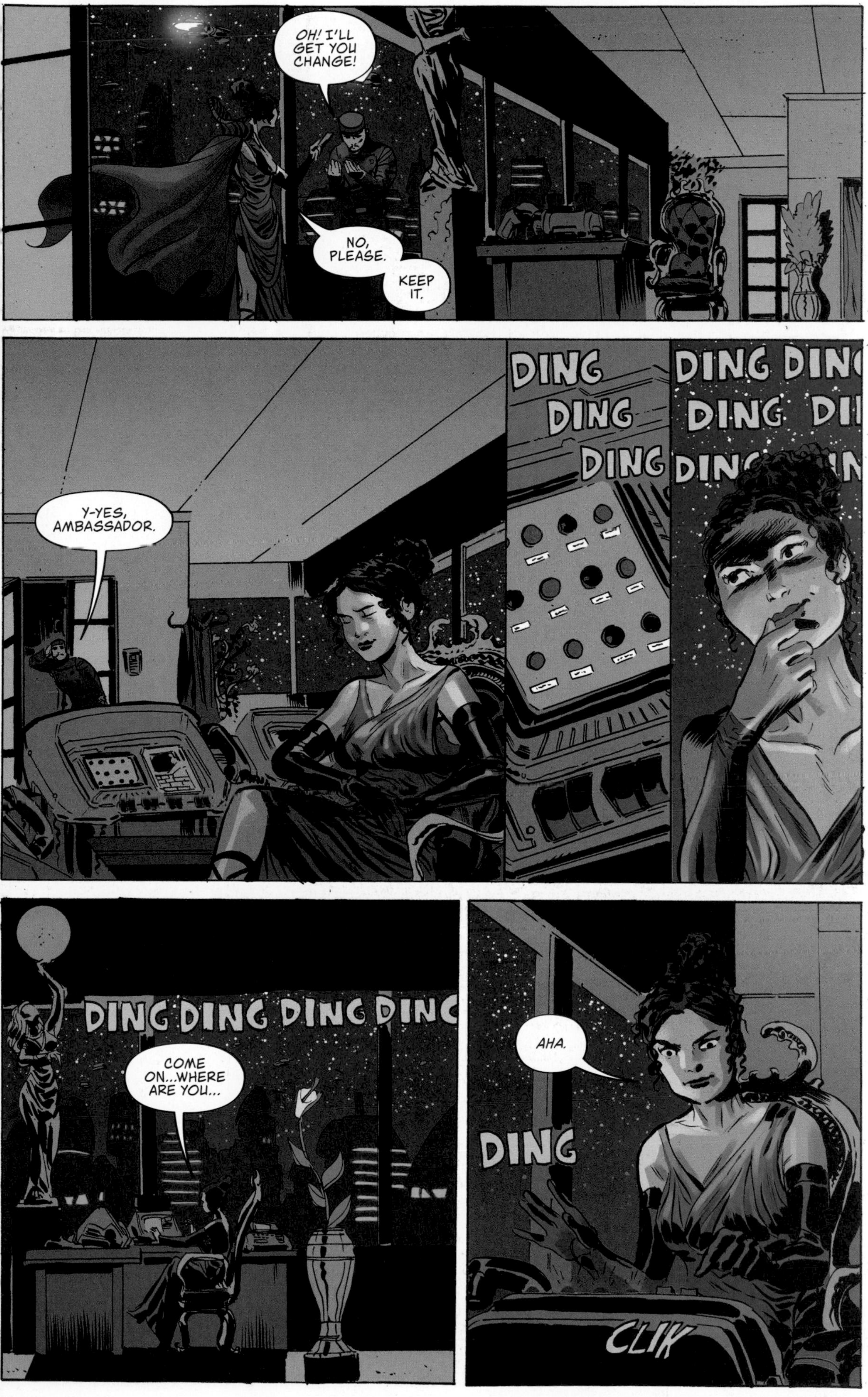
OH! I'LL GET YOU CHANGE!
NO, PLEASE.
KEEP IT.
Y-YES, AMBASSADOR.
DING
DING
DING
DING DING
DING
COME ON...WHERE ARE YOU...
DING DING DING
AHA.
DING
CLIK

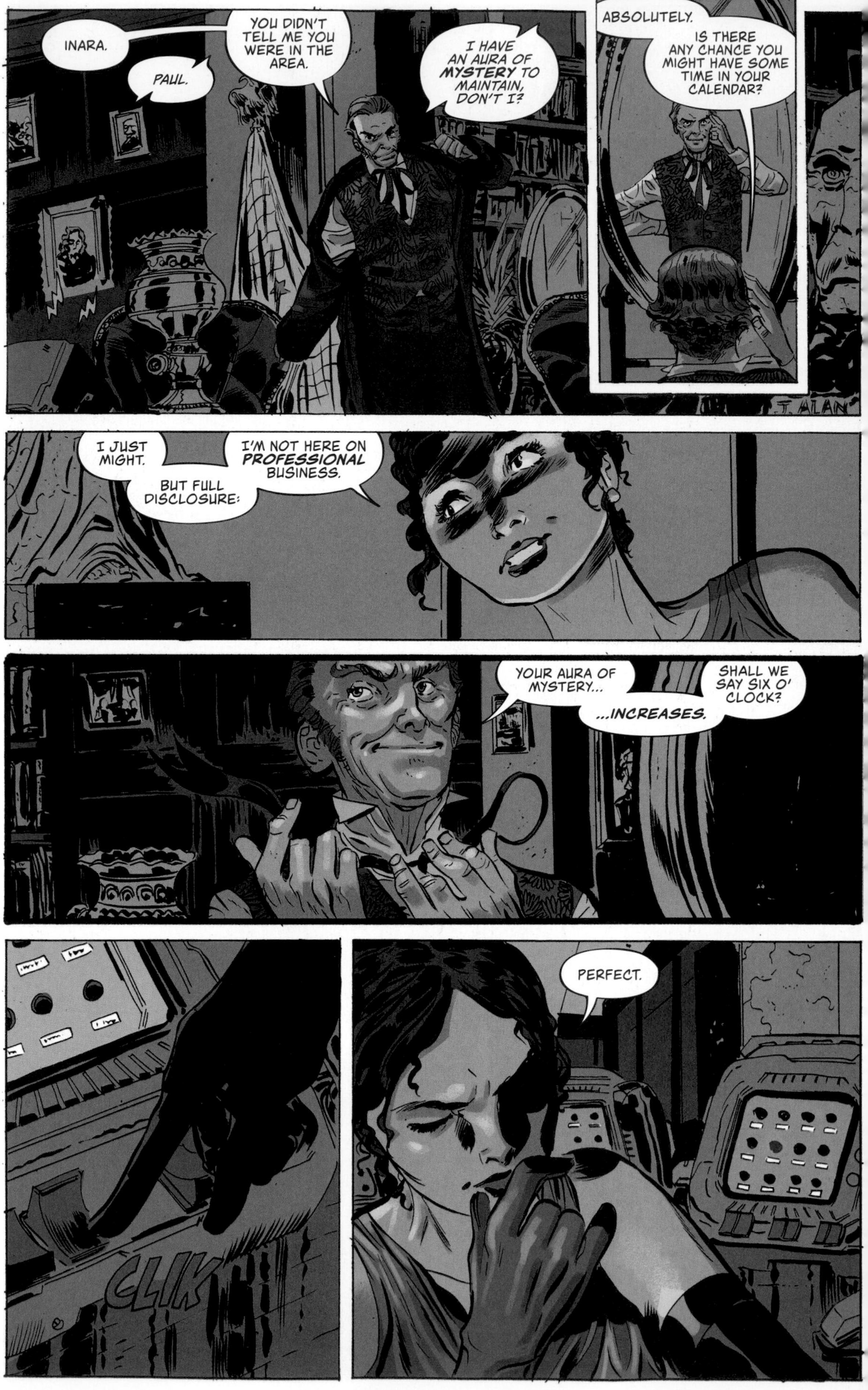
INARA.
PAUL.
YOU DIDN'T TELL ME YOU WERE IN THE AREA.
I HAVE AN AURA OF MYSTERY TO MAINTAIN, DON'T I?
ABSOLUTELY.
IS THERE ANY CHANCE YOU MIGHT HAVE SOME TIME IN YOUR CALENDAR?
J. ALAN
I JUST MIGHT.
BUT FULL DISCLOSURE:
I'M NOT HERE ON PROFESSIONAL BUSINESS.
YOUR AURA OF MYSTERY...
...INCREASES.
SHALL WE SAY SIX O' CLOCK?
CLIK
PERFECT.

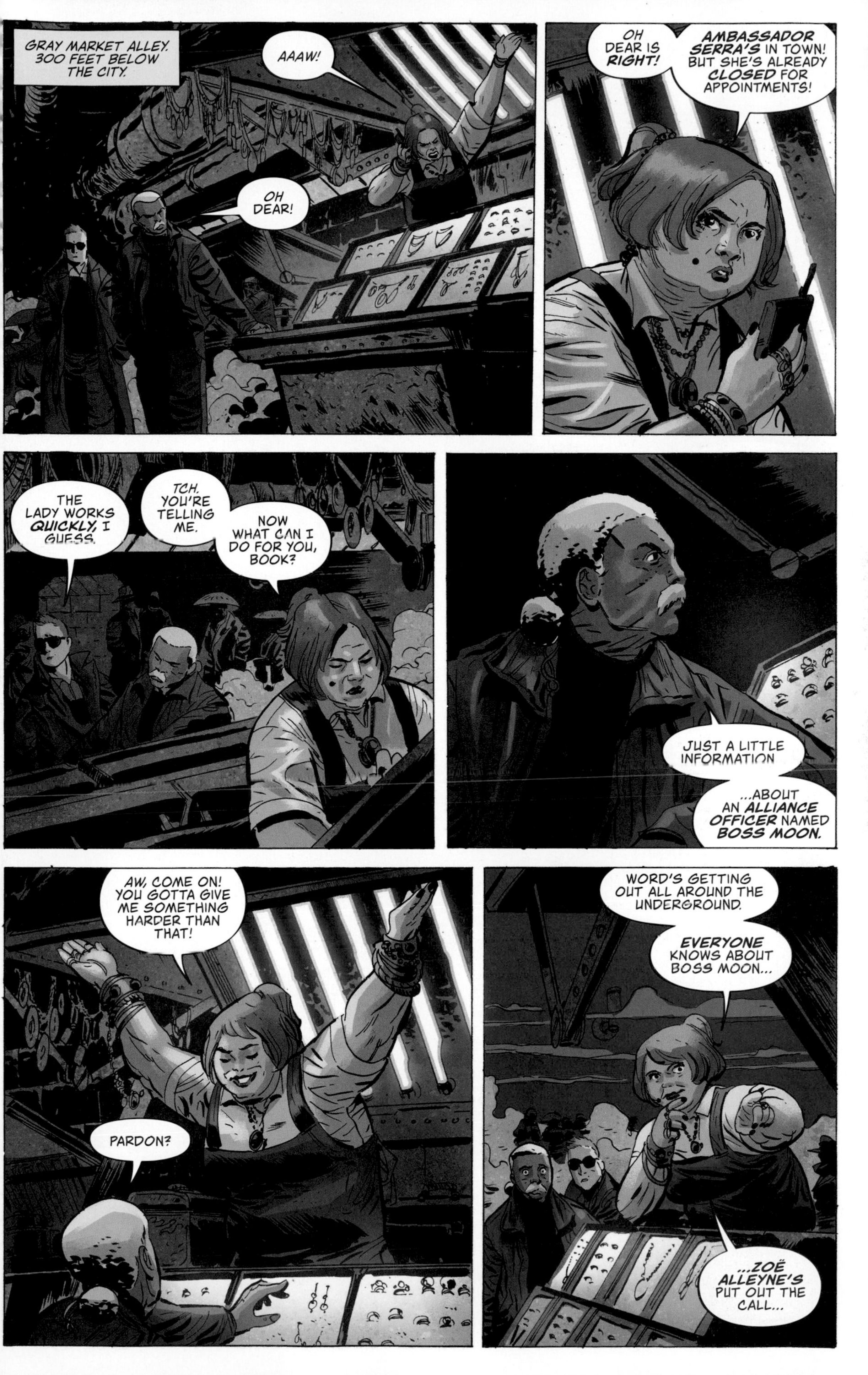
GRAY MARKET ALLEY. 300 FEET BELOW THE CITY.
AAAW!
OH DEAR!
OH DEAR IS RIGHT!
AMBASSADOR SERRA'S IN TOWN! BUT SHE'S ALREADY CLOSED FOR APPOINTMENTS!
THE LADY WORKS QUICKLY, I GUESS.
TCH. YOU'RE TELLING ME.
NOW WHAT CAN I DO FOR YOU, BOOK?
JUST A LITTLE INFORMATION
...ABOUT AN ALLIANCE OFFICER NAMED BOSS MOON.
AW, COME ON! YOU GOTTA GIVE ME SOMETHING HARDER THAN THAT!
PARDON?
WORD'S GETTING OUT ALL AROUND THE UNDERGROUND.
EVERYONE KNOWS ABOUT BOSS MOON...
...ZOË ALLEYNE'S PUT OUT THE CALL...

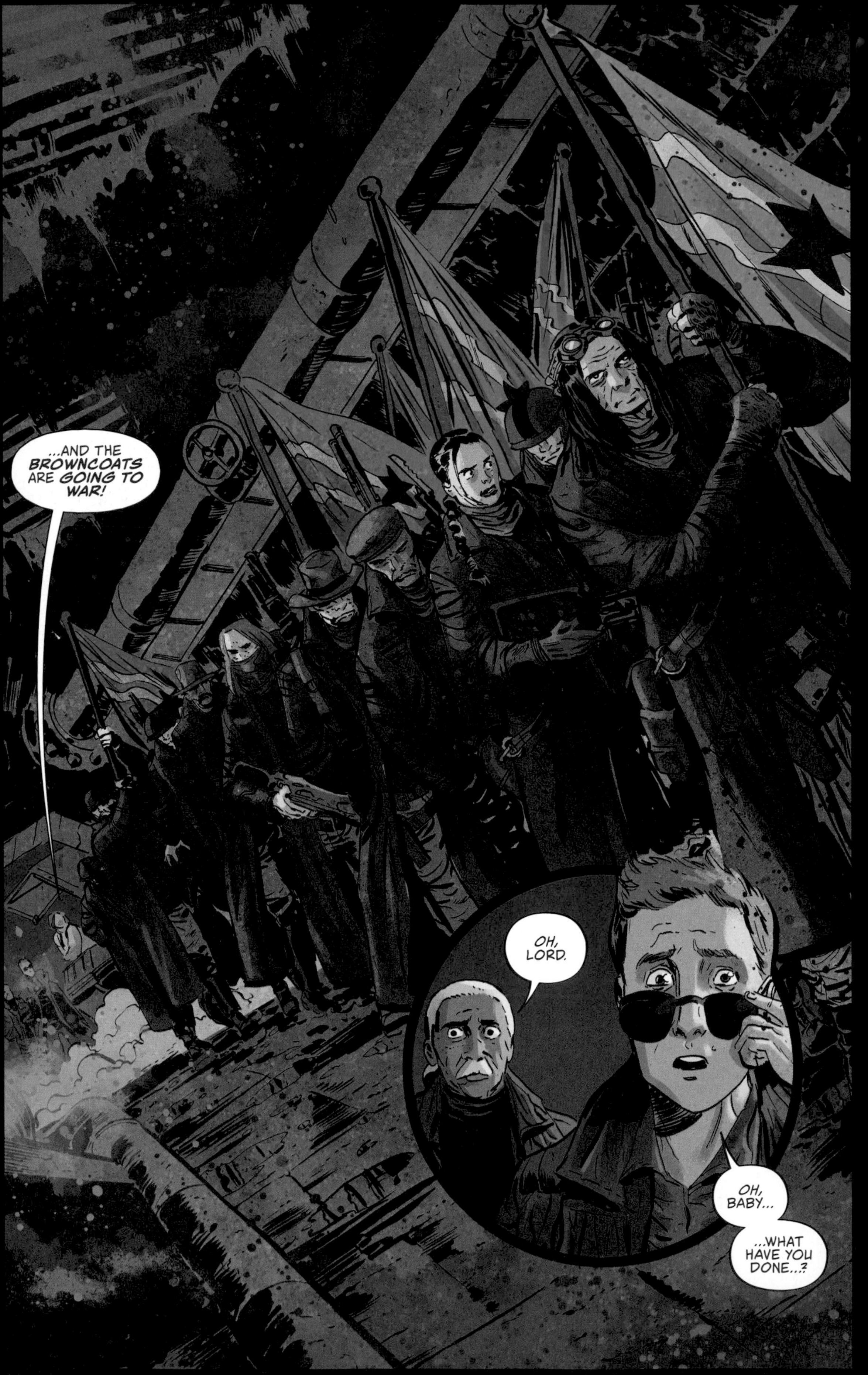
...AND THE BROWNCOATS ARE GOING TO WAR!
OH, LORD.
OH, BABY...
...WHAT HAVE YOU DONE...?

WE'VE GOT US SOME CRIME TO BE DONE.

THAT MAKES US SPE...

...spot, sir. She still has the...

...ow why? Because we are so very pretty. We are just too pretty for God to let us die.

I don't believe there's a power in the 'Verse can stop Kaylee from being cheerful. Sometimes you just w...

And I'm thinking you weren't burdened with an overabundance of schooling. So why don't we just...

Ship like this will be with you 'til the day you die. That's cause it's a death trap.

Sir, I think you have a problem with your brain being missing.

Seems to me the last time there was a chance for a little palaver we were all manner of...

This ain't bad. There's a trick to it. Wood alcohol. Now we're favored guests treated to...

YOU'RE LOS...

WE ALL AR...

喧闹 起来

...D IN MY AWFUL SKY.

This is why w... lost, you kno...

SUPE...

INEVITABLE BETRAYAL.

WE'D BE DEAD.

Curse your sudden but...

Can't get paid if you're dead.

喧闹 起...

CA... HA... YO... SH...

It's a real burden... BEING RIGHT

...US SO

fruity oaty bar!

FINEST IN BEVERAGES THAT MAKE YOU...

喧闹 起来

What did I say to you about barging into my shuttle? The...

I brought you some supper. But if you'd prefer a lecture I have a few very catchy ones prepped.

MANLY AN...

IMPULSIVE...

BLUE SUN

青日

Preacher, don't th... pretty specific thi... Quite specific...

SIN AND HELLFIRE. ONE HAS LEPERS.

旅

DEN OF THI...

MAN OF HO...

Only I think you're still a sergeant, see?

Big, tough veteran. Now you go...

Sergeant Malcolm R...

That big...

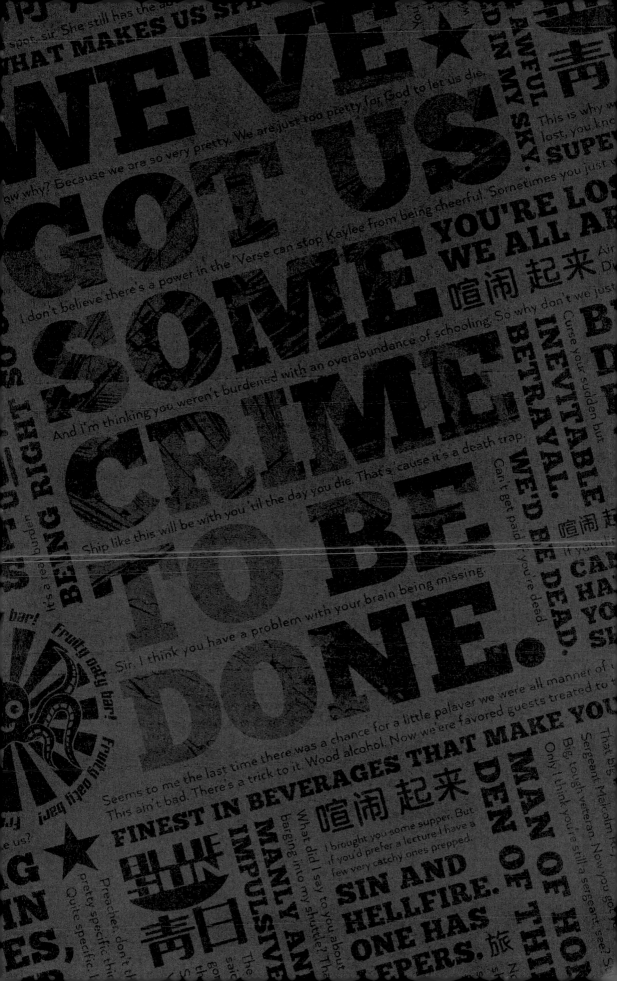

CHAPTER EIGHT

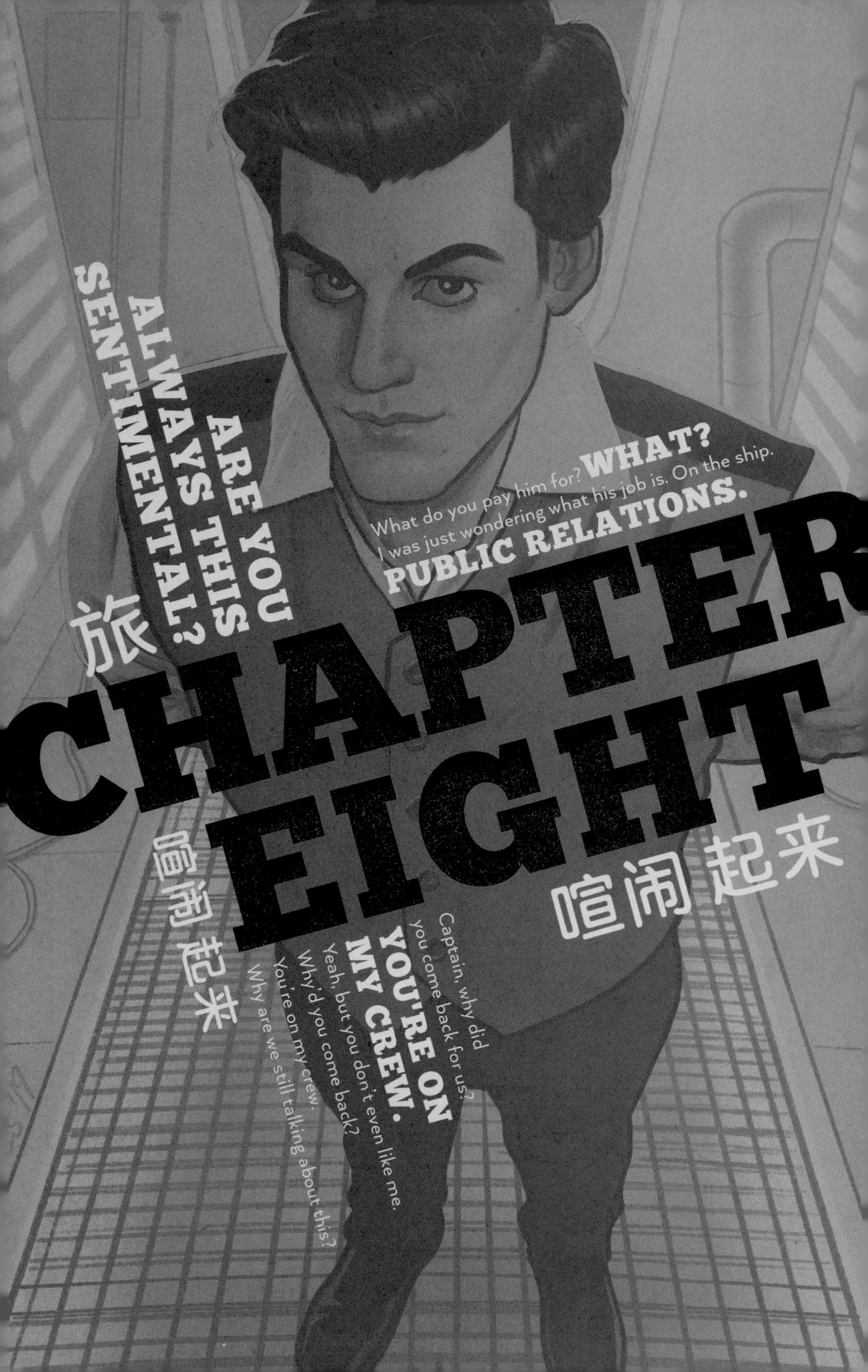

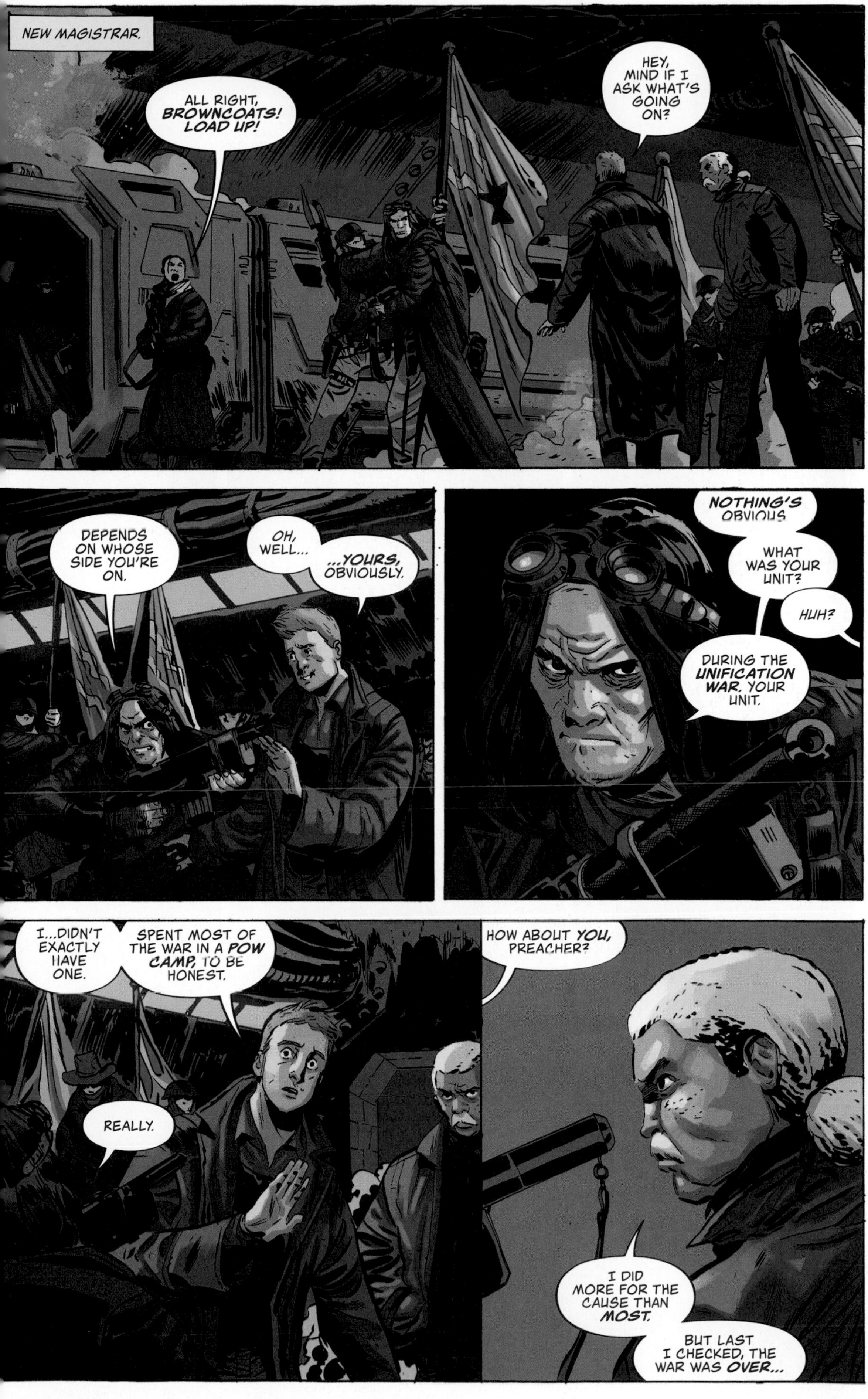
NEW MAGISTRAR.
ALL RIGHT, BROWNCOATS! LOAD UP!
HEY, MIND IF I ASK WHAT'S GOING ON?
DEPENDS ON WHOSE SIDE YOU'RE ON.
OH, WELL...
...YOURS, OBVIOUSLY.
NOTHING'S OBVIOUS.
WHAT WAS YOUR UNIT?
HUH?
DURING THE UNIFICATION WAR. YOUR UNIT.
I...DIDN'T EXACTLY HAVE ONE.
SPENT MOST OF THE WAR IN A POW CAMP, TO BE HONEST.
REALLY.
HOW ABOUT YOU, PREACHER?
I DID MORE FOR THE CAUSE THAN MOST.
BUT LAST I CHECKED, THE WAR WAS OVER...

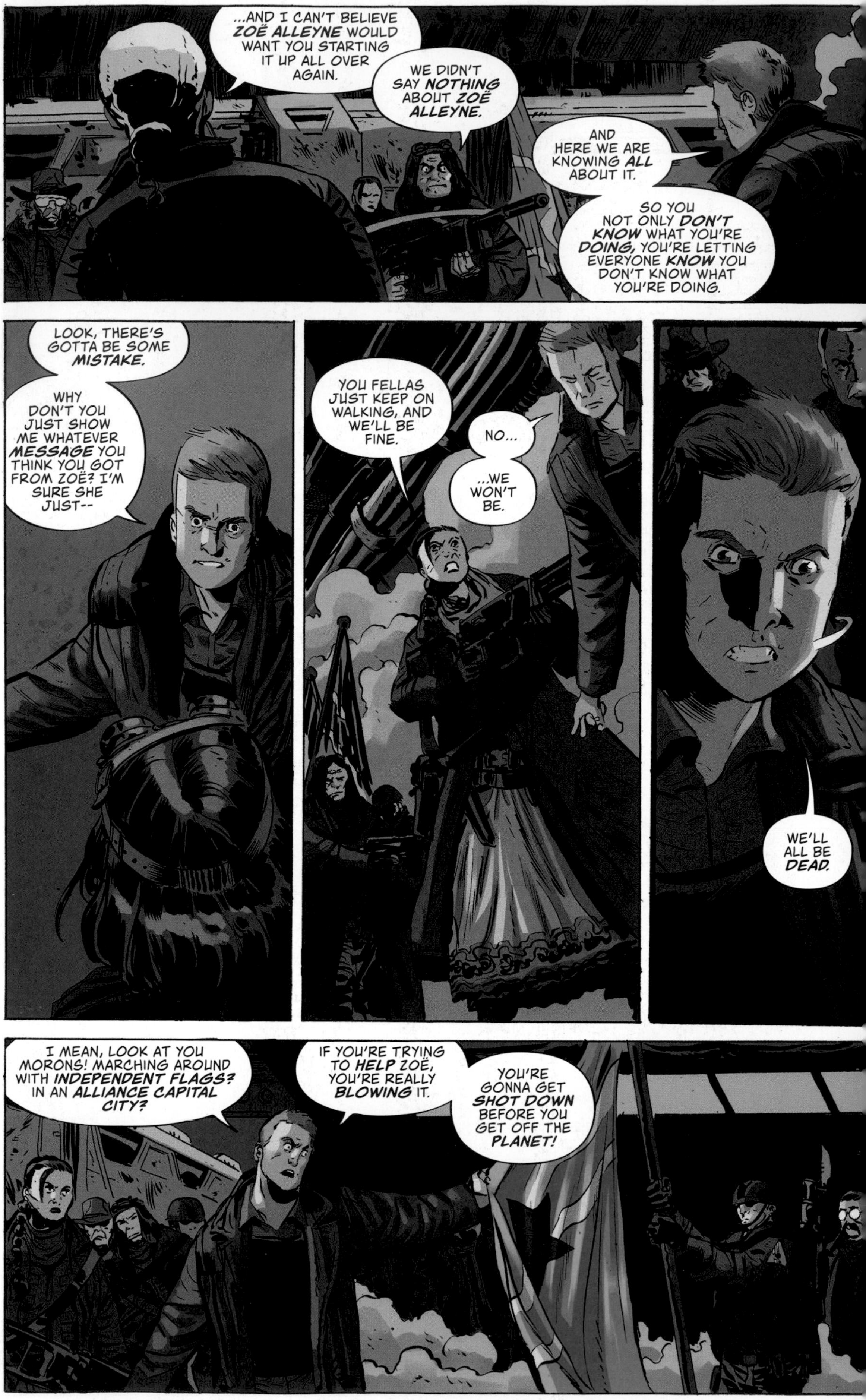
...AND I CAN'T BELIEVE ZOË ALLEYNE WOULD WANT YOU STARTING IT UP ALL OVER AGAIN.
WE DIDN'T SAY NOTHING ABOUT ZOË ALLEYNE.
AND HERE WE ARE KNOWING ALL ABOUT IT.
SO YOU NOT ONLY DON'T KNOW WHAT YOU'RE DOING, YOU'RE LETTING EVERYONE KNOW YOU DON'T KNOW WHAT YOU'RE DOING.
LOOK, THERE'S GOTTA BE SOME MISTAKE.
WHY DON'T YOU JUST SHOW ME WHATEVER MESSAGE YOU THINK YOU GOT FROM ZOË? I'M SURE SHE JUST--
YOU FELLAS JUST KEEP ON WALKING, AND WE'LL BE FINE.
NO...
...WE WON'T BE.
WE'LL ALL BE DEAD.
I MEAN, LOOK AT YOU MORONS! MARCHING AROUND WITH INDEPENDENT FLAGS? IN AN ALLIANCE CAPITAL CITY?
IF YOU'RE TRYING TO HELP ZOË, YOU'RE REALLY BLOWING IT.
YOU'RE GONNA GET SHOT DOWN BEFORE YOU GET OFF THE PLANET!

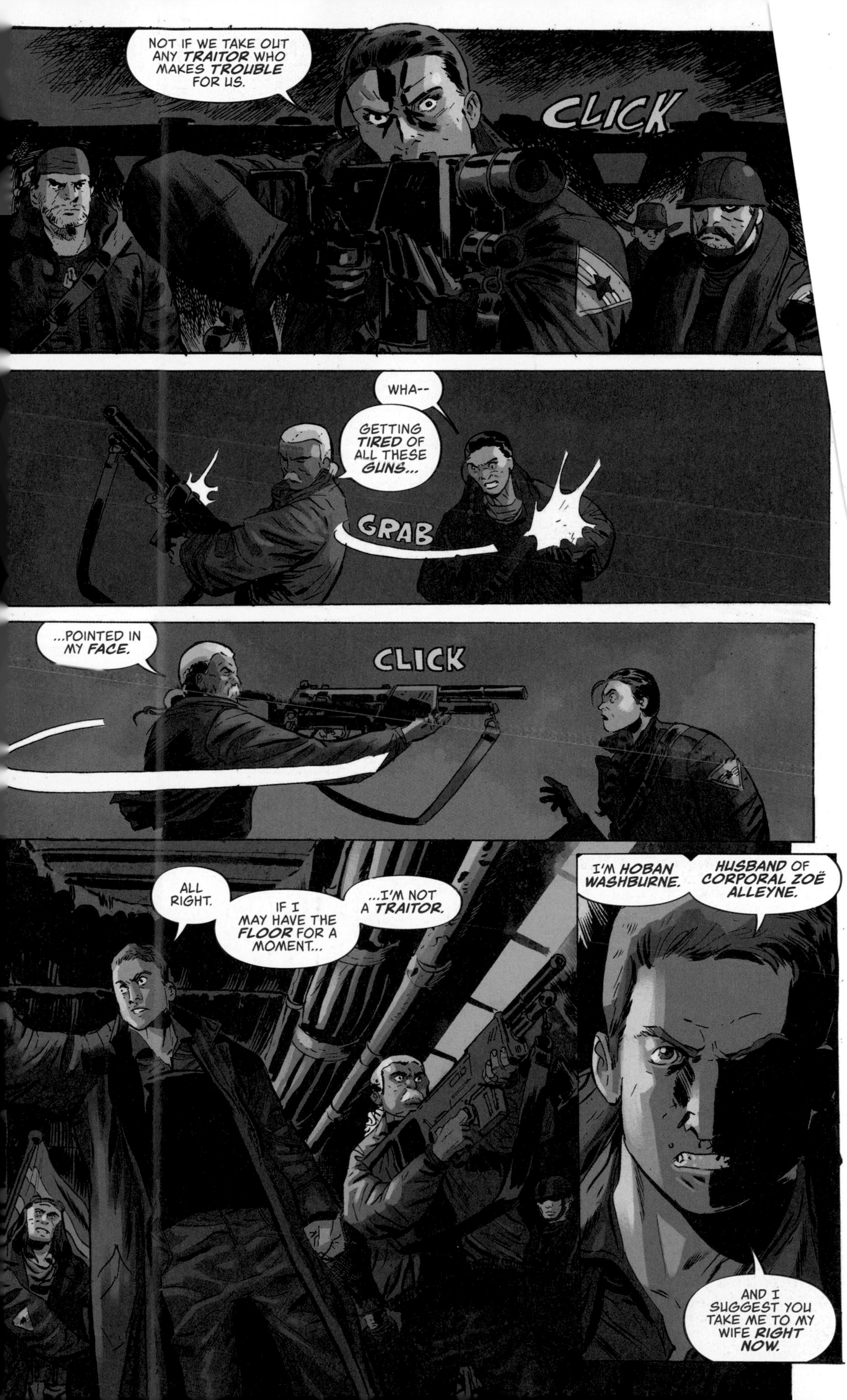
NOT IF WE TAKE OUT ANY TRAITOR WHO MAKES TROUBLE FOR US.
CLICK
WHA--
GETTING TIRED OF ALL THESE GUNS...
GRAB
...POINTED IN MY FACE.
CLICK
ALL RIGHT.
IF I MAY HAVE THE FLOOR FOR A MOMENT...
...I'M NOT A TRAITOR.
I'M HOBAN WASHBURNE.
HUSBAND OF CORPORAL ZOË ALLEYNE.
AND I SUGGEST YOU TAKE ME TO MY WIFE RIGHT NOW.

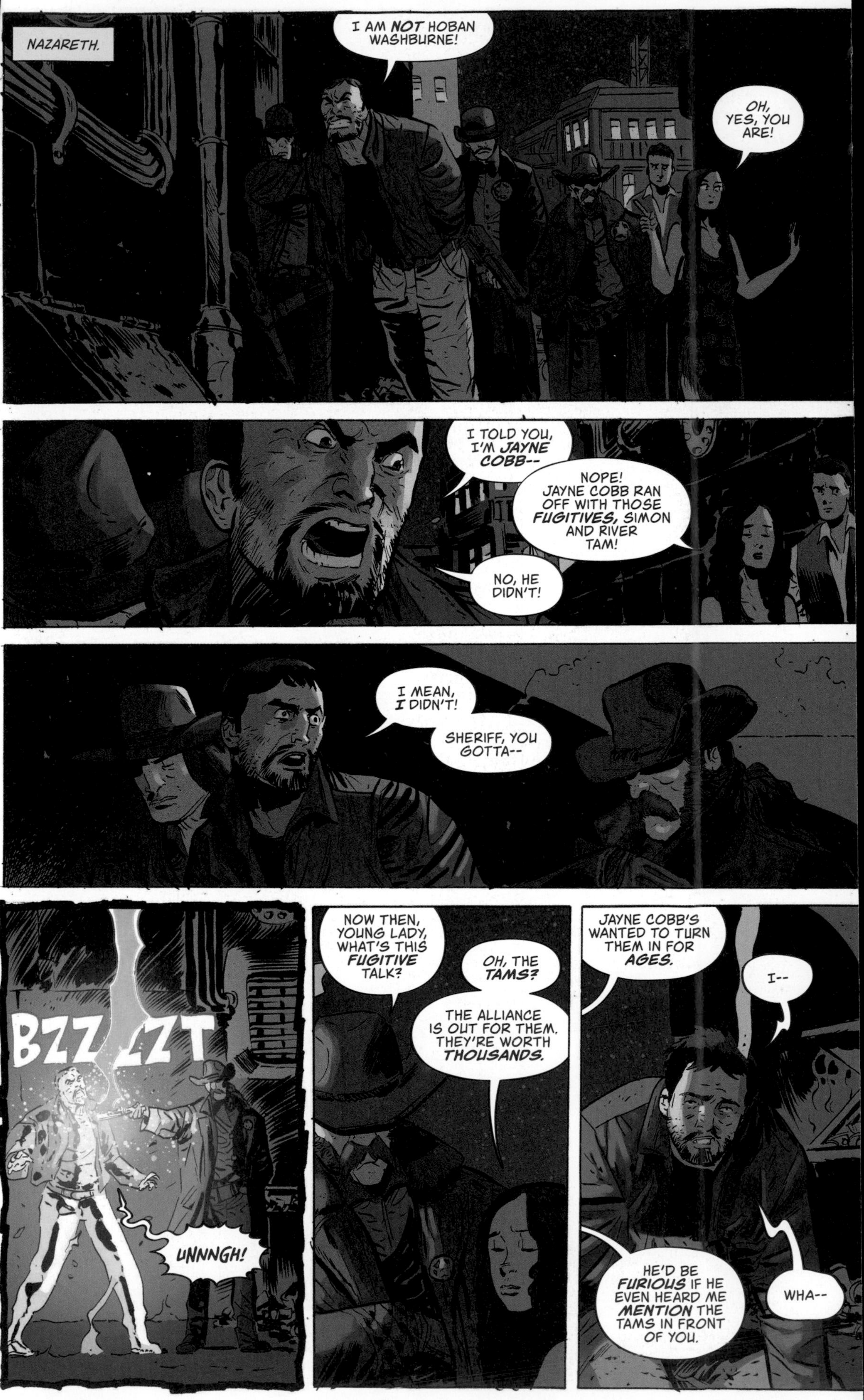
NAZARETH.
I AM NOT HOBAN WASHBURNE!
OH, YES, YOU ARE!
I TOLD YOU, I'M JAYNE COBB--
NOPE! JAYNE COBB RAN OFF WITH THOSE FUGITIVES, SIMON AND RIVER TAM!
NO, HE DIDN'T!
I MEAN, I DIDN'T!
SHERIFF, YOU GOTTA--
BZZZZT
UNNNGH!
NOW THEN, YOUNG LADY, WHAT'S THIS FUGITIVE TALK?
OH, THE TAMS?
THE ALLIANCE IS OUT FOR THEM. THEY'RE WORTH THOUSANDS.
JAYNE COBB'S WANTED TO TURN THEM IN FOR AGES.
I--
HE'D BE FURIOUS IF HE EVEN HEARD ME MENTION THE TAMS IN FRONT OF YOU.
WHA--

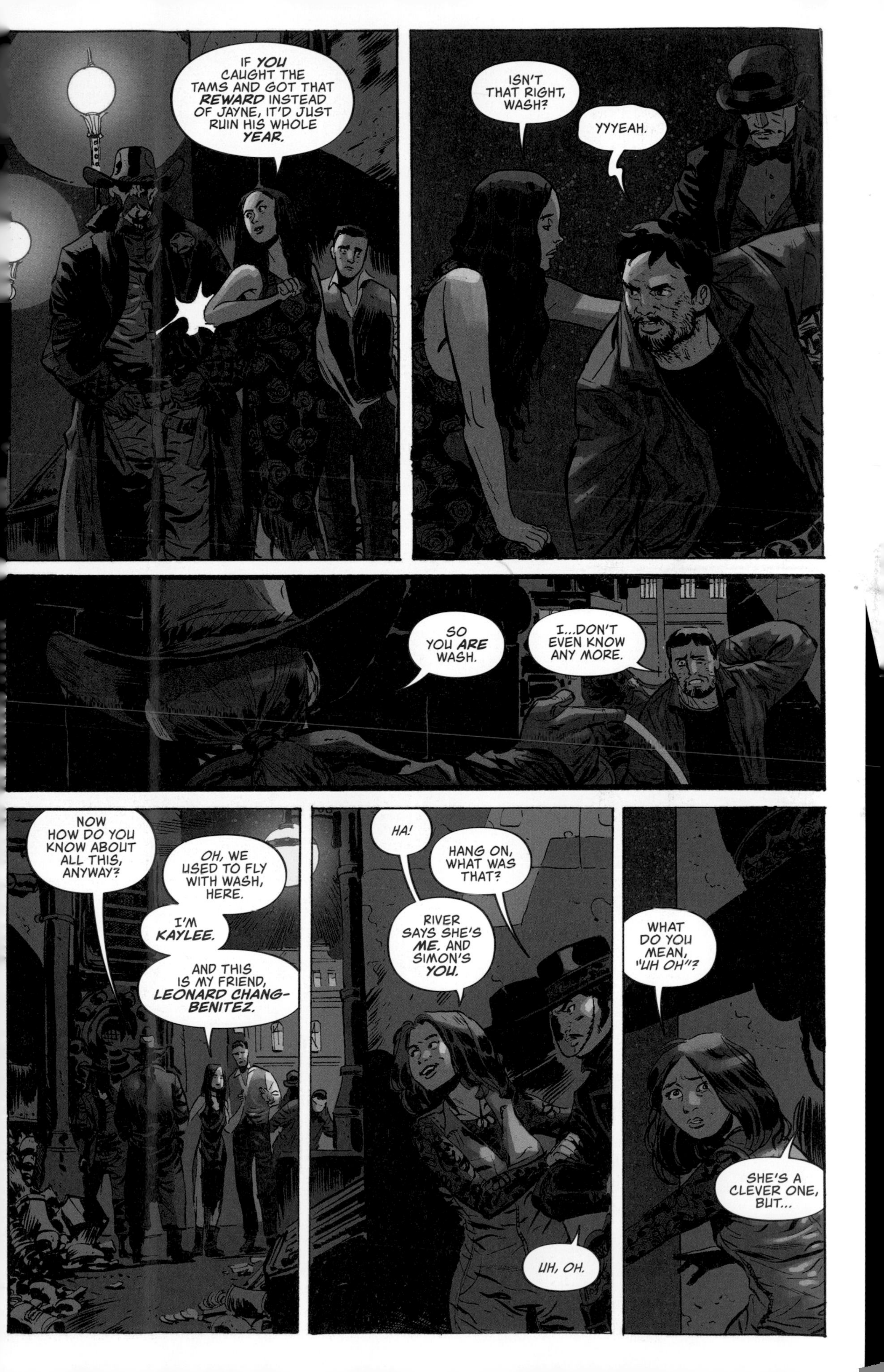
IF YOU CAUGHT THE TAMS AND GOT THAT REWARD INSTEAD OF JAYNE, IT'D JUST RUIN HIS WHOLE YEAR.
ISN'T THAT RIGHT, WASH?
YYYEAH.
SO YOU ARE WASH.
I...DON'T EVEN KNOW ANY MORE.
NOW HOW DO YOU KNOW ABOUT ALL THIS, ANYWAY?
OH, WE USED TO FLY WITH WASH, HERE.
I'M KAYLEE.
AND THIS IS MY FRIEND, LEONARD CHANG-BENITEZ.
HA!
HANG ON, WHAT WAS THAT?
RIVER SAYS SHE'S ME. AND SIMON'S YOU.
UH, OH.
WHAT DO YOU MEAN, "UH OH"?
SHE'S A CLEVER ONE, BUT...

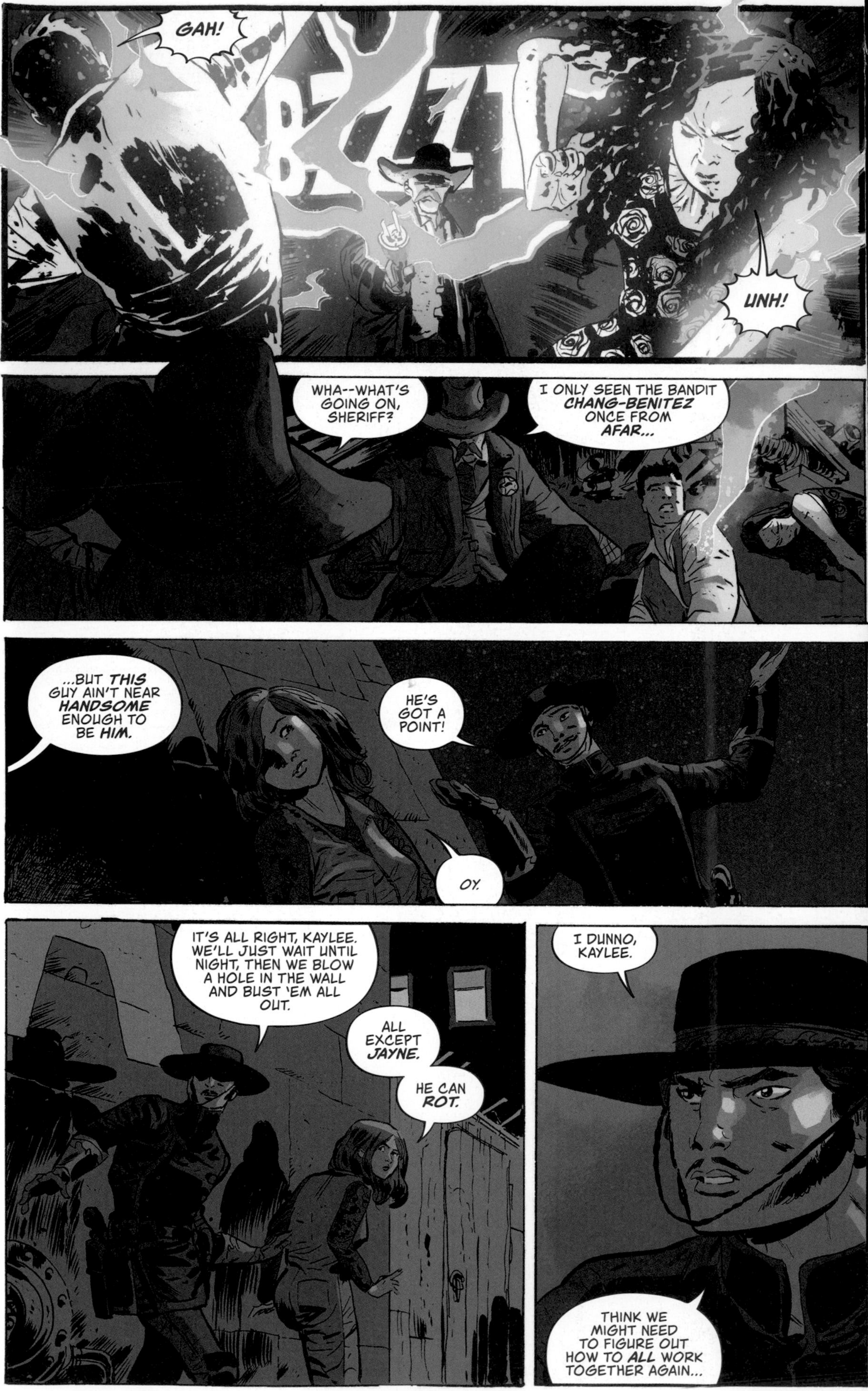
GAH!
BZZT!
UNH!
WHA--WHAT'S GOING ON, SHERIFF?
I ONLY SEEN THE BANDIT CHANG-BENITEZ ONCE FROM AFAR...
...BUT THIS GUY AIN'T NEAR HANDSOME ENOUGH TO BE HIM.
HE'S GOT A POINT!
OY.
IT'S ALL RIGHT, KAYLEE. WE'LL JUST WAIT UNTIL NIGHT, THEN WE BLOW A HOLE IN THE WALL AND BUST 'EM ALL OUT.
ALL EXCEPT JAYNE.
HE CAN ROT.
I DUNNO, KAYLEE.
THINK WE MIGHT NEED TO FIGURE OUT HOW TO ALL WORK TOGETHER AGAIN...

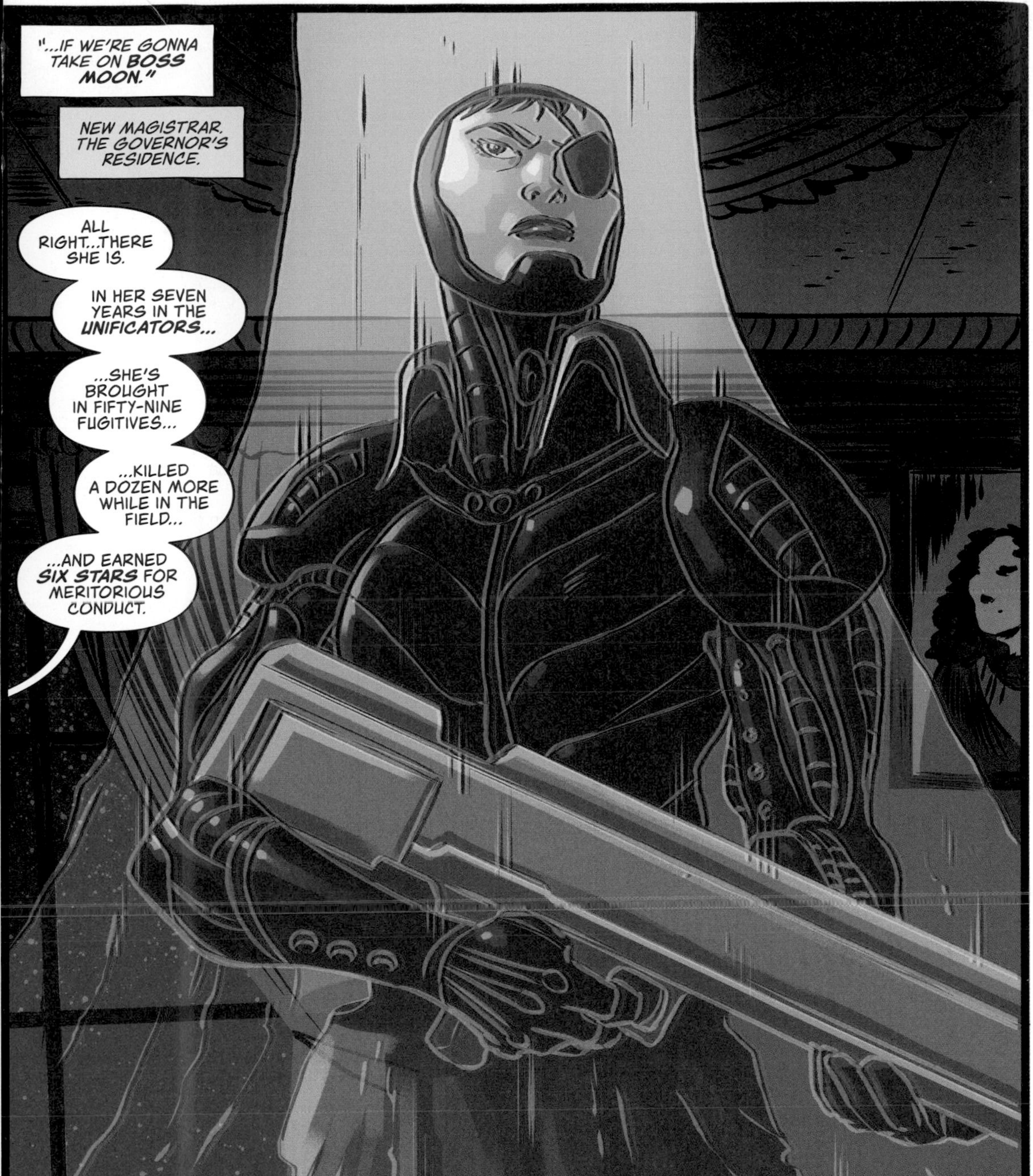
"...IF WE'RE GONNA TAKE ON **BOSS MOON.**"
NEW MAGISTRAR. THE GOVERNOR'S RESIDENCE.
ALL RIGHT...THERE SHE IS.
IN HER SEVEN YEARS IN THE ***UNIFICATORS...***
...SHE'S BROUGHT IN FIFTY-NINE FUGITIVES...
...KILLED A DOZEN MORE WHILE IN THE FIELD...
...AND EARNED ***SIX STARS*** FOR MERITORIOUS CONDUCT.

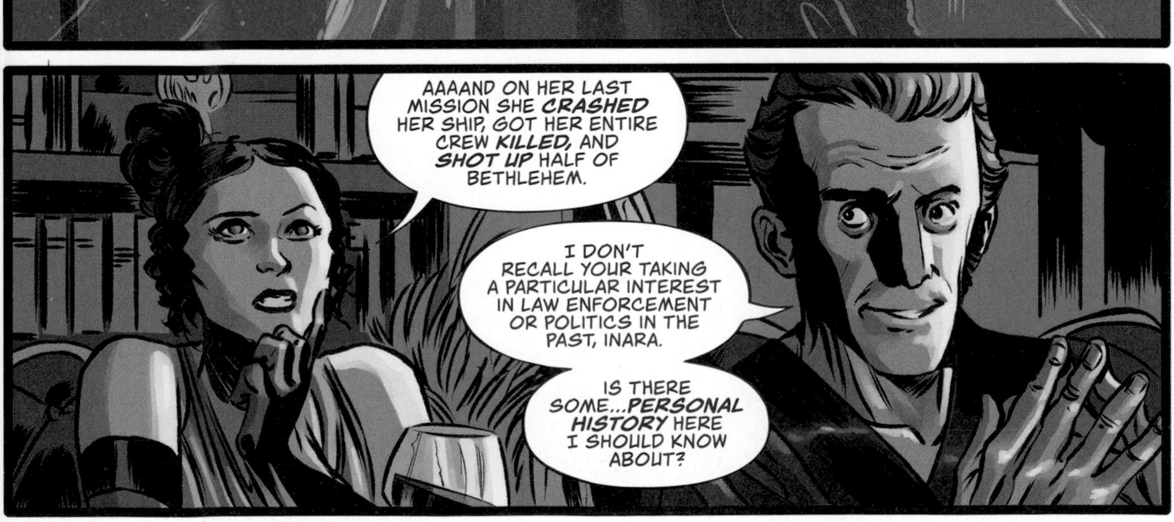
AAAAND ON HER LAST MISSION SHE ***CRASHED*** HER SHIP, GOT HER ENTIRE CREW ***KILLED,*** AND ***SHOT UP*** HALF OF BETHLEHEM.
I DON'T RECALL YOUR TAKING A PARTICULAR INTEREST IN LAW ENFORCEMENT OR POLITICS IN THE PAST, INARA.
IS THERE SOME...***PERSONAL HISTORY*** HERE I SHOULD KNOW ABOUT?

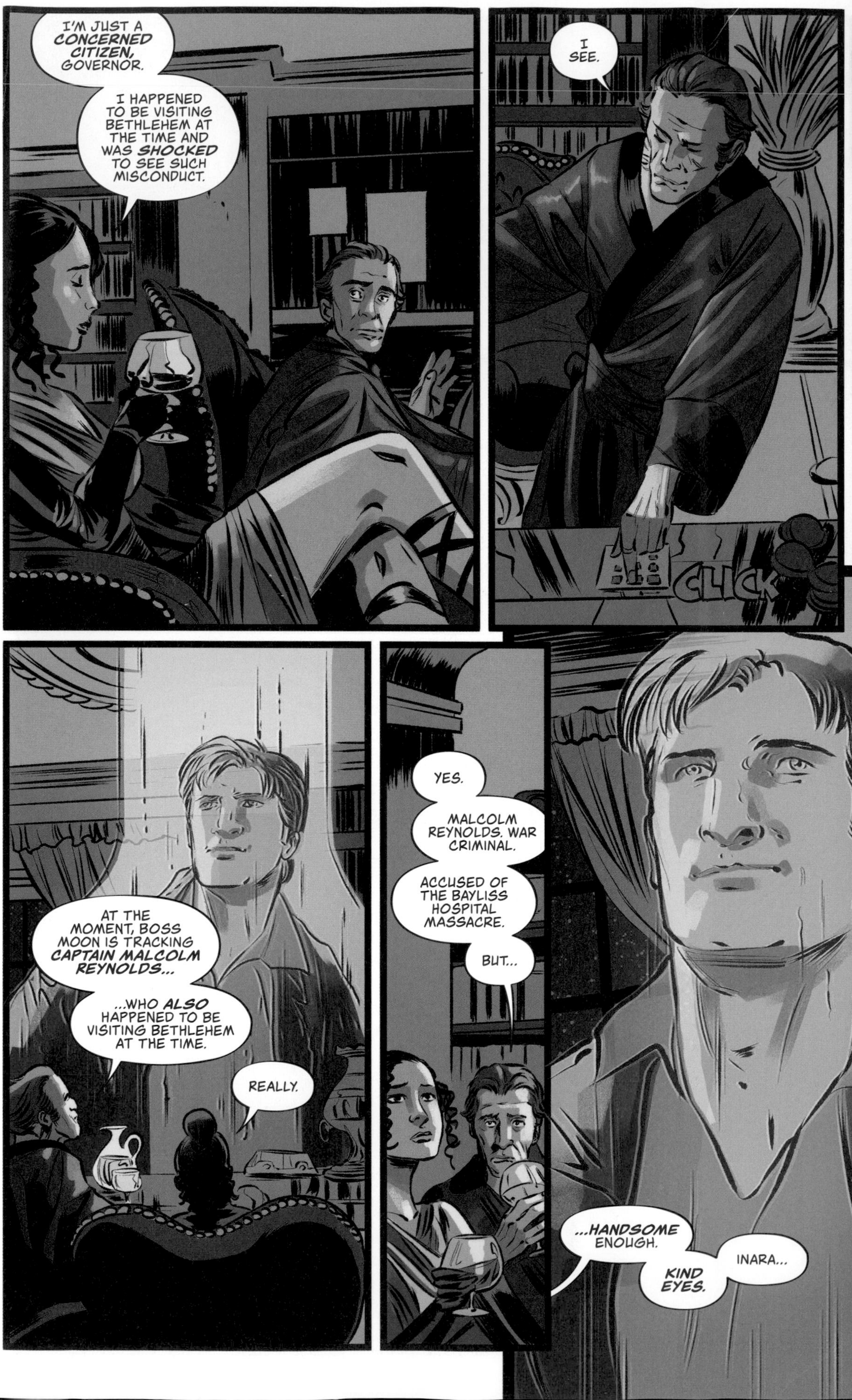
I'M JUST A CONCERNED CITIZEN, GOVERNOR.
I HAPPENED TO BE VISITING BETHLEHEM AT THE TIME AND WAS SHOCKED TO SEE SUCH MISCONDUCT.
I SEE.
CLICK
AT THE MOMENT, BOSS MOON IS TRACKING CAPTAIN MALCOLM REYNOLDS...
...WHO ALSO HAPPENED TO BE VISITING BETHLEHEM AT THE TIME.
REALLY.
YES.
MALCOLM REYNOLDS. WAR CRIMINAL.
ACCUSED OF THE BAYLISS HOSPITAL MASSACRE.
BUT...
...HANDSOME ENOUGH.
KIND EYES.
INARA...

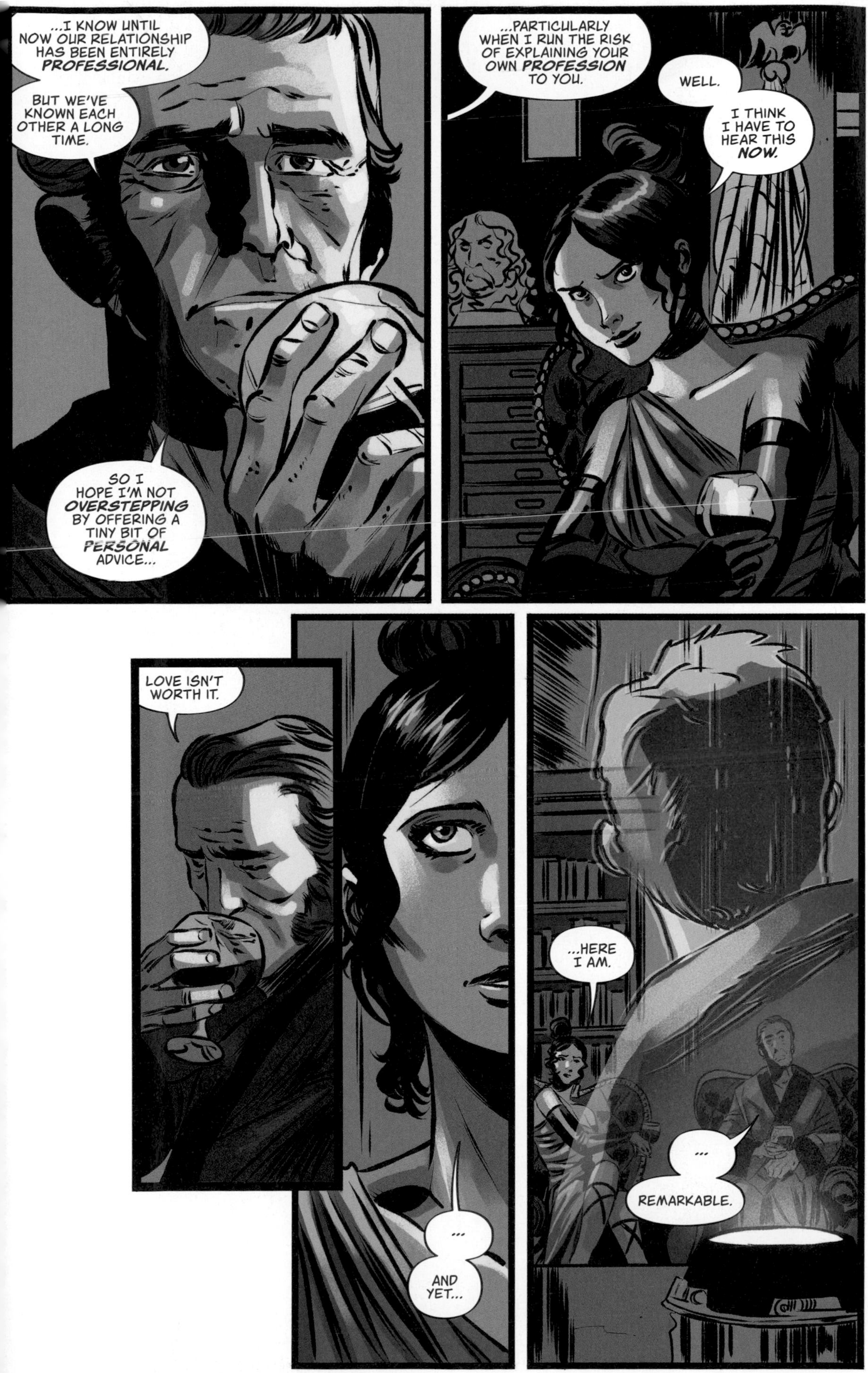
...I KNOW UNTIL NOW OUR RELATIONSHIP HAS BEEN ENTIRELY PROFESSIONAL.
BUT WE'VE KNOWN EACH OTHER A LONG TIME.
SO I HOPE I'M NOT OVERSTEPPING BY OFFERING A TINY BIT OF PERSONAL ADVICE...
...PARTICULARLY WHEN I RUN THE RISK OF EXPLAINING YOUR OWN PROFESSION TO YOU.
WELL.
I THINK I HAVE TO HEAR THIS NOW.
LOVE ISN'T WORTH IT.
...
AND YET...
...HERE I AM.
...
REMARKABLE.

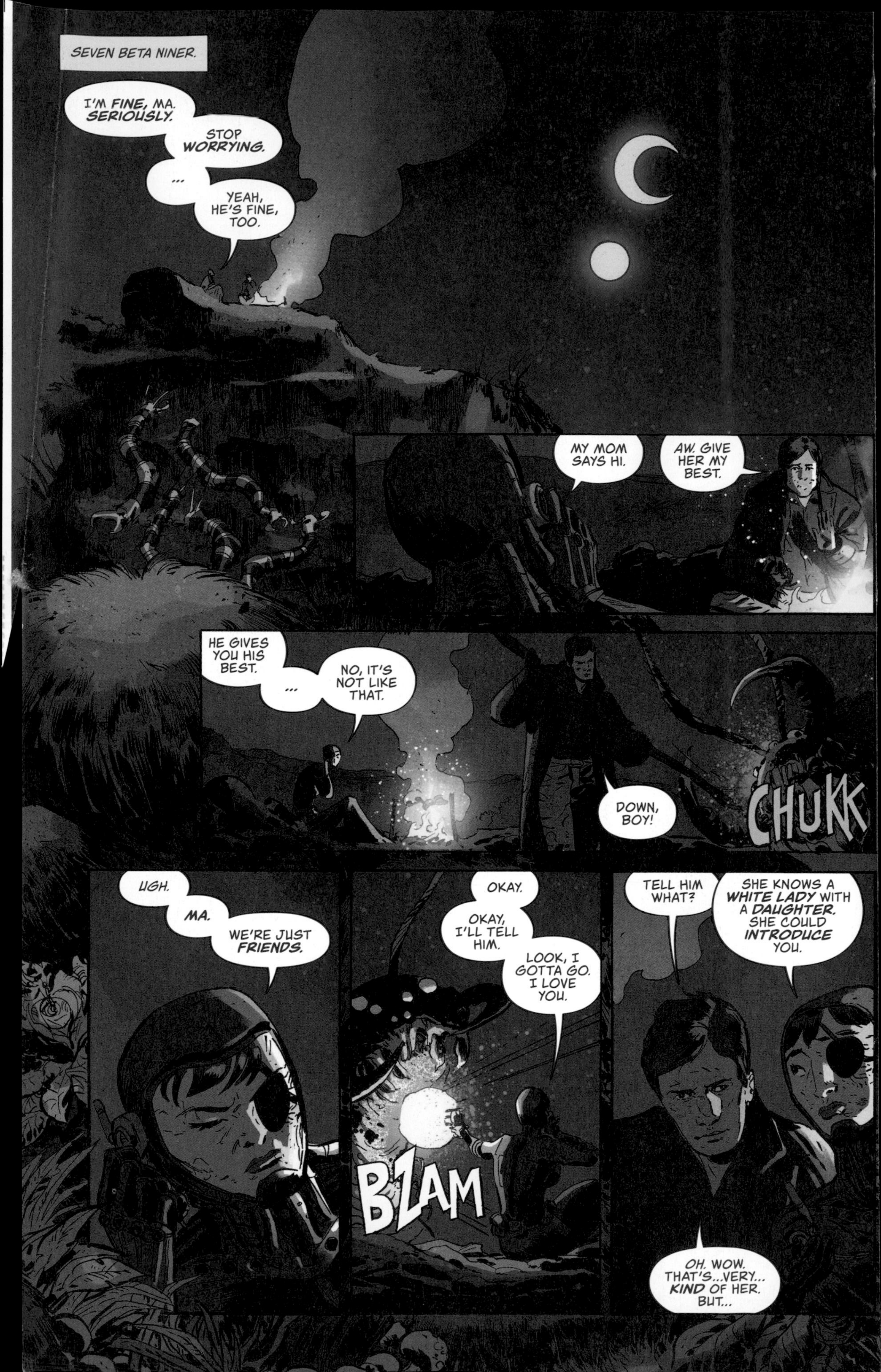
SEVEN BETA NINER.
I'M FINE, MA. SERIOUSLY.
STOP WORRYING.
...
YEAH, HE'S FINE, TOO.
MY MOM SAYS HI.
AW. GIVE HER MY BEST.
HE GIVES YOU HIS BEST.
...
NO, IT'S NOT LIKE THAT.
DOWN, BOY!
CHUKK
UGH.
MA.
WE'RE JUST FRIENDS.
OKAY.
OKAY, I'LL TELL HIM.
LOOK, I GOTTA GO. I LOVE YOU.
BZAM
TELL HIM WHAT?
SHE KNOWS A WHITE LADY WITH A DAUGHTER. SHE COULD INTRODUCE YOU.
OH. WOW. THAT'S...VERY... KIND OF HER. BUT...

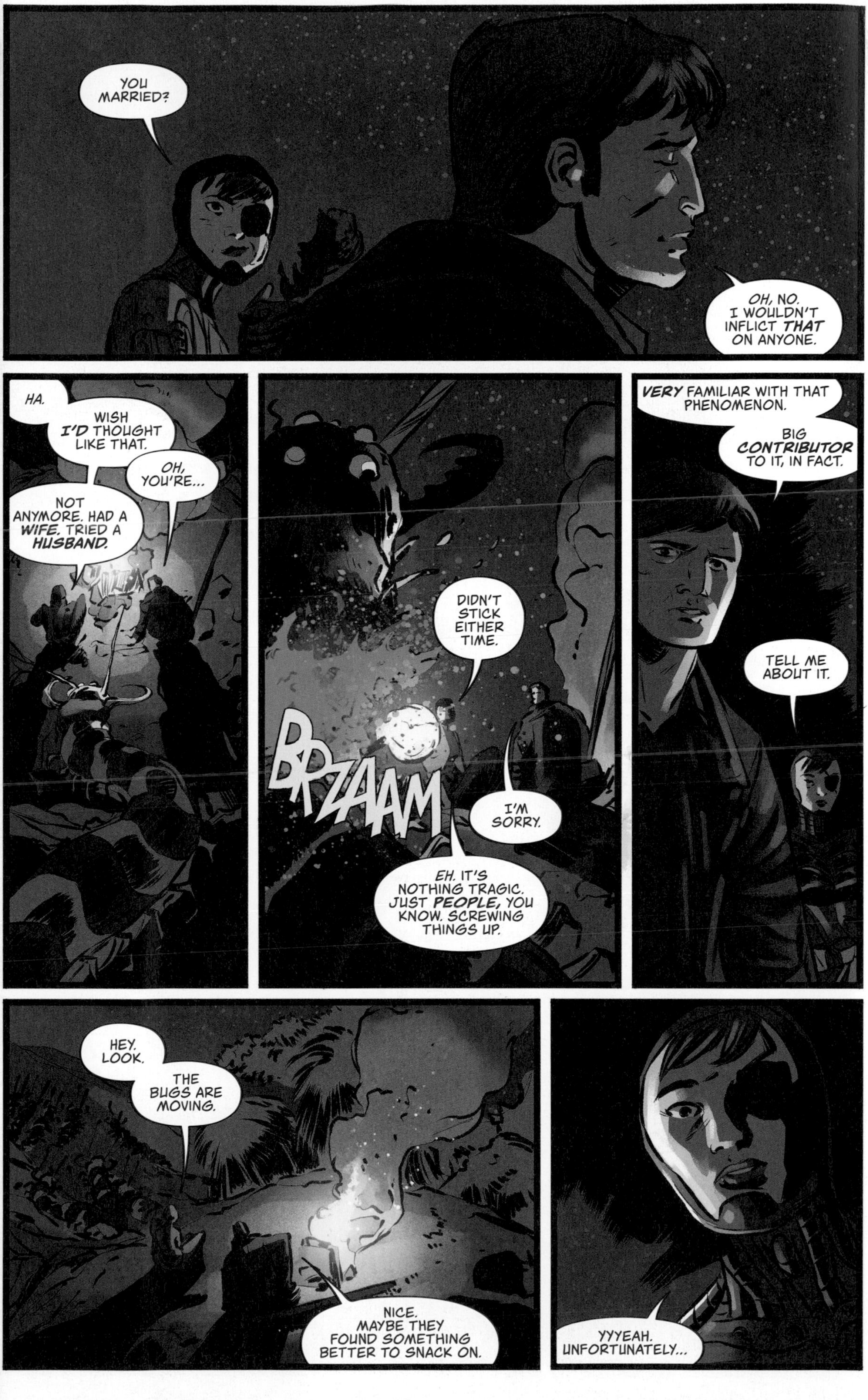

YOU MARRIED?
OH, NO. I WOULDN'T INFLICT THAT ON ANYONE.
HA.
WISH I'D THOUGHT LIKE THAT.
OH, YOU'RE...
NOT ANYMORE. HAD A WIFE. TRIED A HUSBAND.
DIDN'T STICK EITHER TIME.
BRZAAM
I'M SORRY.
EH. IT'S NOTHING TRAGIC. JUST PEOPLE, YOU KNOW. SCREWING THINGS UP.
VERY FAMILIAR WITH THAT PHENOMENON.
BIG CONTRIBUTOR TO IT, IN FACT.
TELL ME ABOUT IT.
HEY. LOOK.
THE BUGS ARE MOVING.
NICE. MAYBE THEY FOUND SOMETHING BETTER TO SNACK ON.
YYYEAH. UNFORTUNATELY...

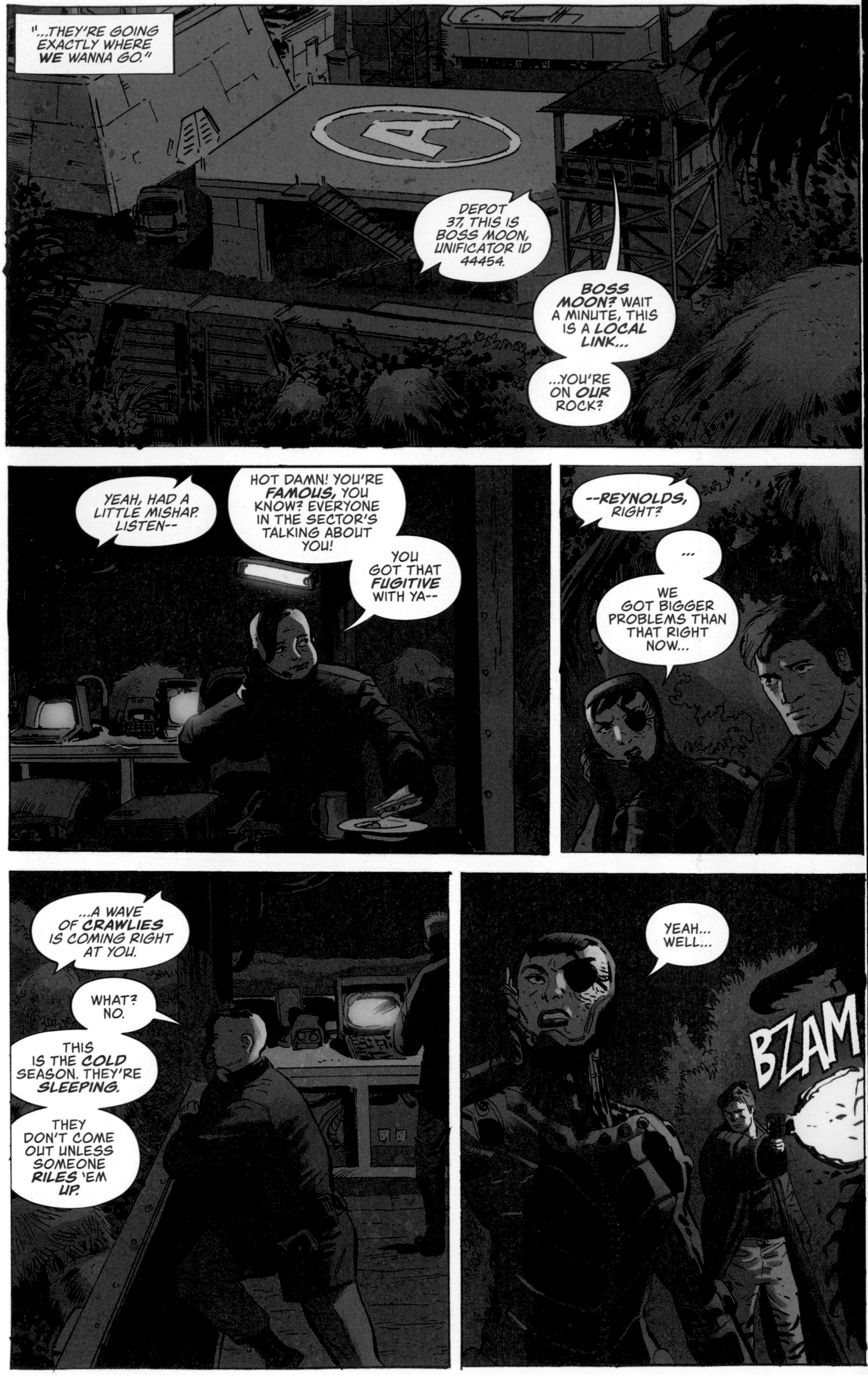
"...THEY'RE GOING EXACTLY WHERE **WE** WANNA GO."
DEPOT 37, THIS IS BOSS MOON, UNIFICATOR ID 44454.
BOSS MOON? WAIT A MINUTE, THIS IS A **LOCAL LINK...**
...YOU'RE ON **OUR** ROCK?
YEAH, HAD A LITTLE MISHAP. LISTEN--
HOT DAMN! YOU'RE **FAMOUS,** YOU KNOW? EVERYONE IN THE SECTOR'S TALKING ABOUT YOU!
YOU GOT THAT **FUGITIVE** WITH YA--
--REYNOLDS, RIGHT?
...
WE GOT BIGGER PROBLEMS THAN THAT RIGHT NOW...
...A WAVE OF **CRAWLIES** IS COMING RIGHT AT YOU.
WHAT? NO.
THIS IS THE **COLD** SEASON. THEY'RE **SLEEPING.**
THEY DON'T COME OUT UNLESS SOMEONE **RILES** 'EM **UP.**
YEAH... WELL...
BZAM

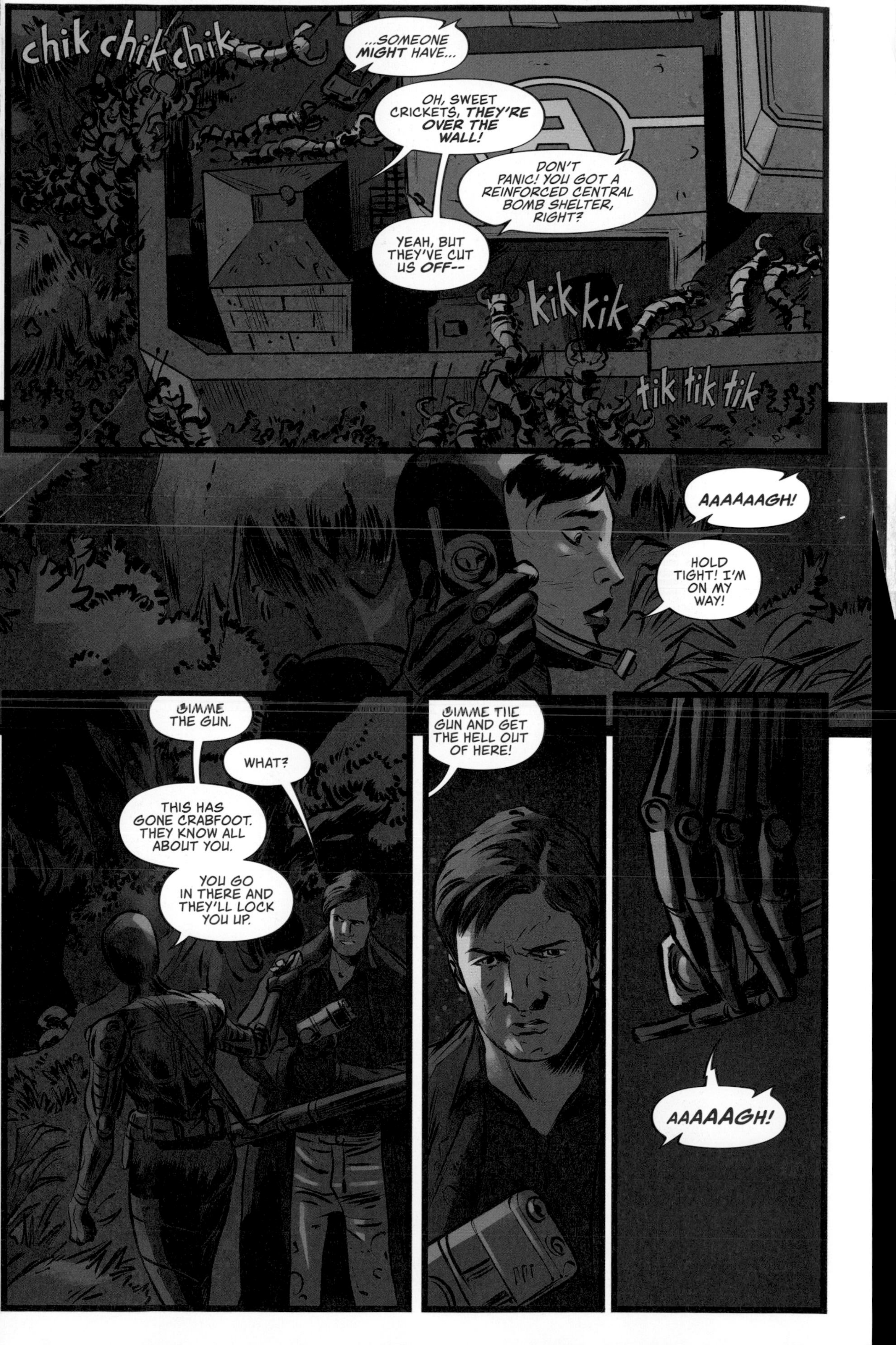
chik chik chik
...SOMEONE MIGHT HAVE...
OH, SWEET CRICKETS, THEY'RE OVER THE WALL!
DON'T PANIC! YOU GOT A REINFORCED CENTRAL BOMB SHELTER, RIGHT?
YEAH, BUT THEY'VE CUT US OFF--
kik kik
tik tik tik
AAAAAAGH!
HOLD TIGHT! I'M ON MY WAY!
GIMME THE GUN.
WHAT?
THIS HAS GONE CRABFOOT. THEY KNOW ALL ABOUT YOU.
YOU GO IN THERE AND THEY'LL LOCK YOU UP.
GIMME THE GUN AND GET THE HELL OUT OF HERE!
AAAAAGH!

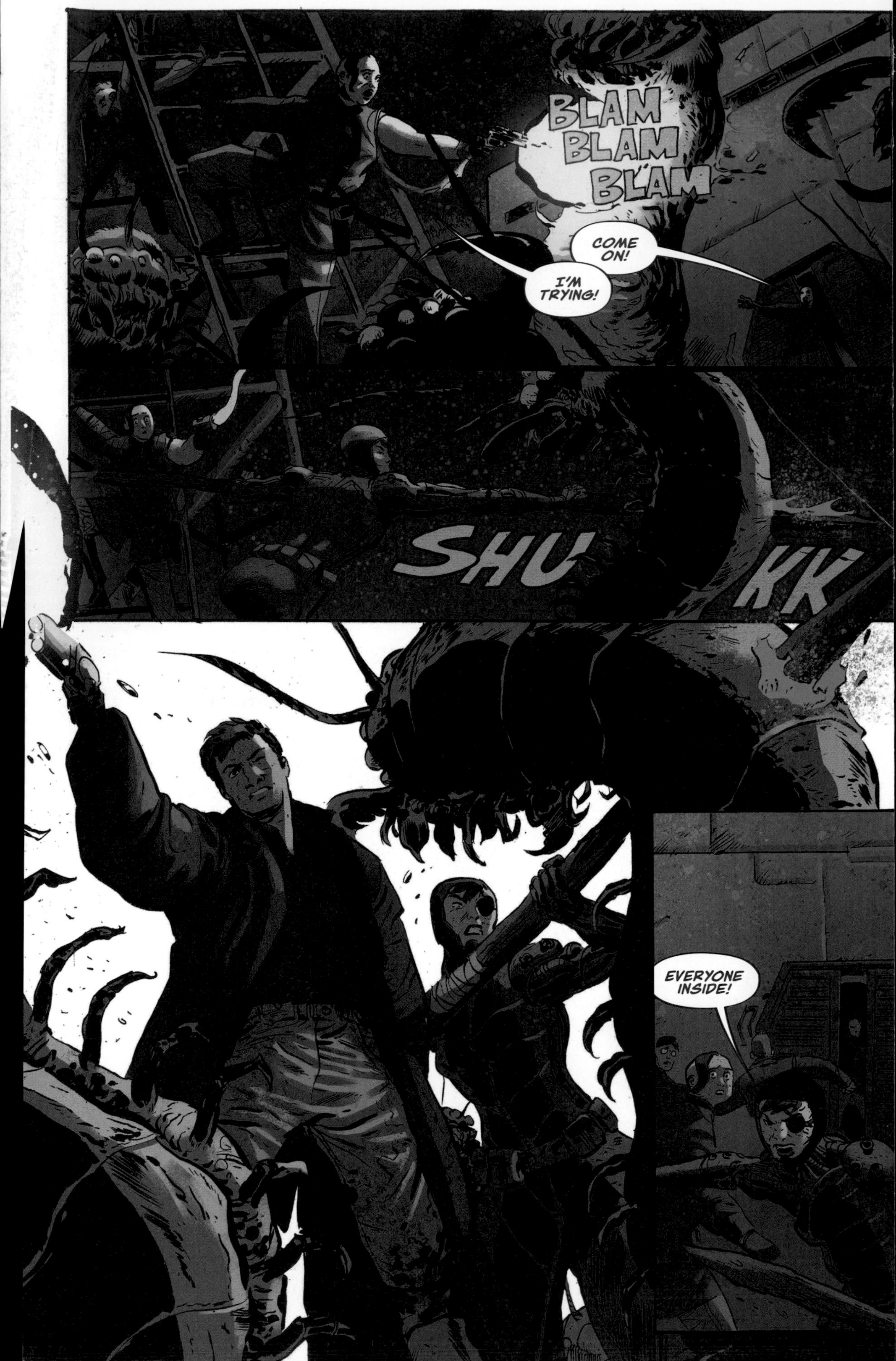
BLAM
BLAM
BLAM
COME ON!
I'M TRYING!
SHU
KK
EVERYONE INSIDE!

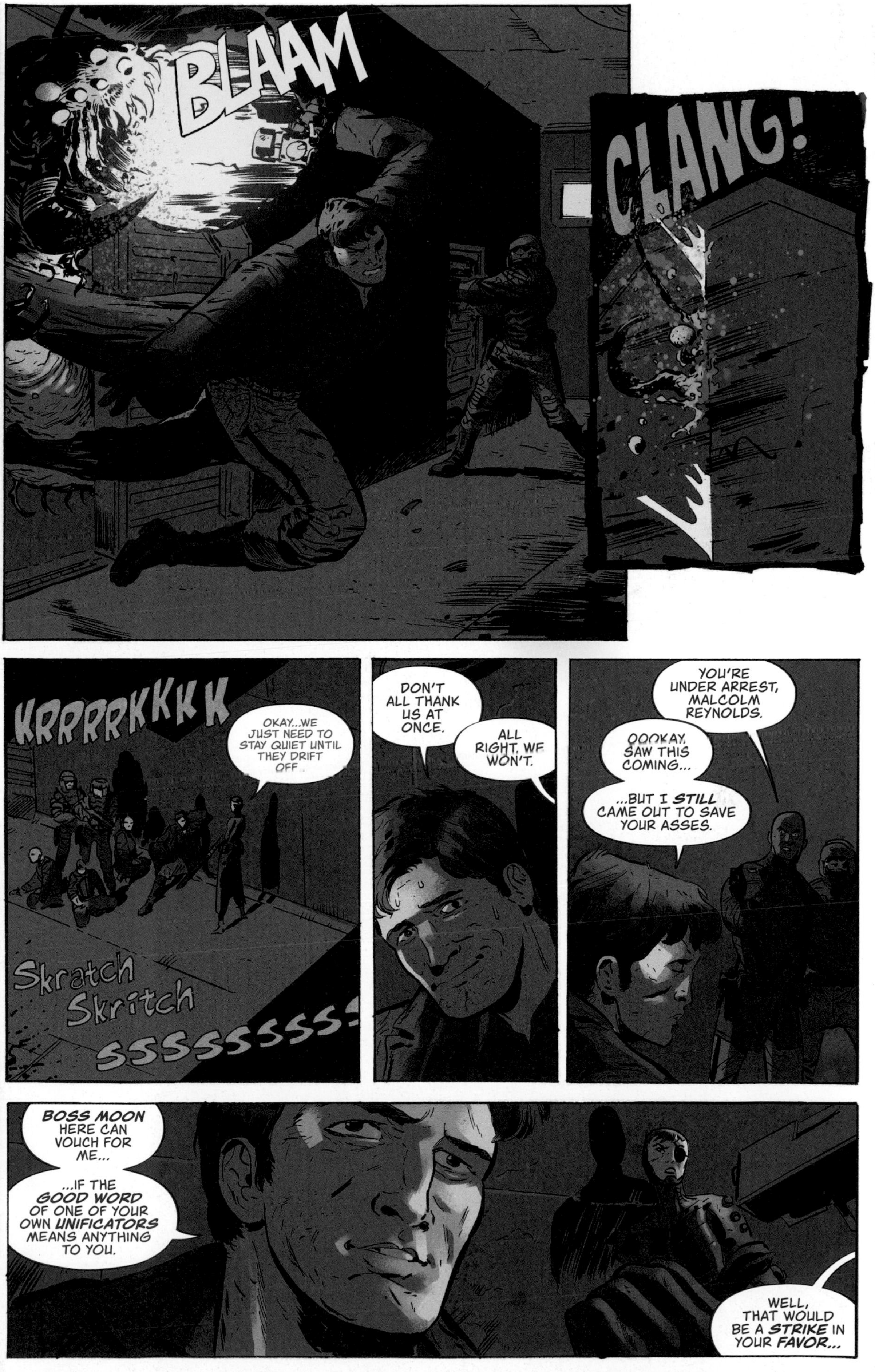

BLAAM
CLANG!
KRRRRKKKK
OKAY...WE JUST NEED TO STAY QUIET UNTIL THEY DRIFT OFF.
Skratch
Skritch
SSSSSSSSS
DON'T ALL THANK US AT ONCE.
ALL RIGHT, WE WON'T.
YOU'RE UNDER ARREST, MALCOLM REYNOLDS.
OOOKAY. SAW THIS COMING...
...BUT I STILL CAME OUT TO SAVE YOUR ASSES.
BOSS MOON HERE CAN VOUCH FOR ME...
...IF THE GOOD WORD OF ONE OF YOUR OWN UNIFICATORS MEANS ANYTHING TO YOU.
WELL, THAT WOULD BE A STRIKE IN YOUR FAVOR...

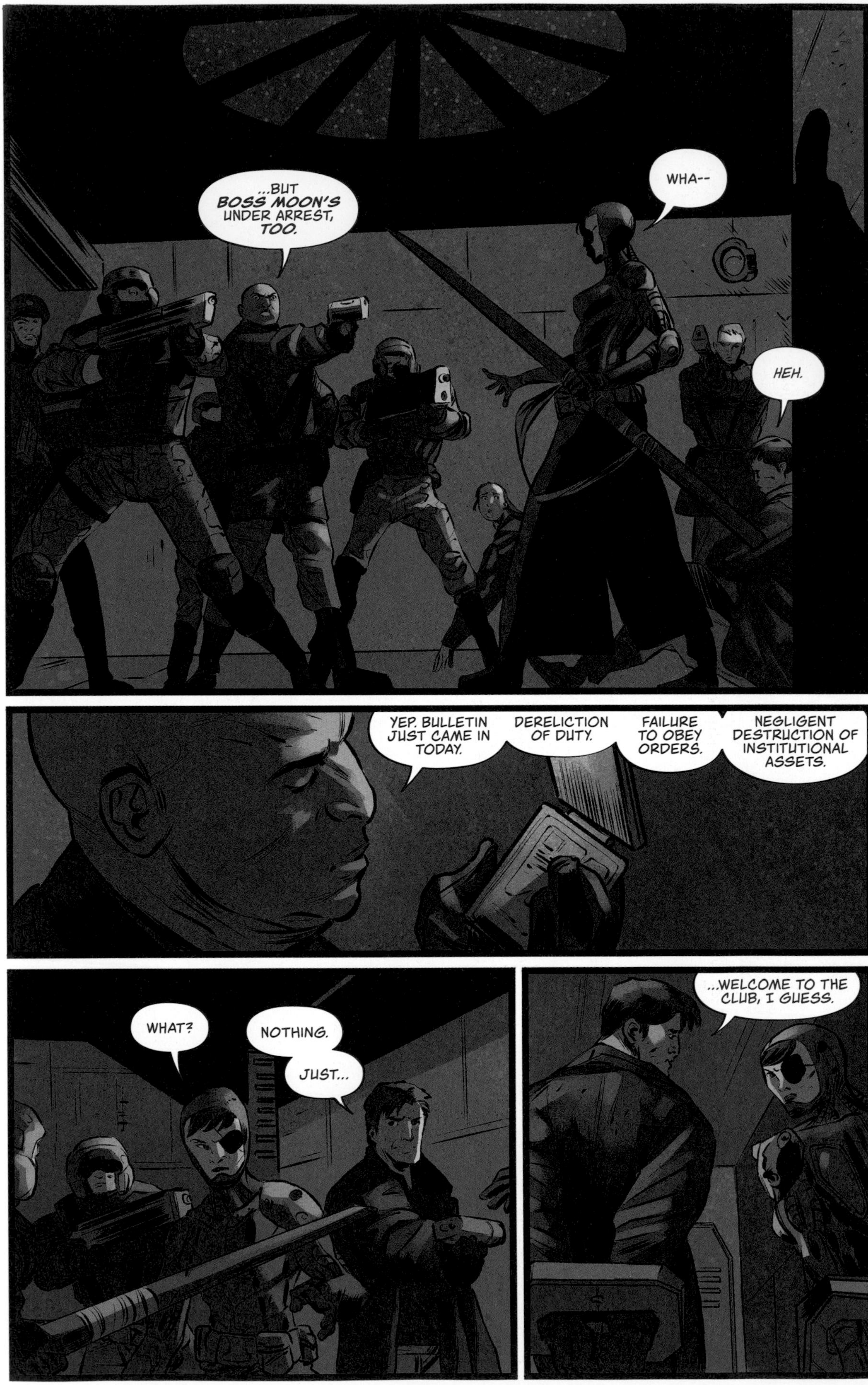
...BUT BOSS MOON'S UNDER ARREST, TOO.
WHA--
HEH.
YEP. BULLETIN JUST CAME IN TODAY.
DERELICTION OF DUTY.
FAILURE TO OBEY ORDERS.
NEGLIGENT DESTRUCTION OF INSTITUTIONAL ASSETS.
WHAT?
NOTHING.
JUST...
...WELCOME TO THE CLUB, I GUESS.

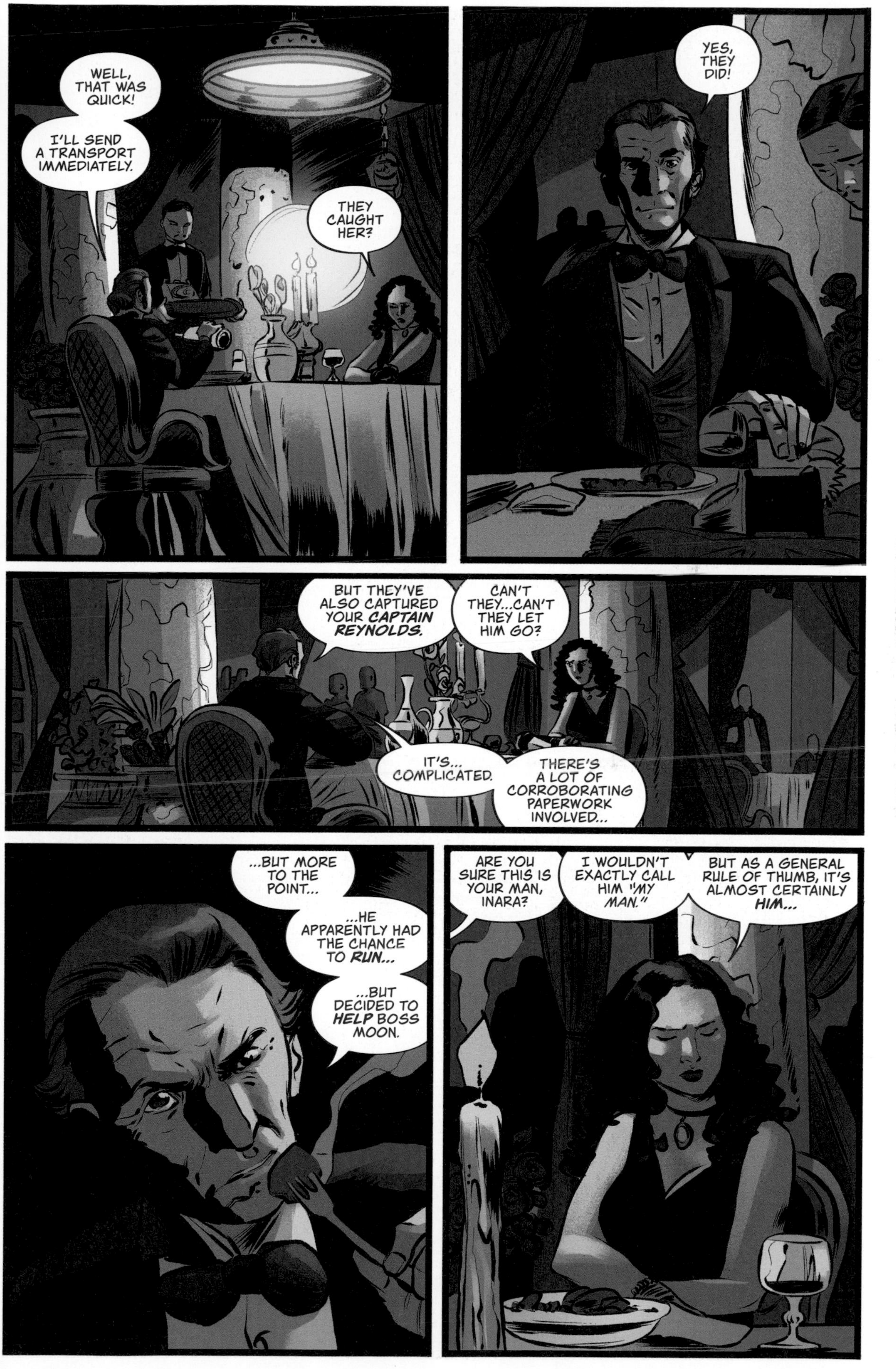
WELL, THAT WAS QUICK!
I'LL SEND A TRANSPORT IMMEDIATELY.
THEY CAUGHT HER?
YES, THEY DID!
BUT THEY'VE ALSO CAPTURED YOUR CAPTAIN REYNOLDS.
CAN'T THEY...CAN'T THEY LET HIM GO?
IT'S... COMPLICATED.
THERE'S A LOT OF CORROBORATING PAPERWORK INVOLVED...
...BUT MORE TO THE POINT...
...HE APPARENTLY HAD THE CHANCE TO RUN...
...BUT DECIDED TO HELP BOSS MOON.
ARE YOU SURE THIS IS YOUR MAN, INARA?
I WOULDN'T EXACTLY CALL HIM "MY MAN."
BUT AS A GENERAL RULE OF THUMB, IT'S ALMOST CERTAINLY HIM...

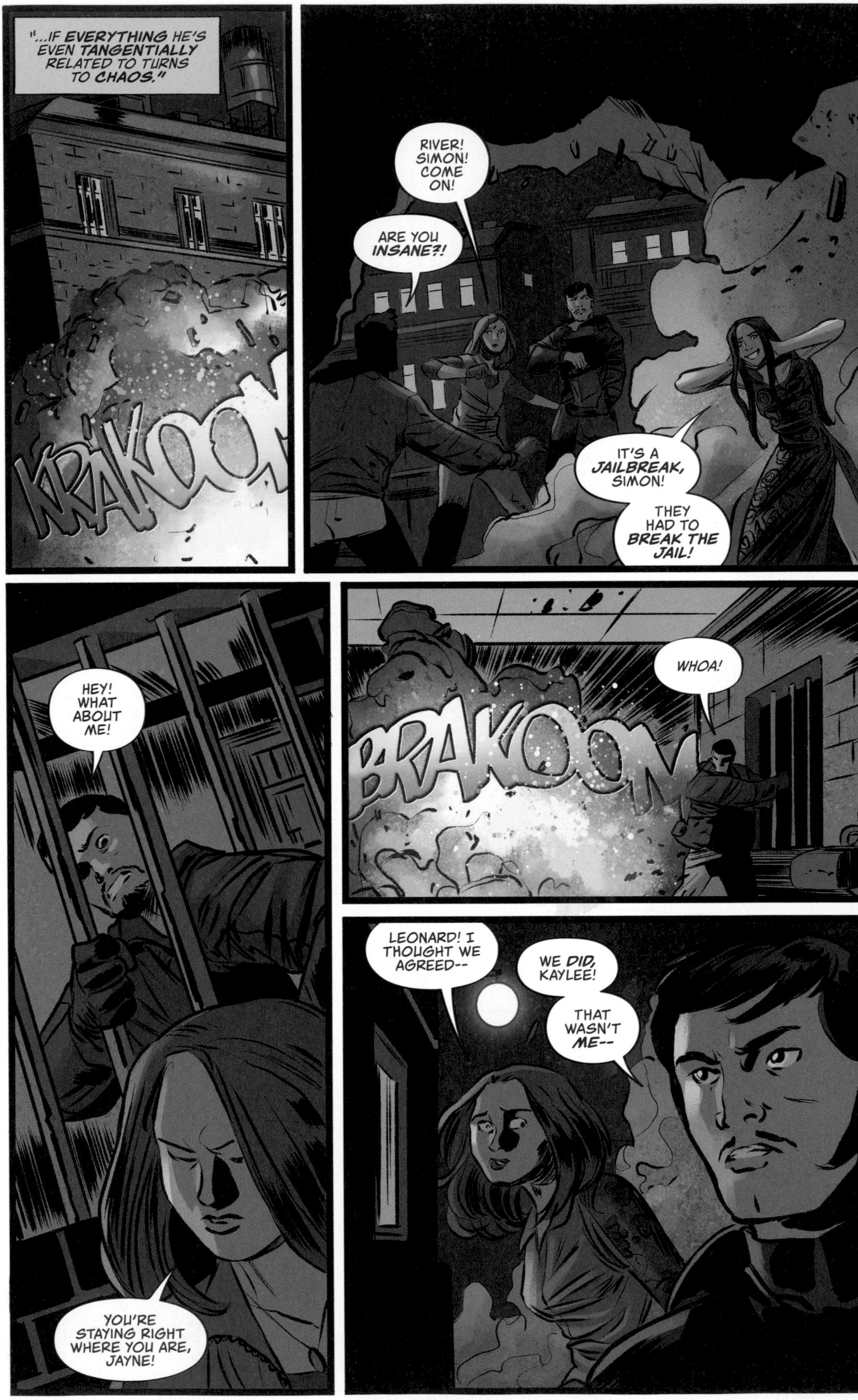
"...IF EVERYTHING HE'S EVEN TANGENTIALLY RELATED TO TURNS TO CHAOS."
KRAKOOM
RIVER! SIMON! COME ON!
ARE YOU INSANE?!
IT'S A JAILBREAK, SIMON!
THEY HAD TO BREAK THE JAIL!
HEY! WHAT ABOUT ME!
YOU'RE STAYING RIGHT WHERE YOU ARE, JAYNE!
BRAKOOM
WHOA!
LEONARD! I THOUGHT WE AGREED--
WE DID, KAYLEE!
THAT WASN'T ME--

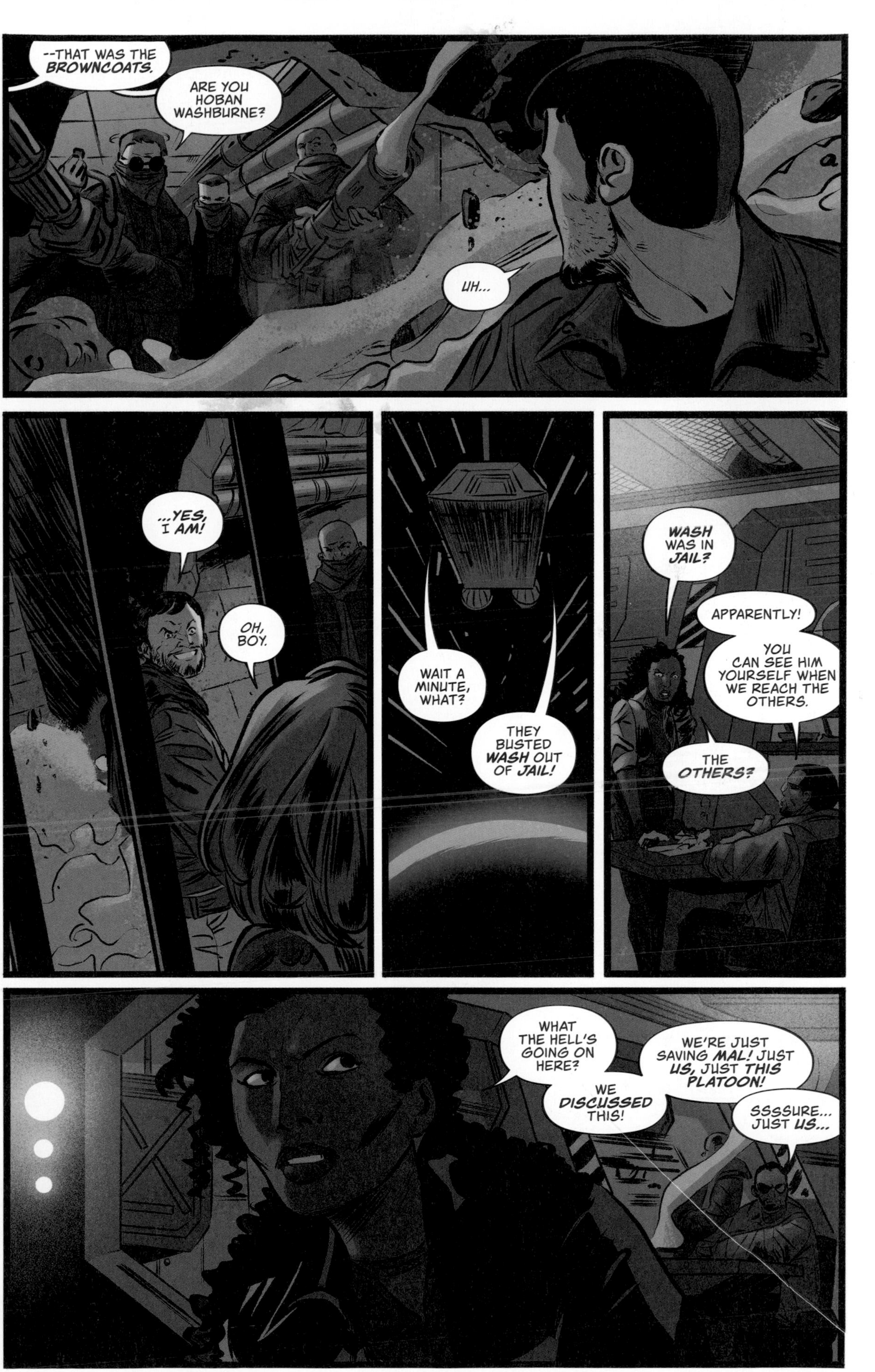
--THAT WAS THE BROWNCOATS.
ARE YOU HOBAN WASHBURNE?
UH...
...YES, I AM!
OH, BOY.
WAIT A MINUTE, WHAT?
THEY BUSTED WASH OUT OF JAIL!
WASH WAS IN JAIL?
APPARENTLY!
YOU CAN SEE HIM YOURSELF WHEN WE REACH THE OTHERS.
THE OTHERS?
WHAT THE HELL'S GOING ON HERE?
WE DISCUSSED THIS!
WE'RE JUST SAVING MAL! JUST US, JUST THIS PLATOON!
SSSSURE... JUST US...

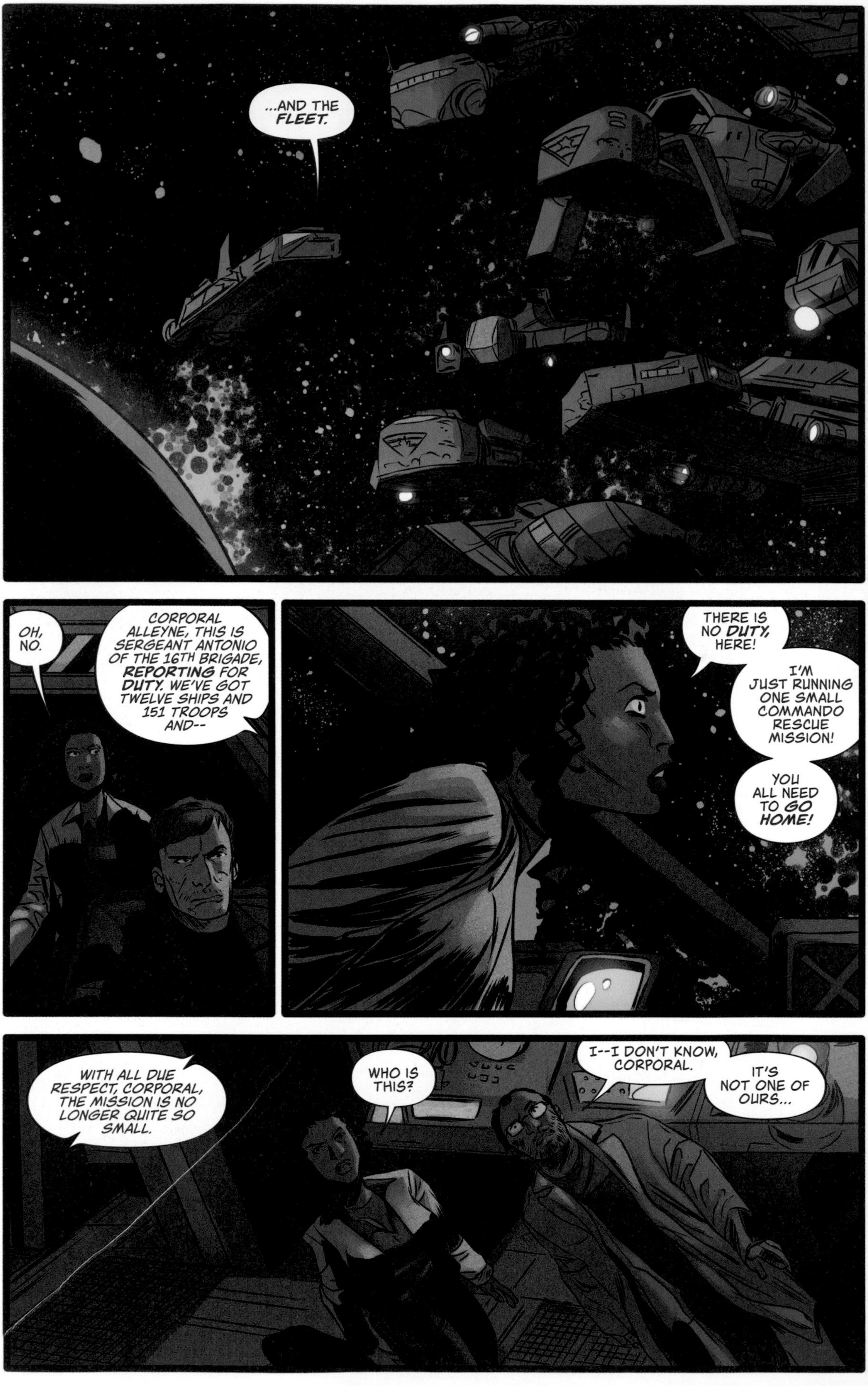
...AND THE FLEET.
OH, NO.
CORPORAL ALLEYNE, THIS IS SERGEANT ANTONIO OF THE 16TH BRIGADE, REPORTING FOR DUTY. WE'VE GOT TWELVE SHIPS AND 151 TROOPS AND--
THERE IS NO DUTY, HERE!
I'M JUST RUNNING ONE SMALL COMMANDO RESCUE MISSION!
YOU ALL NEED TO GO HOME!
WITH ALL DUE RESPECT, CORPORAL, THE MISSION IS NO LONGER QUITE SO SMALL.
WHO IS THIS?
I--I DON'T KNOW, CORPORAL.
IT'S NOT ONE OF OURS...

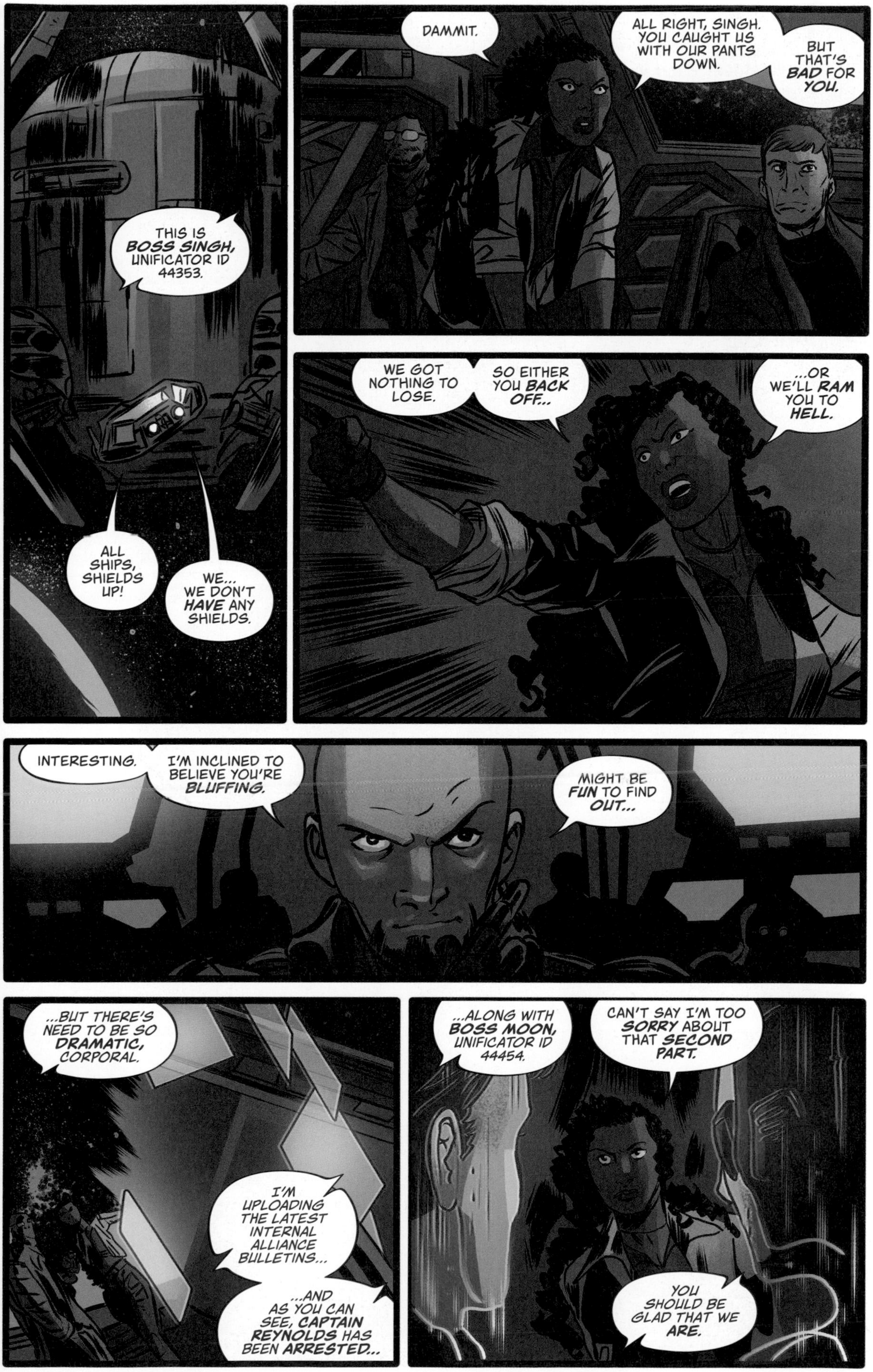
THIS IS BOSS SINGH, UNIFICATOR ID 44353.
ALL SHIPS, SHIELDS UP!
WE... WE DON'T HAVE ANY SHIELDS.
DAMMIT.
ALL RIGHT, SINGH. YOU CAUGHT US WITH OUR PANTS DOWN.
BUT THAT'S BAD FOR YOU.
WE GOT NOTHING TO LOSE.
SO EITHER YOU BACK OFF...
...OR WE'LL RAM YOU TO HELL.
INTERESTING.
I'M INCLINED TO BELIEVE YOU'RE BLUFFING.
MIGHT BE FUN TO FIND OUT...
...BUT THERE'S NEED TO BE SO DRAMATIC, CORPORAL.
I'M UPLOADING THE LATEST INTERNAL ALLIANCE BULLETINS...
...AND AS YOU CAN SEE, CAPTAIN REYNOLDS HAS BEEN ARRESTED...
...ALONG WITH BOSS MOON, UNIFICATOR ID 44454.
CAN'T SAY I'M TOO SORRY ABOUT THAT SECOND PART.
YOU SHOULD BE GLAD THAT WE ARE.

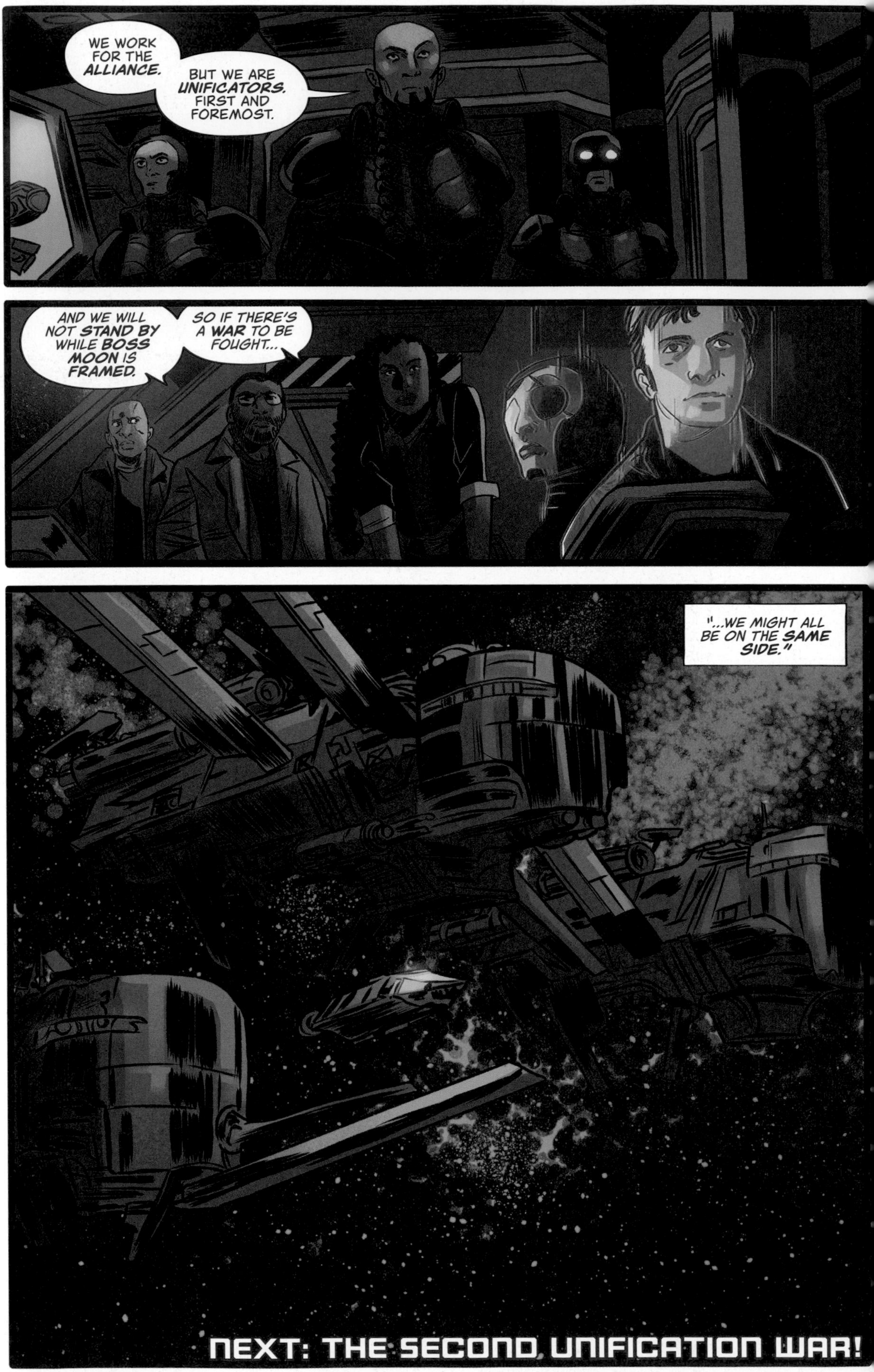
WE WORK FOR THE ALLIANCE.
BUT WE ARE UNIFICATORS. FIRST AND FOREMOST.
AND WE WILL NOT STAND BY WHILE BOSS MOON IS FRAMED.
SO IF THERE'S A WAR TO BE FOUGHT...
"...WE MIGHT ALL BE ON THE SAME SIDE."
NEXT: THE SECOND UNIFICATION WAR!

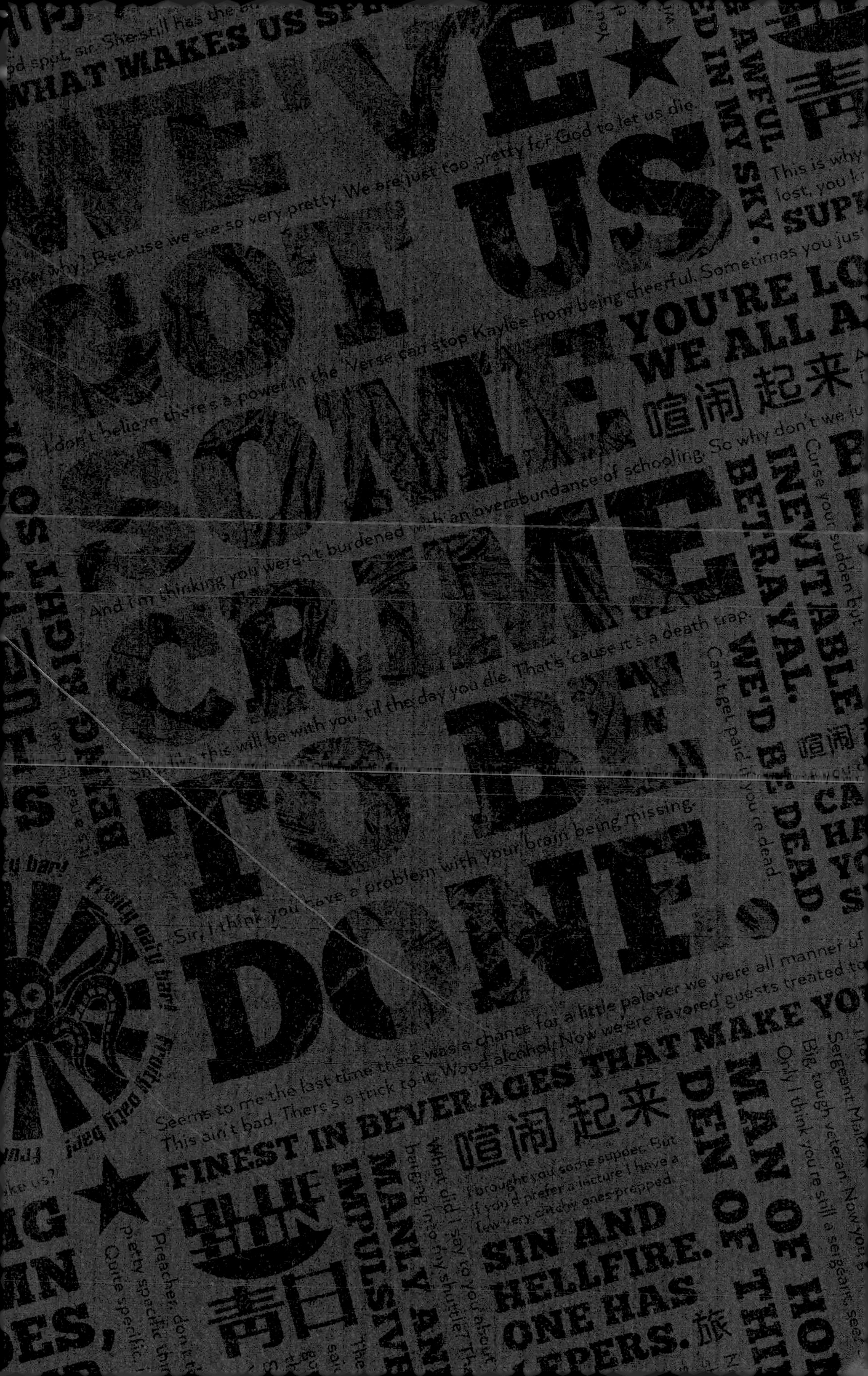

WE'VE GOT US SOME CRIME TO BE DONE.
WHAT MAKES US SP
Because we are so very pretty. We are just too pretty for God to let us die.
Nothing can stop Kaylee from being cheerful. Sometimes you just
I don't believe there's a power in the 'Verse can stop Kaylee from being cheerful.
And I'm thinking you weren't burdened with an overabundance of schooling. So why don't we just
this will be with you til the day you die. That's 'cause it's a death trap.
Sir, I think you have a problem with your brain being missing.
Seems to me the last time there was a chance for a little palaver we were all manner of
This ain't bad. There's a trick to it. Wood alcohol. Now we're favored guests treated to
YOU'RE LO
WE ALL A
喧闹起来
ED IN MY SKY.
AWFUL
This is why
lost, you k
SUPE
INEVITABLE
BETRAYAL.
WE'D BE DEAD.
Curse your sudden but
Can't get paid if you're dead
CA
HA
YO
S
FINEST IN BEVERAGES THAT MAKE YOU
喧闹起来
I brought you some supper. But if you'd prefer a lecture I have a few very catchy ones prepped.
SIN AND HELLFIRE.
ONE HAS
EPERS.
旅
MAN OF HO
DEN OF THI
Big, tough veteran. Now you
Only I think you're still a sergeant, see
Sergeant Malc
BLUE SUN
青日
IMPULSIVE
MANLY AN
What did I say to you about
Preacher, don't
Quite specific
pretty specific
Fruity Oaty Bar!

BOSS MOON: BIRTH OF A UNIFICATOR

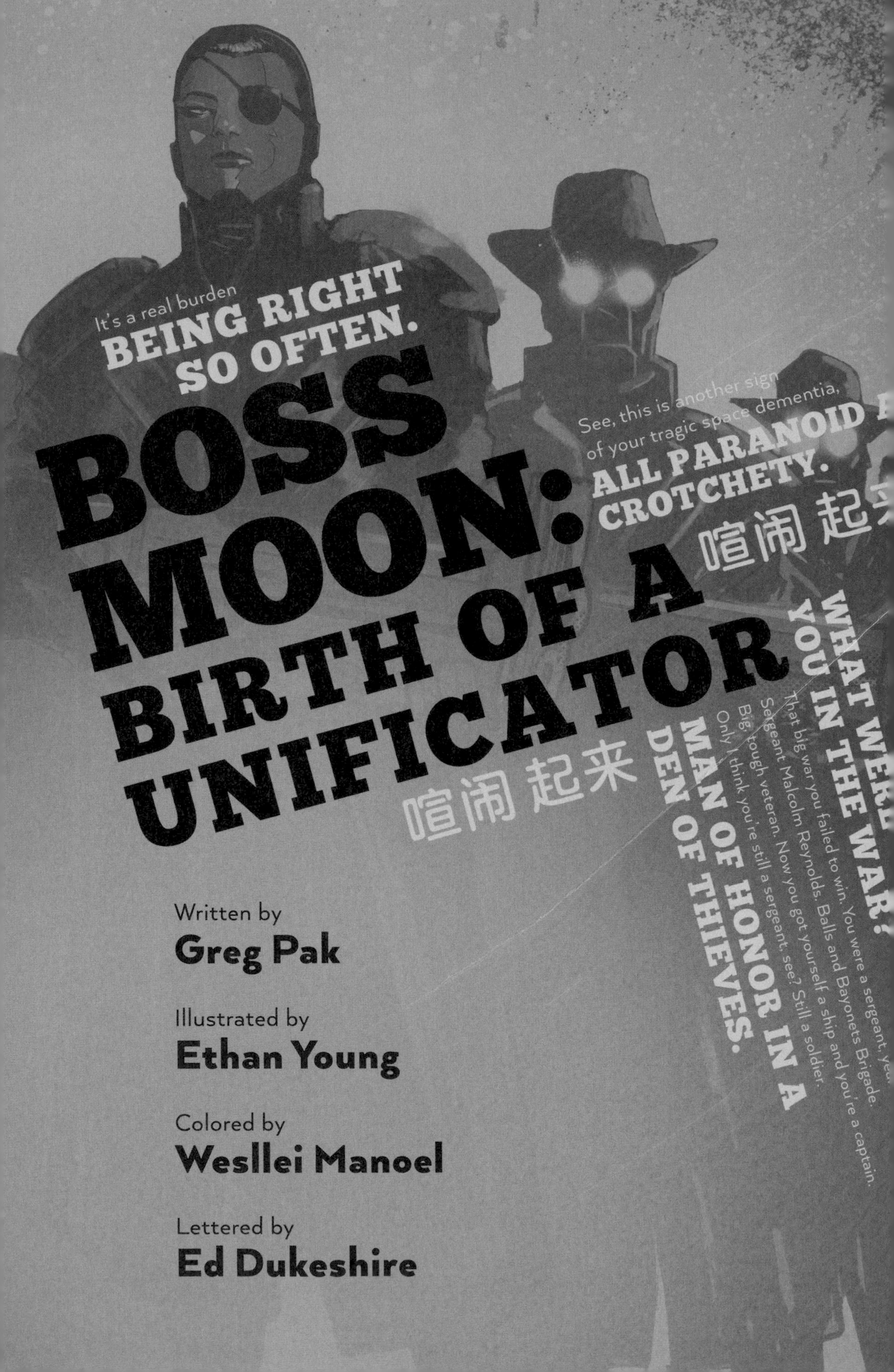
It's a real burden
BEING RIGHT
SO OFTEN.
See, this is another sign
of your tragic space dementia,
ALL PARANOID
CROTCHETY.
喧闹起
喧闹起来
WHAT
YOU IN THE WAR?
That big war you failed to win. You were a sergeant,
Sergeant Malcolm Reynolds. Balls and Bayonets Brigade.
Big, tough veteran. Now you got yourself a ship and you're a captain.
Only I think you're still a sergeant, see? Still a soldier.
MAN OF HONOR IN A
DEN OF THIEVES.

Written by
Greg Pak

Illustrated by
Ethan Young

Colored by
Wesllei Manoel

Lettered by
Ed Dukeshire

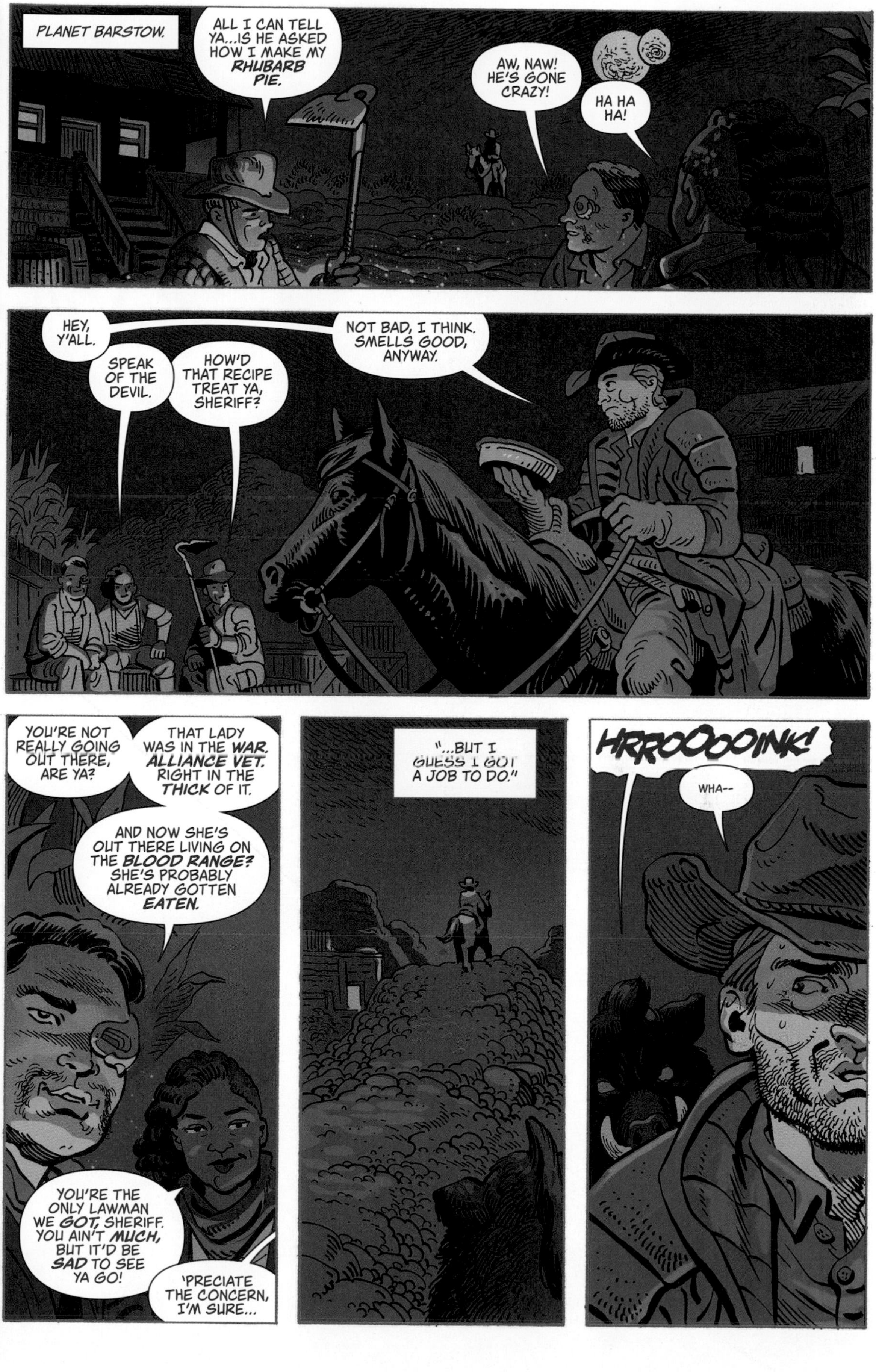
PLANET BARSTOW.
ALL I CAN TELL YA...IS HE ASKED HOW I MAKE MY RHUBARB PIE.
AW, NAW! HE'S GONE CRAZY!
HA HA HA!
HEY, Y'ALL.
NOT BAD, I THINK. SMELLS GOOD, ANYWAY.
SPEAK OF THE DEVIL.
HOW'D THAT RECIPE TREAT YA, SHERIFF?
YOU'RE NOT REALLY GOING OUT THERE, ARE YA?
THAT LADY WAS IN THE WAR. ALLIANCE VET. RIGHT IN THE THICK OF IT.
AND NOW SHE'S OUT THERE LIVING ON THE BLOOD RANGE? SHE'S PROBABLY ALREADY GOTTEN EATEN.
YOU'RE THE ONLY LAWMAN WE GOT, SHERIFF. YOU AIN'T MUCH, BUT IT'D BE SAD TO SEE YA GO!
'PRECIATE THE CONCERN, I'M SURE...
"...BUT I GUESS I GOT A JOB TO DO."
HRROOOOOINK!
WHA--

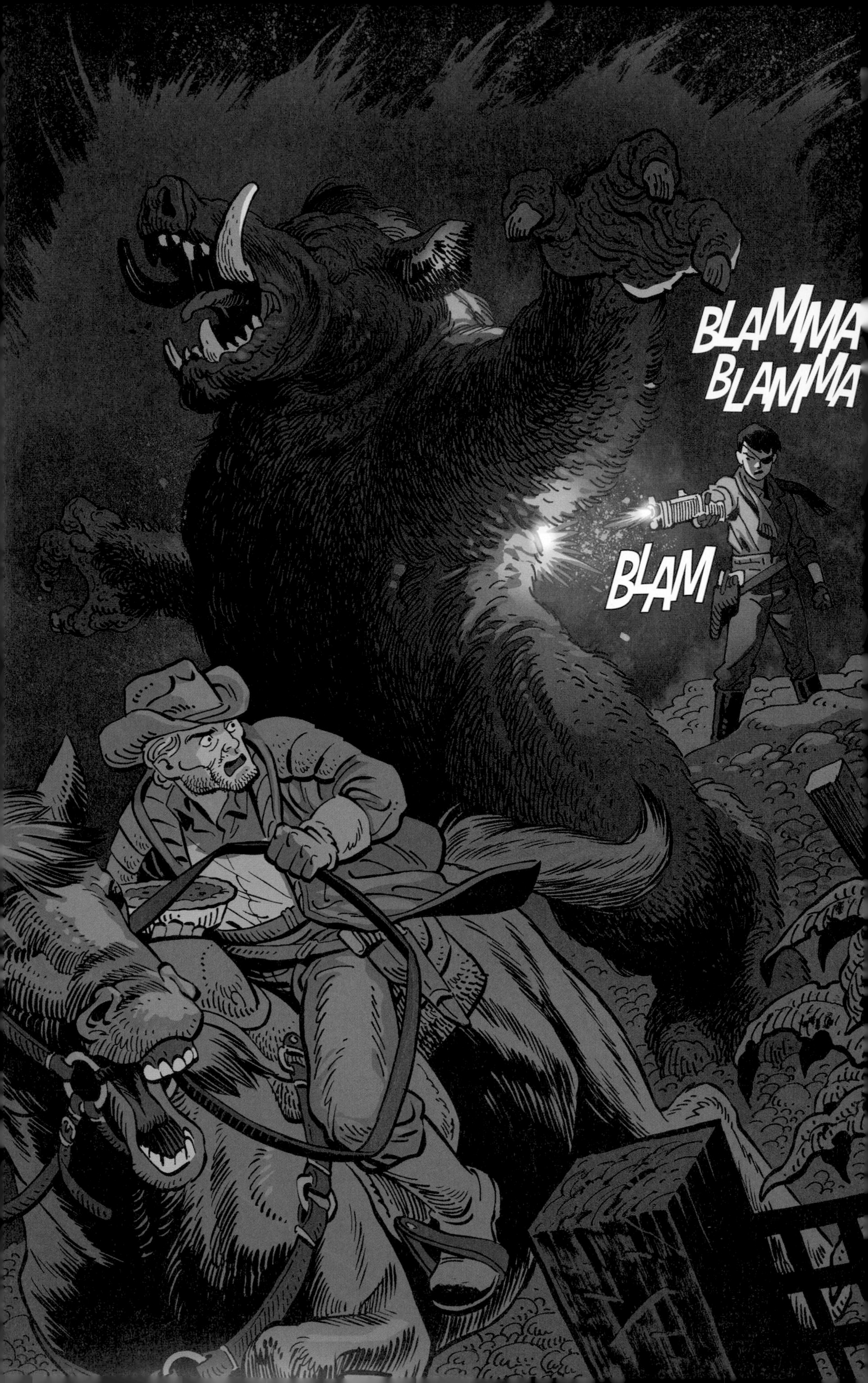
BLAMMA
BLAMMA
BLAM

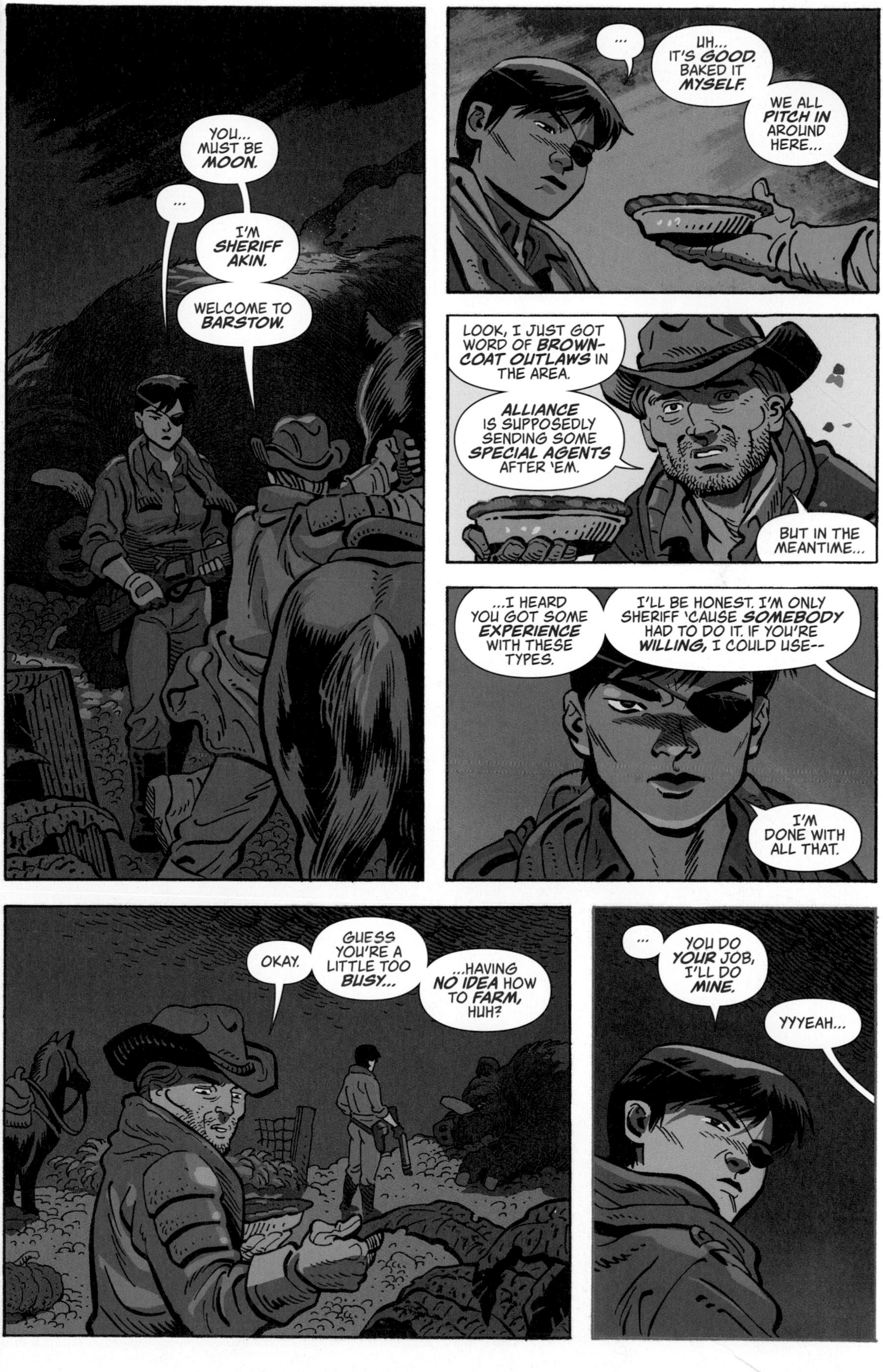
YOU... MUST BE MOON.
...
I'M SHERIFF AKIN.
WELCOME TO BARSTOW.
...
UH... IT'S GOOD. BAKED IT MYSELF.
WE ALL PITCH IN AROUND HERE...
LOOK, I JUST GOT WORD OF BROWN-COAT OUTLAWS IN THE AREA.
ALLIANCE IS SUPPOSEDLY SENDING SOME SPECIAL AGENTS AFTER 'EM.
BUT IN THE MEANTIME...
...I HEARD YOU GOT SOME EXPERIENCE WITH THESE TYPES.
I'LL BE HONEST. I'M ONLY SHERIFF 'CAUSE SOMEBODY HAD TO DO IT. IF YOU'RE WILLING, I COULD USE--
I'M DONE WITH ALL THAT.
OKAY.
GUESS YOU'RE A LITTLE TOO BUSY...
...HAVING NO IDEA HOW TO FARM, HUH?
...
YOU DO YOUR JOB, I'LL DO MINE.
YYYEAH...

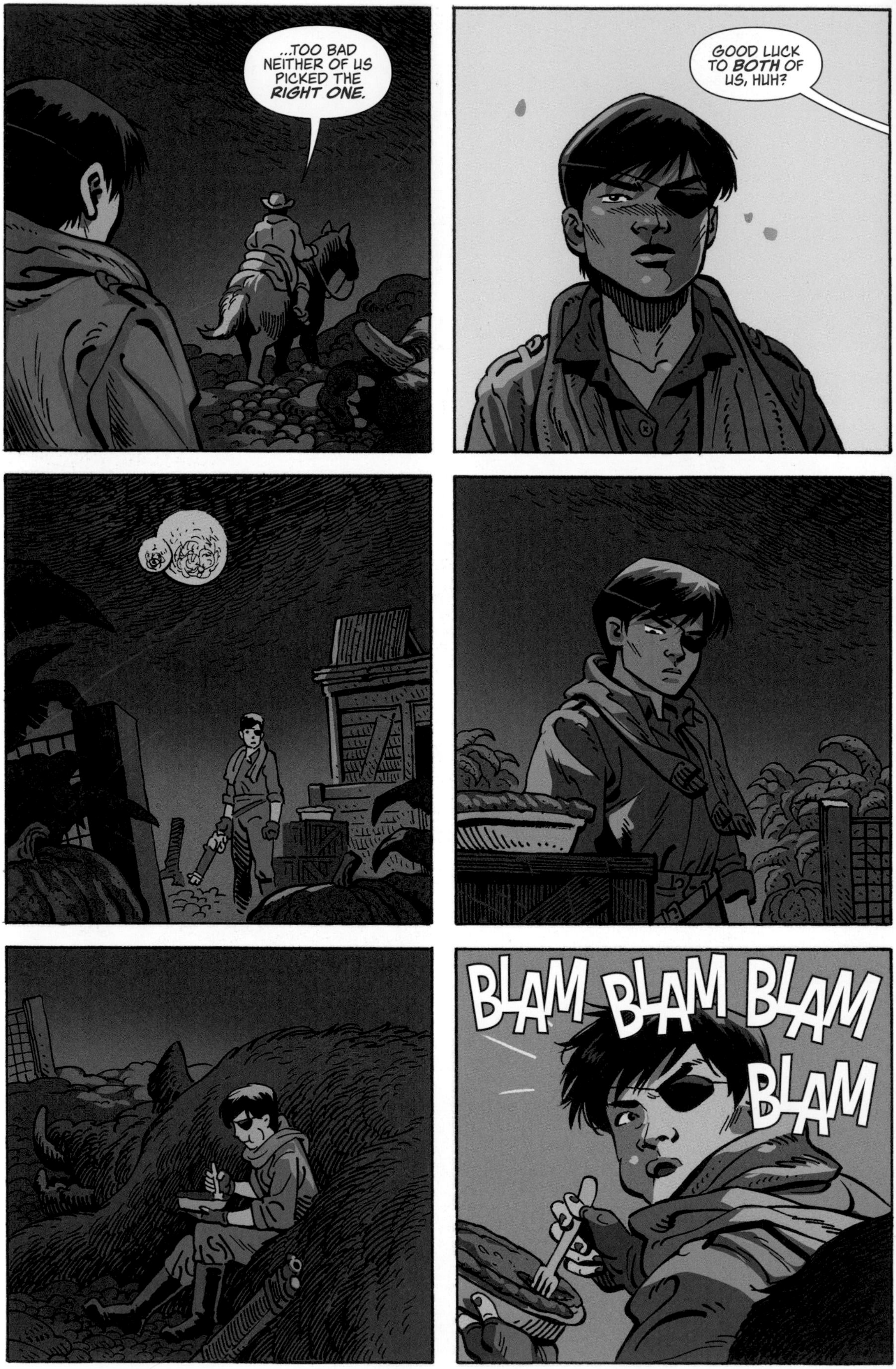
...TOO BAD NEITHER OF US PICKED THE RIGHT ONE.
GOOD LUCK TO BOTH OF US, HUH?
BLAM BLAM BLAM BLAM

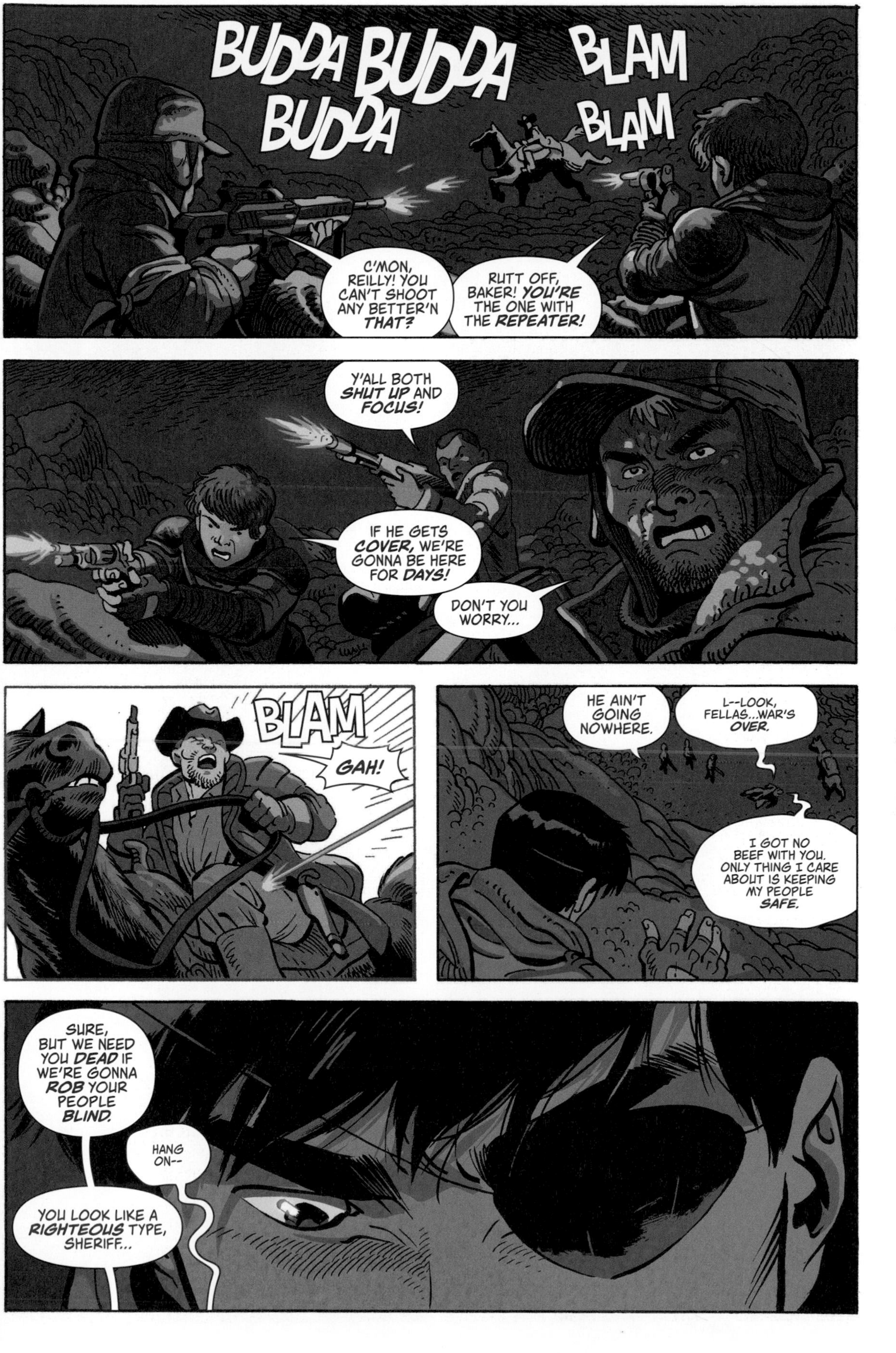
BUDDA BUDDA BUDDA
BLAM BLAM
C'MON, REILLY! YOU CAN'T SHOOT ANY BETTER'N THAT?
RUTT OFF, BAKER! YOU'RE THE ONE WITH THE REPEATER!
Y'ALL BOTH SHUT UP AND FOCUS!
IF HE GETS COVER, WE'RE GONNA BE HERE FOR DAYS!
DON'T YOU WORRY...
BLAM
GAH!
HE AIN'T GOING NOWHERE.
L--LOOK, FELLAS...WAR'S OVER.
I GOT NO BEEF WITH YOU. ONLY THING I CARE ABOUT IS KEEPING MY PEOPLE SAFE.
SURE, BUT WE NEED YOU DEAD IF WE'RE GONNA ROB YOUR PEOPLE BLIND.
HANG ON--
YOU LOOK LIKE A RIGHTEOUS TYPE, SHERIFF...

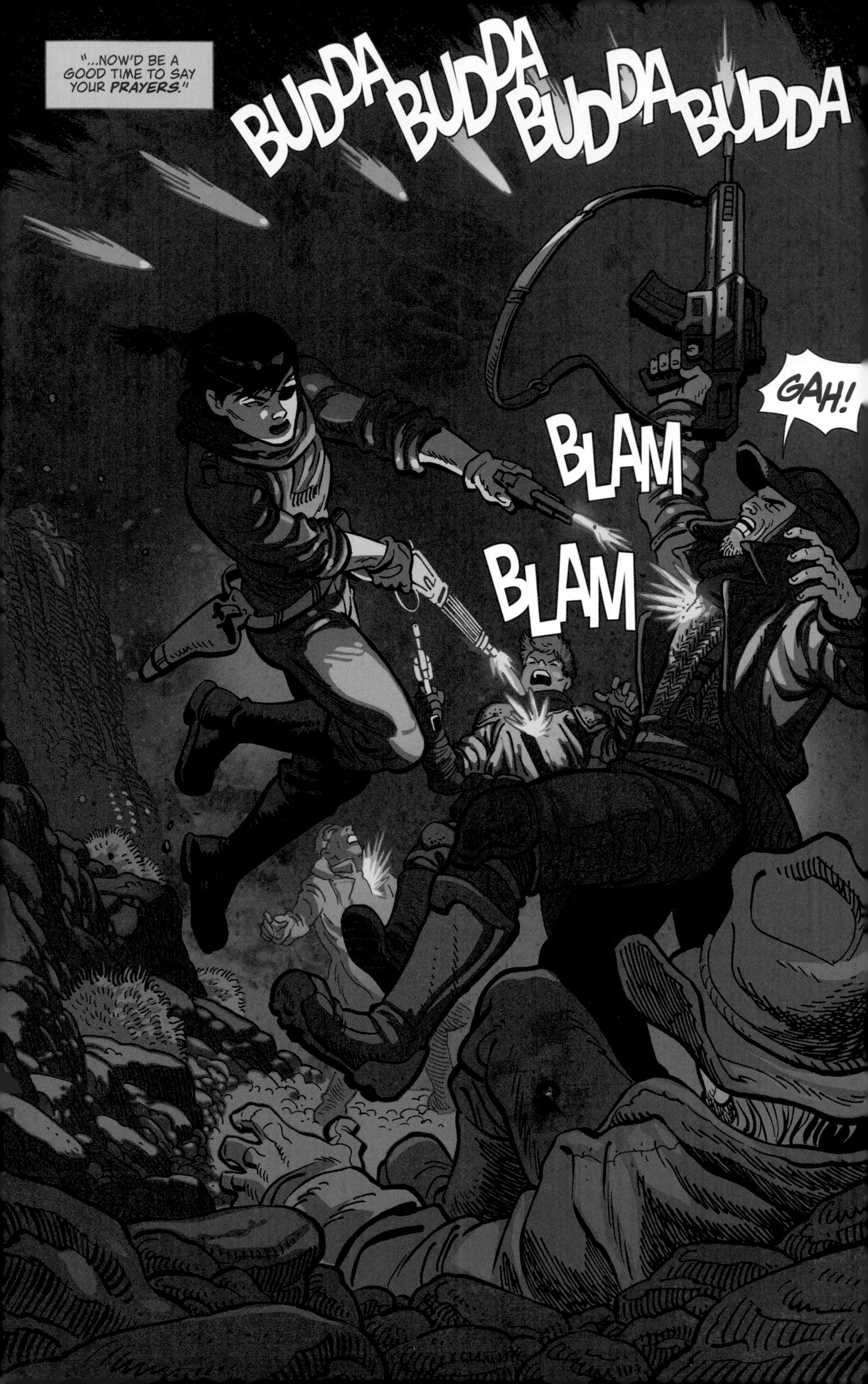
"...NOW'D BE A GOOD TIME TO SAY YOUR PRAYERS."
BUDDA BUDDA BUDDA BUDDA
GAH!
BLAM
BLAM

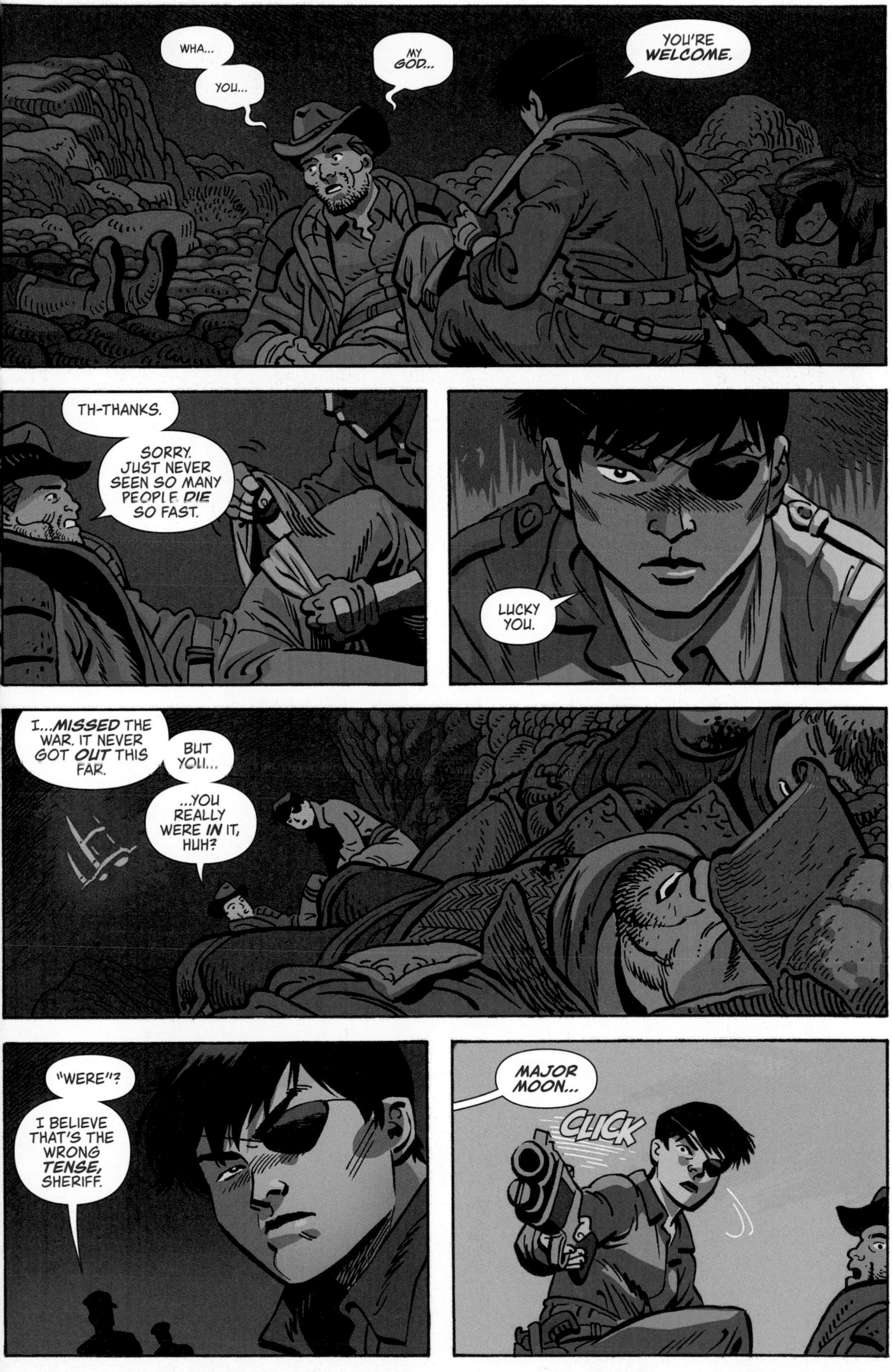
WHA...
YOU...
MY GOD...
YOU'RE WELCOME.
TH-THANKS.
SORRY. JUST NEVER SEEN SO MANY PEOPLE DIE SO FAST.
LUCKY YOU.
I...MISSED THE WAR. IT NEVER GOT OUT THIS FAR.
BUT YOU...
...YOU REALLY WERE IN IT, HUH?
"WERE"?
I BELIEVE THAT'S THE WRONG TENSE, SHERIFF.
MAJOR MOON...
CLICK

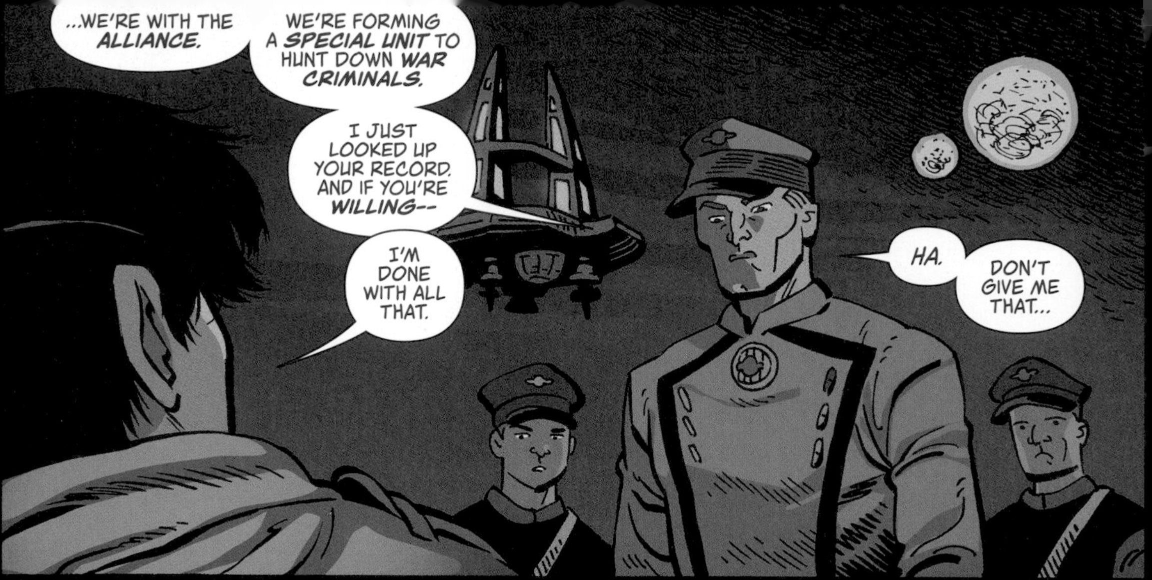
...WE'RE WITH THE ALLIANCE.
WE'RE FORMING A SPECIAL UNIT TO HUNT DOWN WAR CRIMINALS.
I JUST LOOKED UP YOUR RECORD. AND IF YOU'RE WILLING--
I'M DONE WITH ALL THAT.
HA.
DON'T GIVE ME THAT...

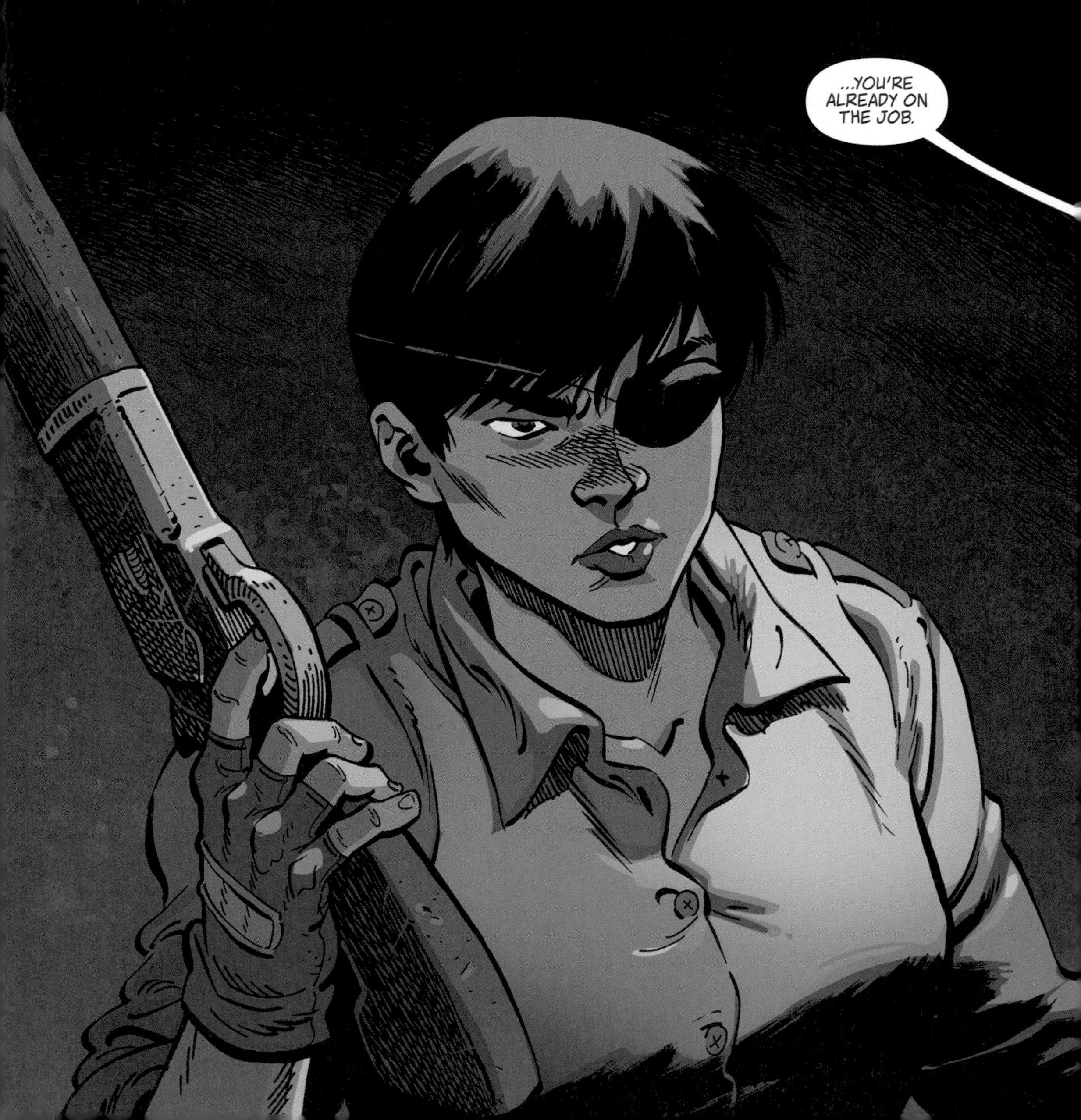
...YOU'RE ALREADY ON THE JOB.

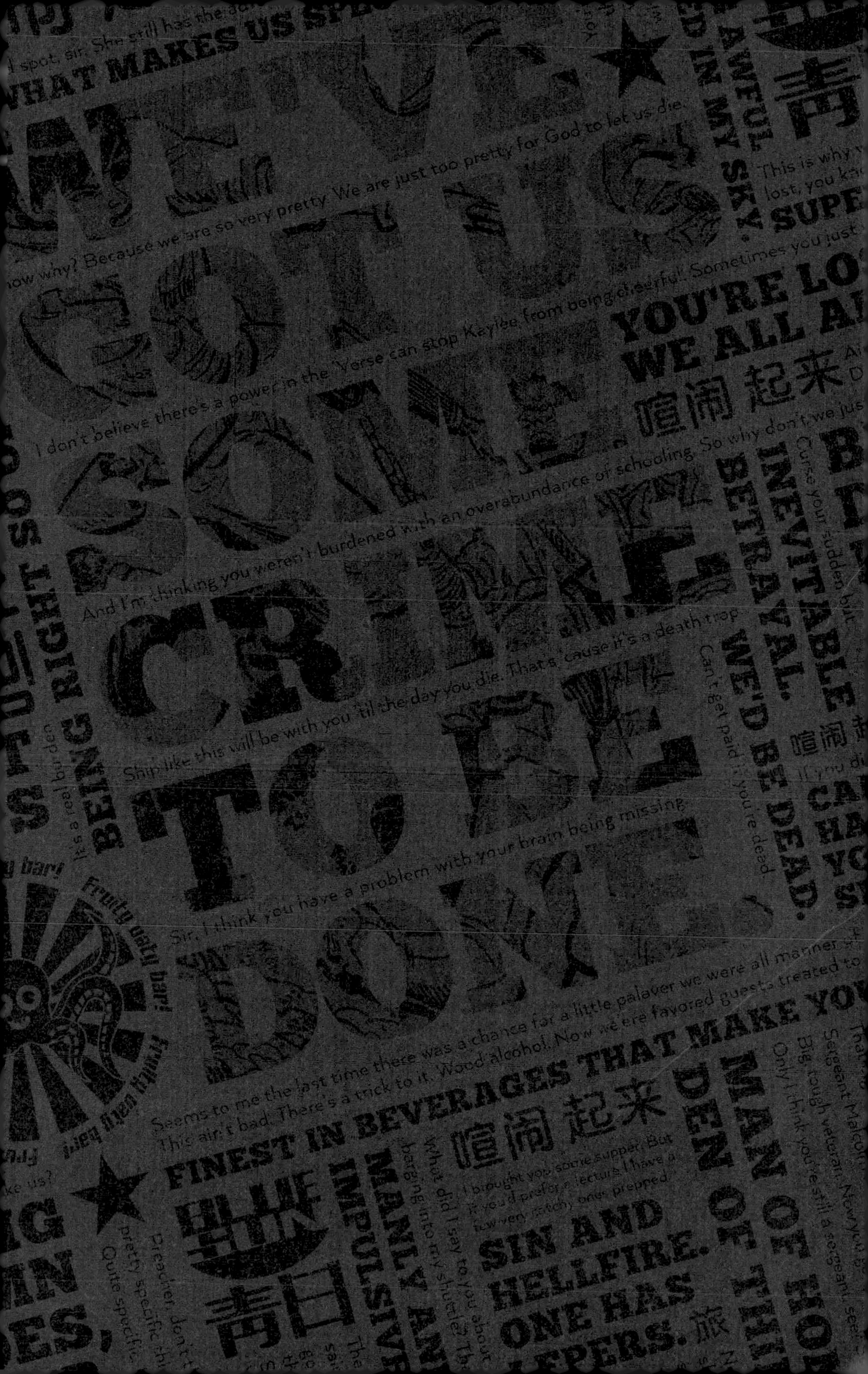
WHAT MAKES US
WE'VE GOT US SOME CRIME TO BE DONE.
Now why? Because we are so very pretty. We are just too pretty for God to let us die.
I don't believe there's a power in the 'Verse can stop Kaylee from being cheerful. Sometimes you just
And I'm thinking you weren't burdened with an overabundance of schooling. So why don't we just
Ship like this will be with you 'til the day you die. That's 'cause it's a death trap
Sir, I think you have a problem with your brain being missing.
Seems to me the last time there was a chance for a little palaver we were all manner of
This ain't bad. There's a trick to it. Wood alcohol. Now we're favored guests treated to
AWFUL
IN MY SKY.
This is why w
SUPE
YOU'RE LO
WE ALL A
喧闹 起来
INEVITABLE
BETRAYAL.
WE'D BE DEAD.
Curse your sudden but
Can't get paid if you're dead
BEING RIGHT
It's a real burden
FINEST IN BEVERAGES THAT MAKE YOU
喧闹 起来
MANLY AN
IMPULSIVE
What did I say to you about
barging into my shuttle?
I brought you some supper. But
if you'd prefer a lecture, I have a
few very catchy ones prepped.
SIN AND
HELLFIRE.
ONE HAS
LEPERS.
DEN
MAN OF THE
Big, tough veteran
Sergeant Malcolm
Only I think you're still a sergeant
Preacher, don't
Quite specific
pretty
Fruity oaty bar!
青

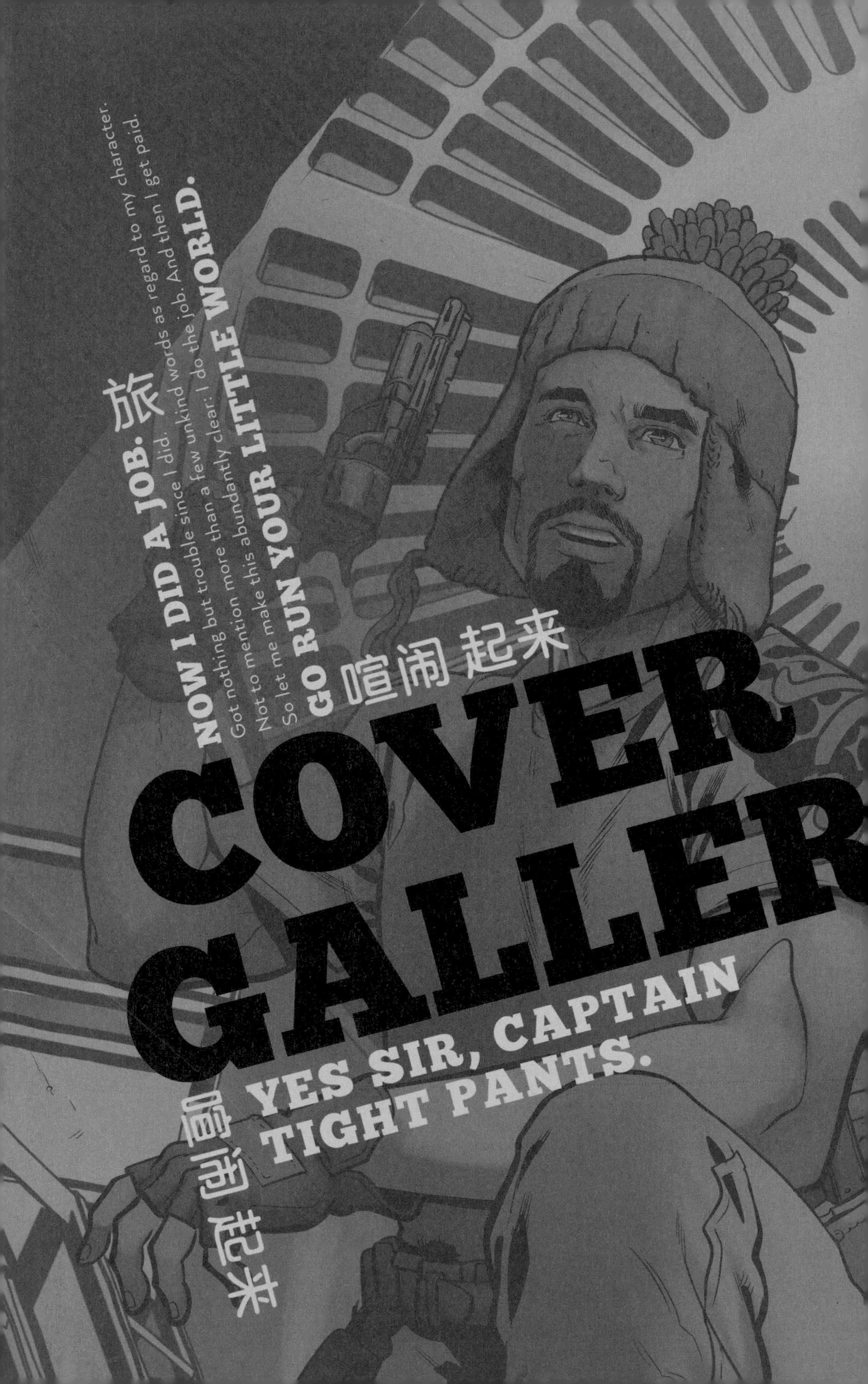

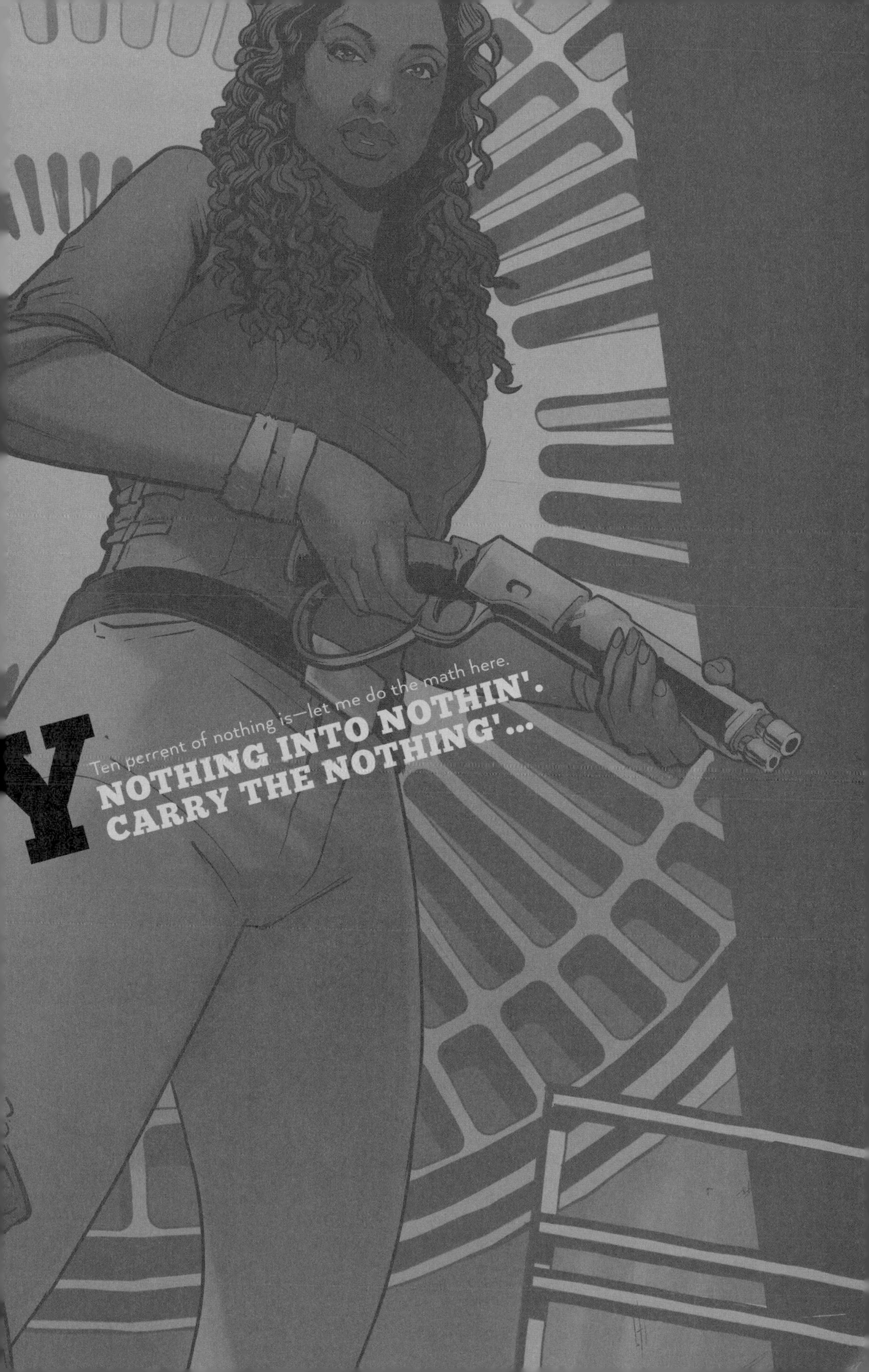
Y
Ten percent of nothing is—let me do the math here.
NOTHING INTO NOTHIN'.
CARRY THE NOTHING'...

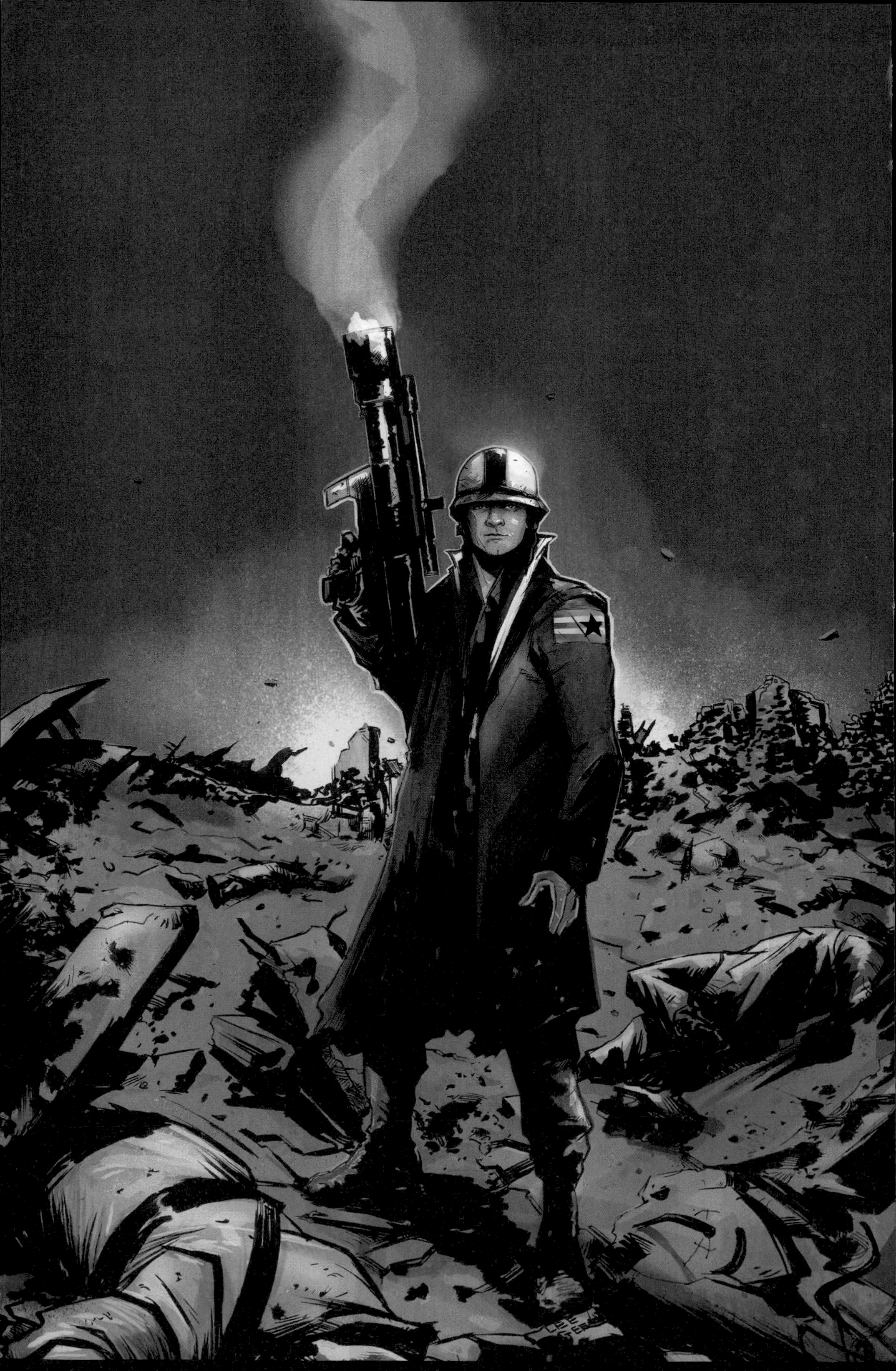

Firefly #5 Cover by **Lee Garbett**

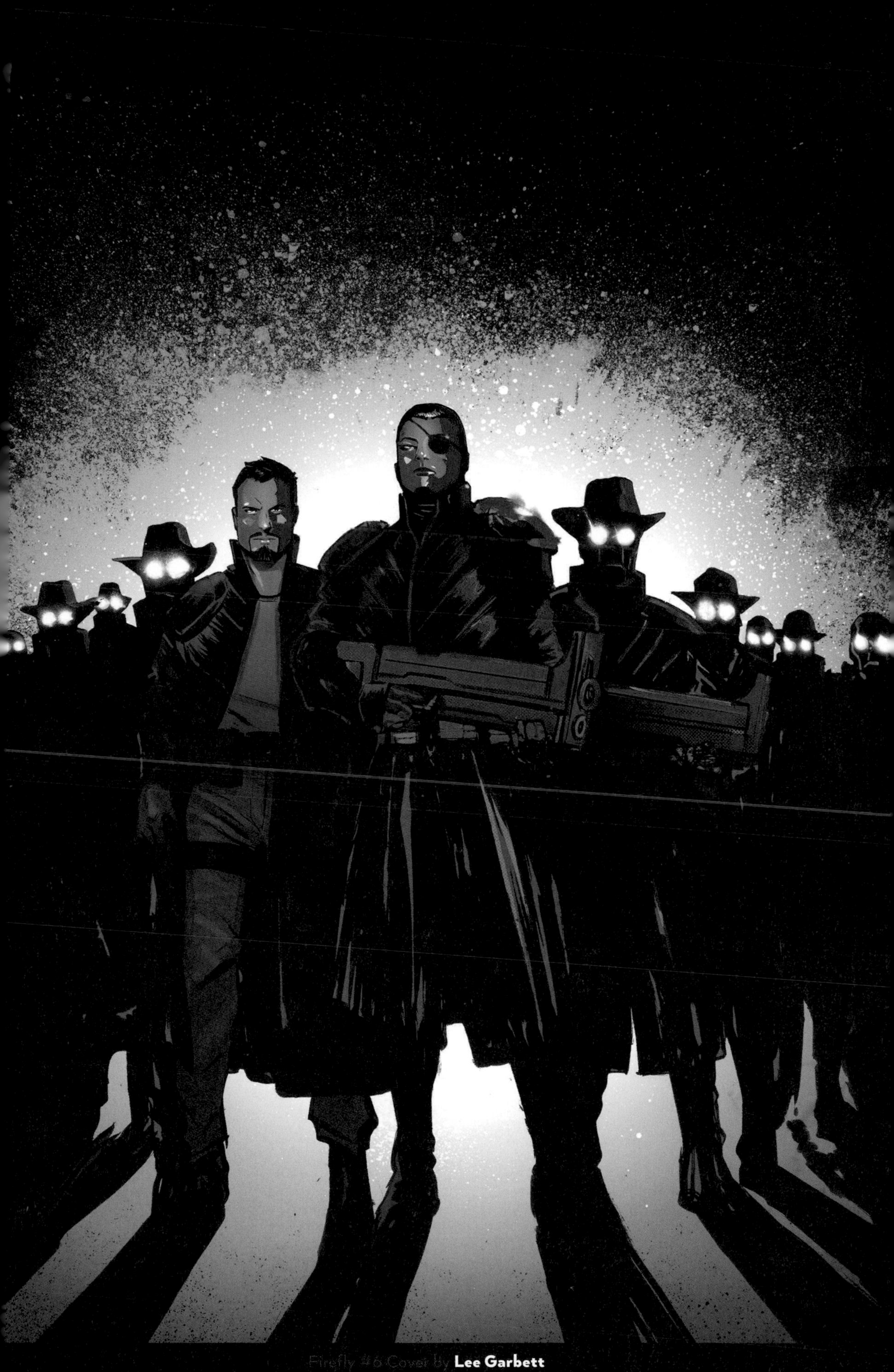

Firefly #6 Cover by **Lee Garbett**

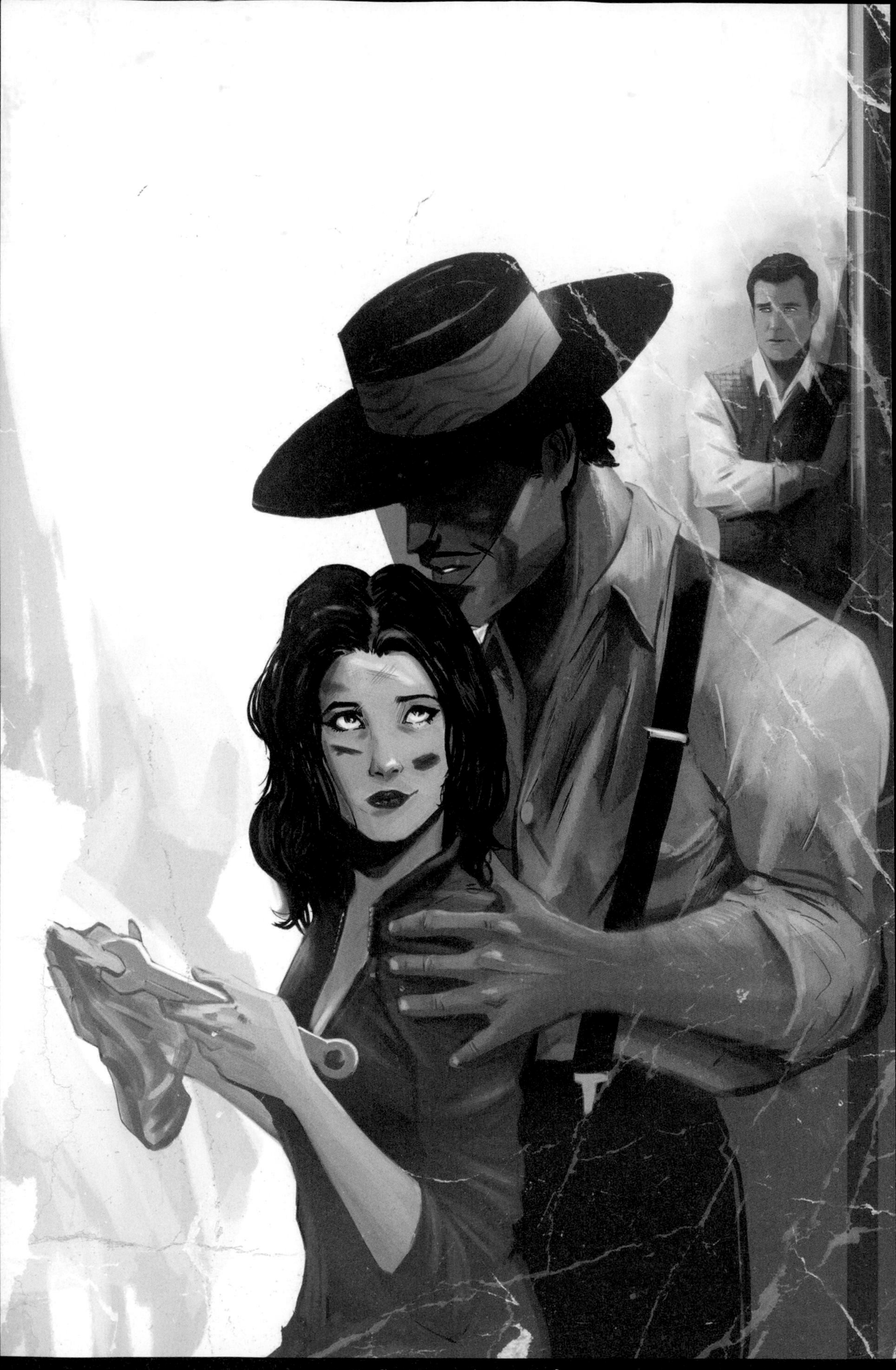

Firefly #7 Cover by **Lee Garbett**

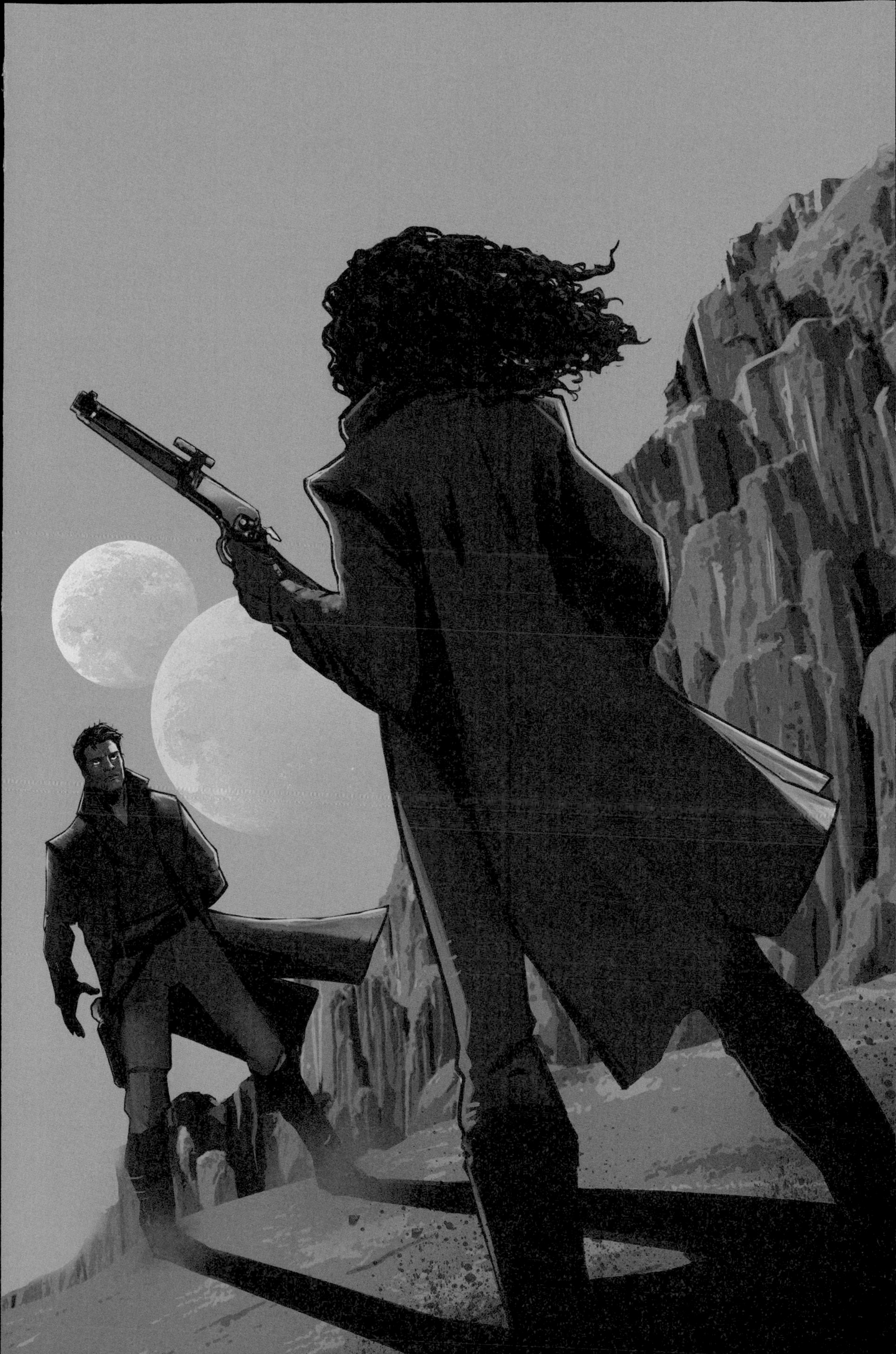

Firefly #8 Cover by **Lee Garbett**

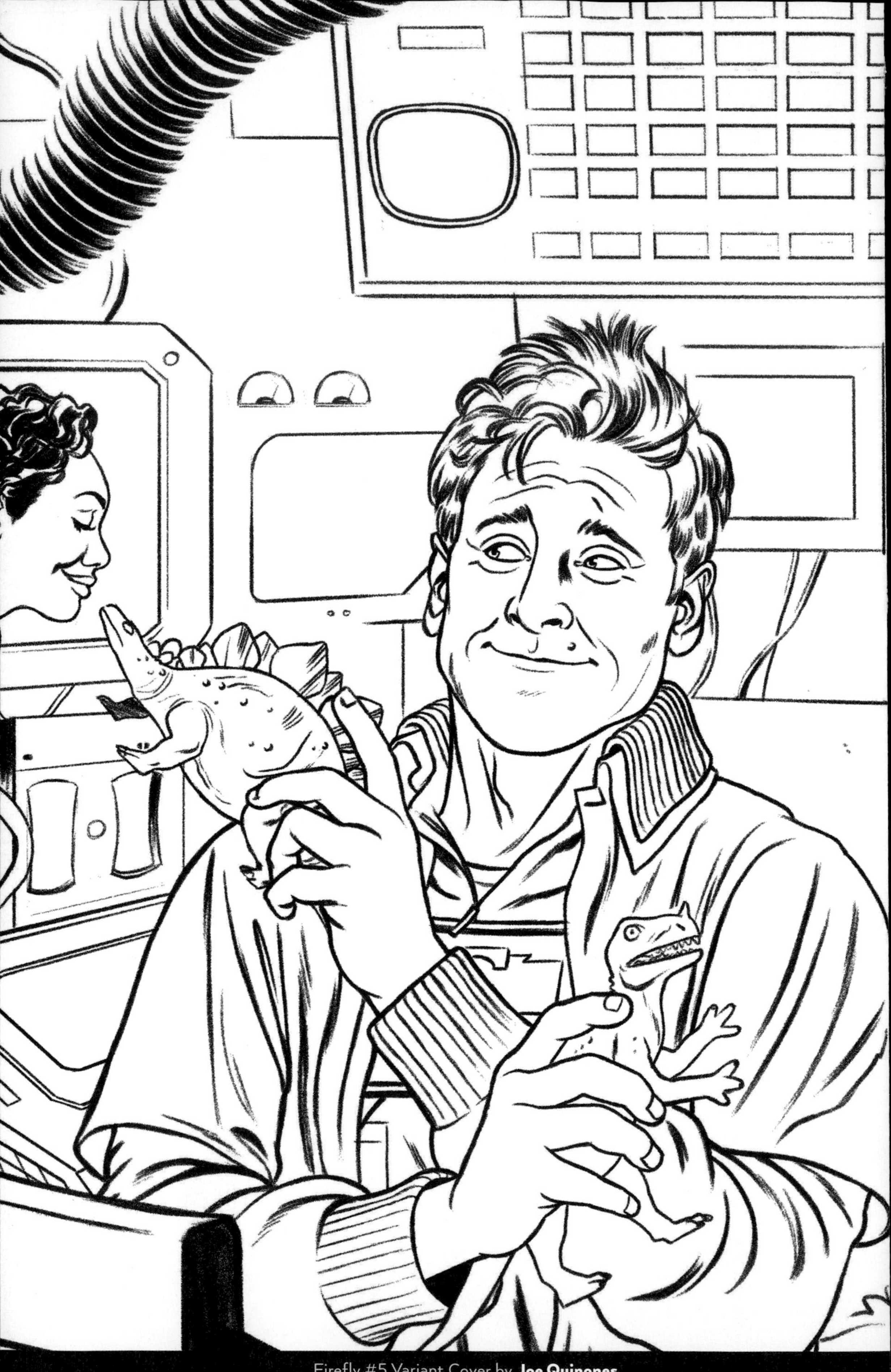

Firefly #5 Variant Cover by **Joe Quinones**

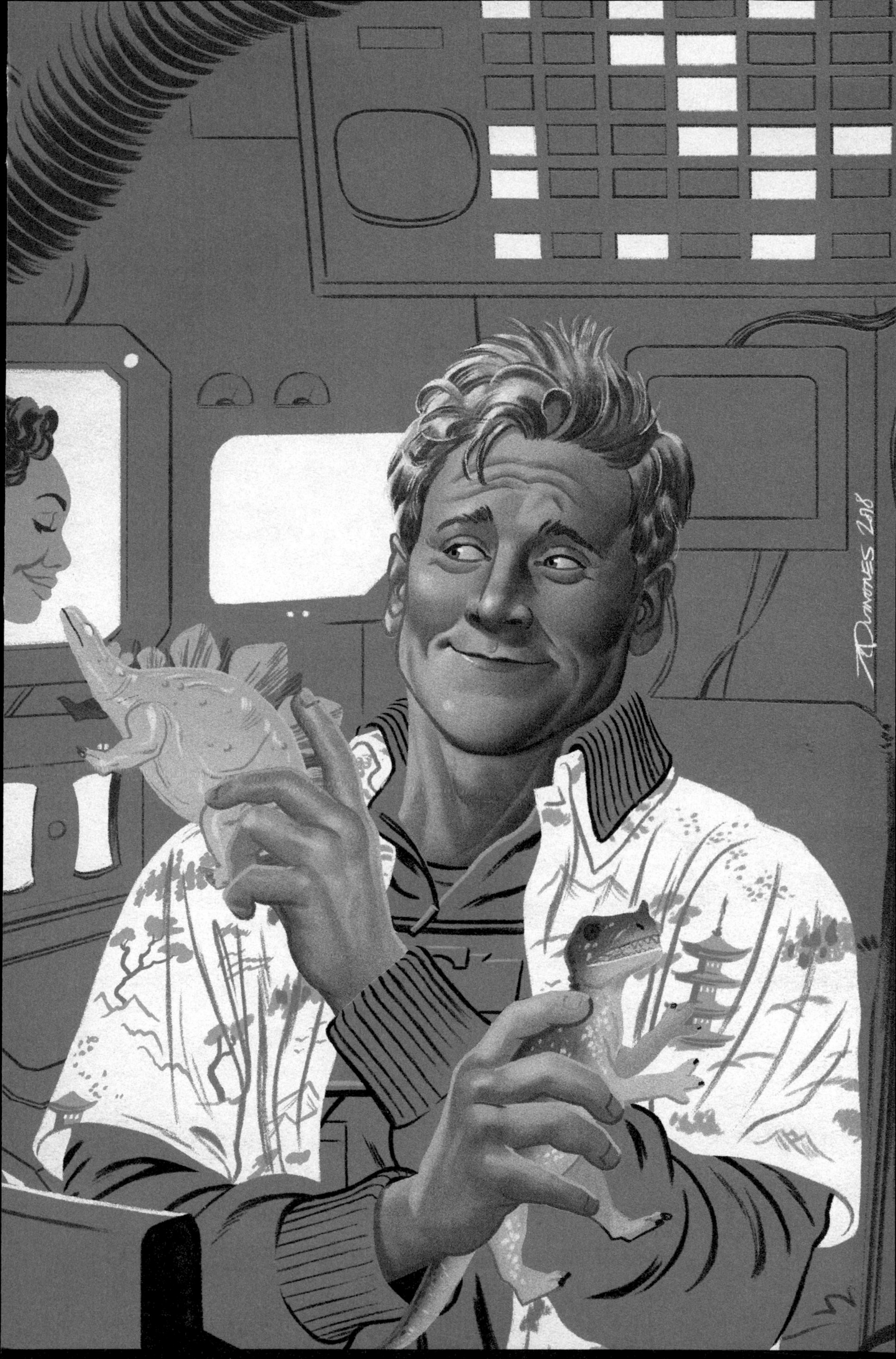
QUINONES 2018

Firefly #5 Preorder Cover by **Joe Quinones**

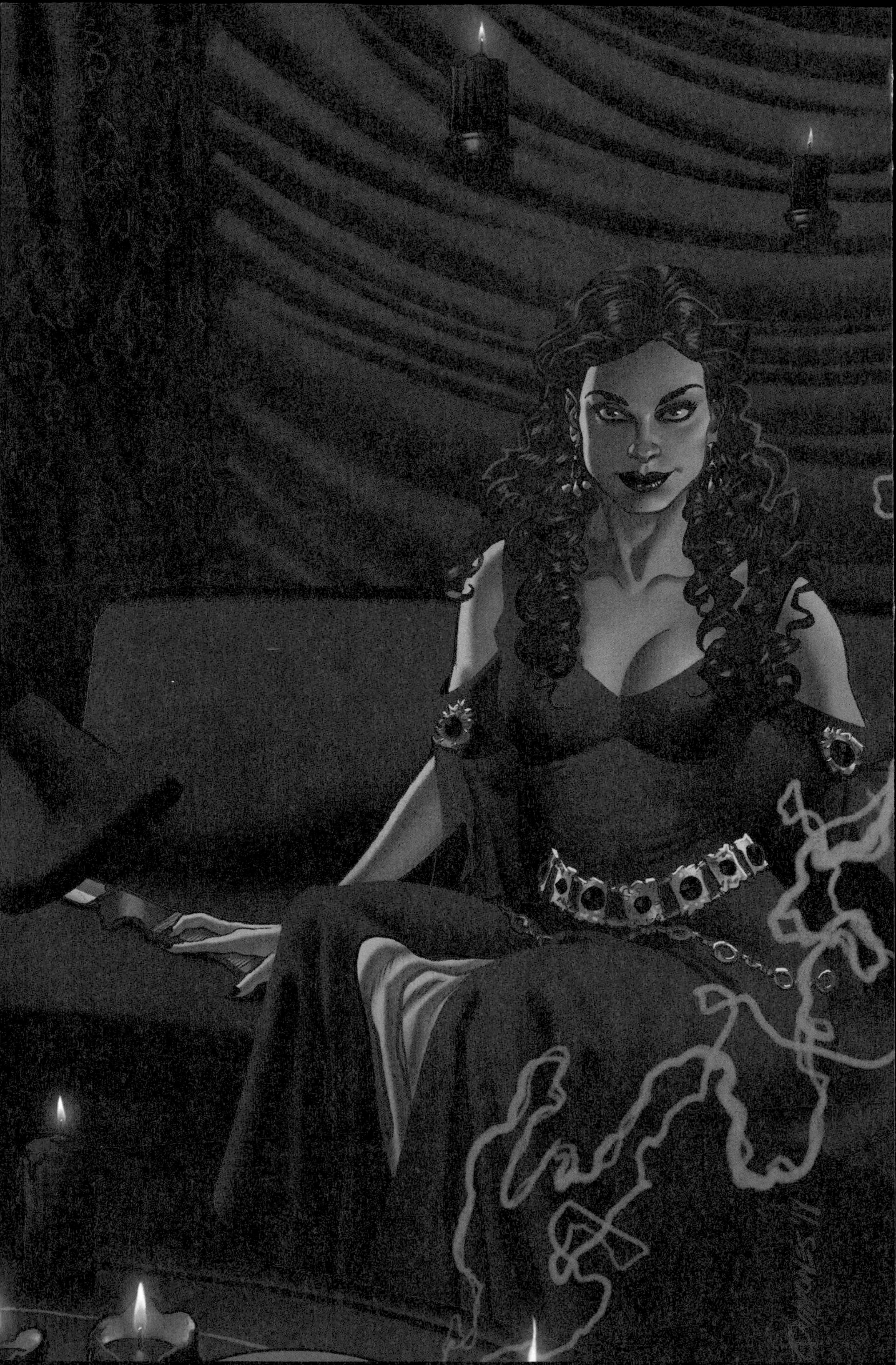

Firefly #6 Preorder Cover by **Joe Quinones**

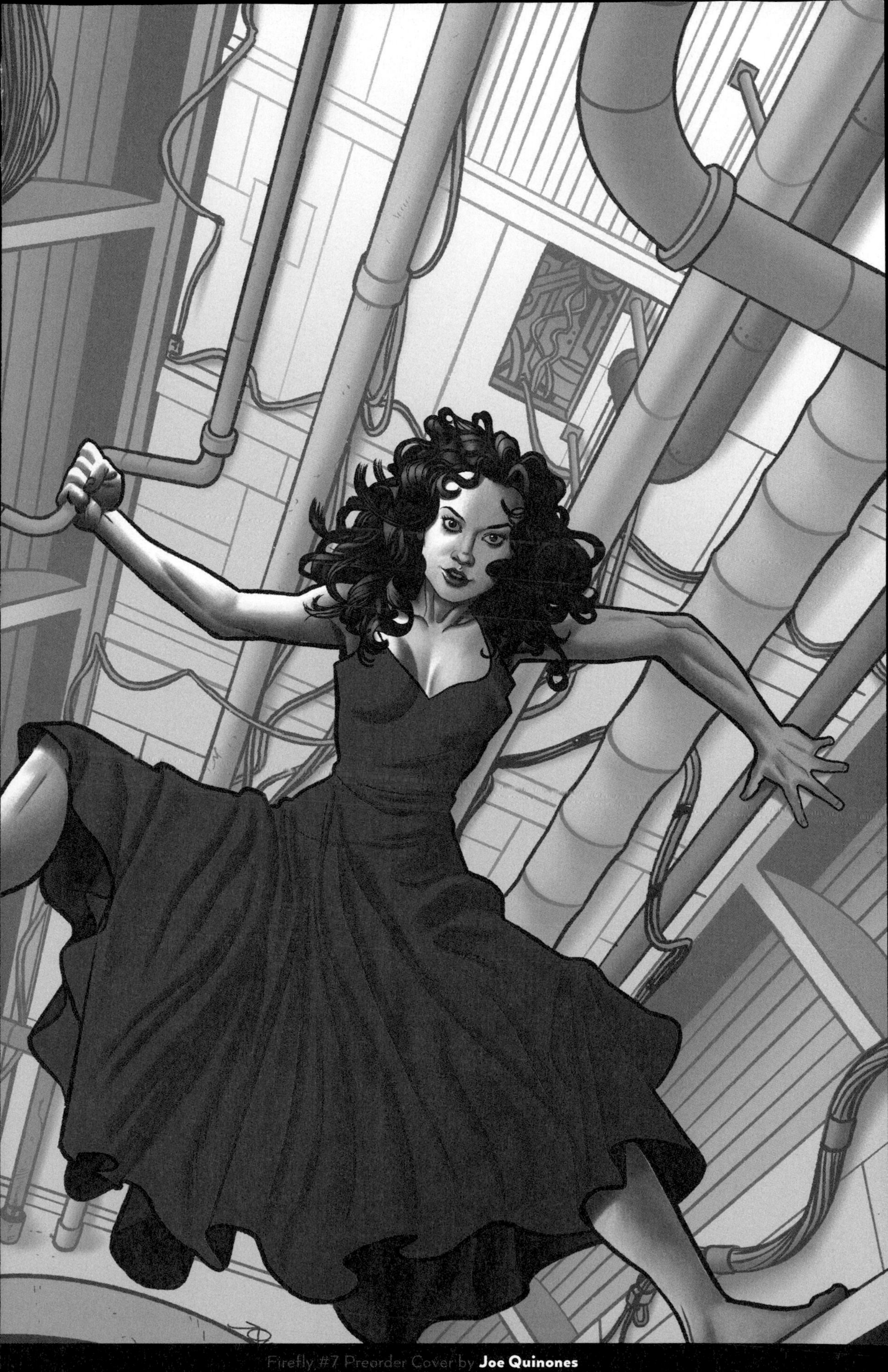

Firefly #7 Preorder Cover by **Joe Quinones**

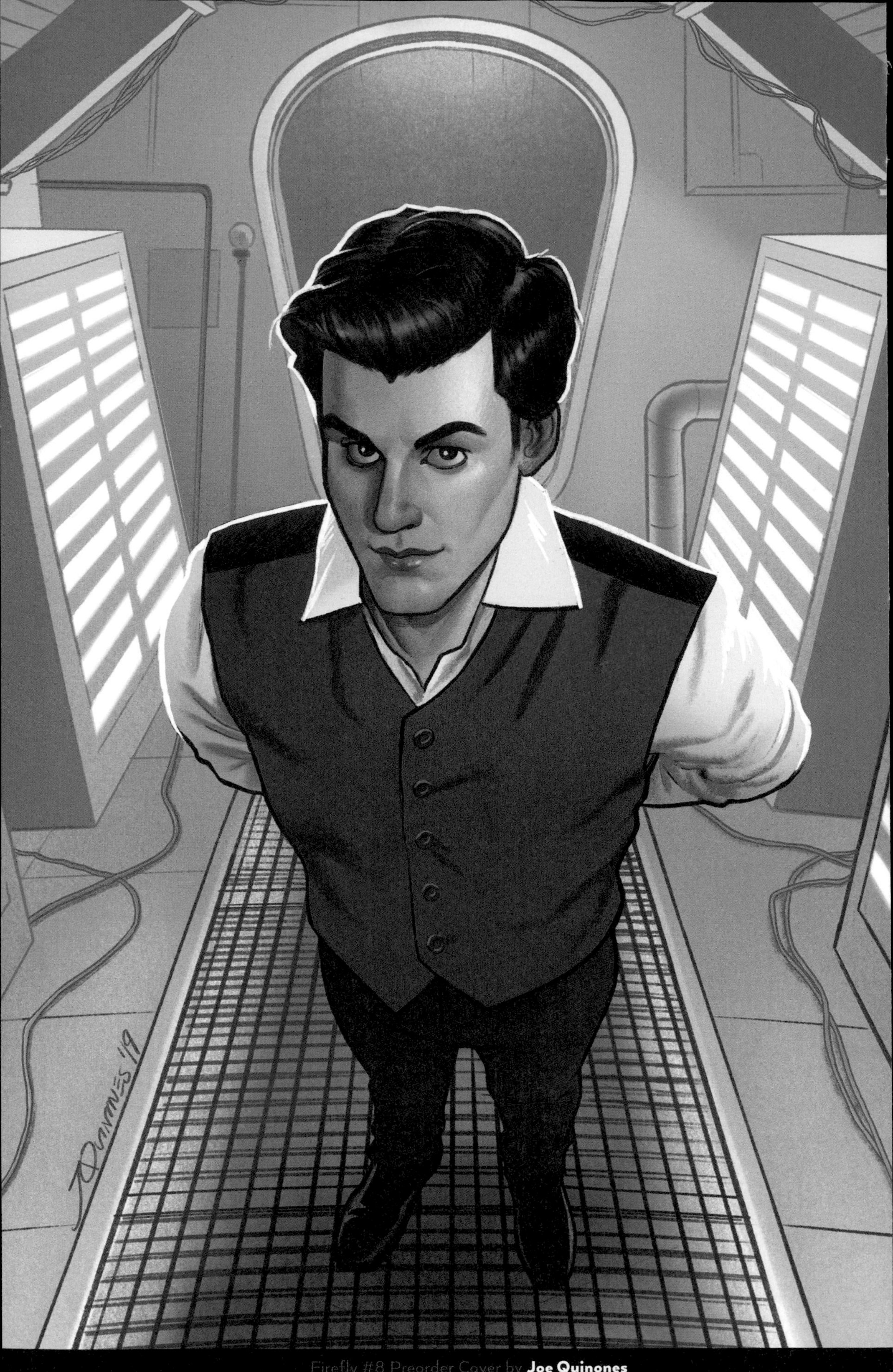

Firefly #8 Preorder Cover by **Joe Quinones**

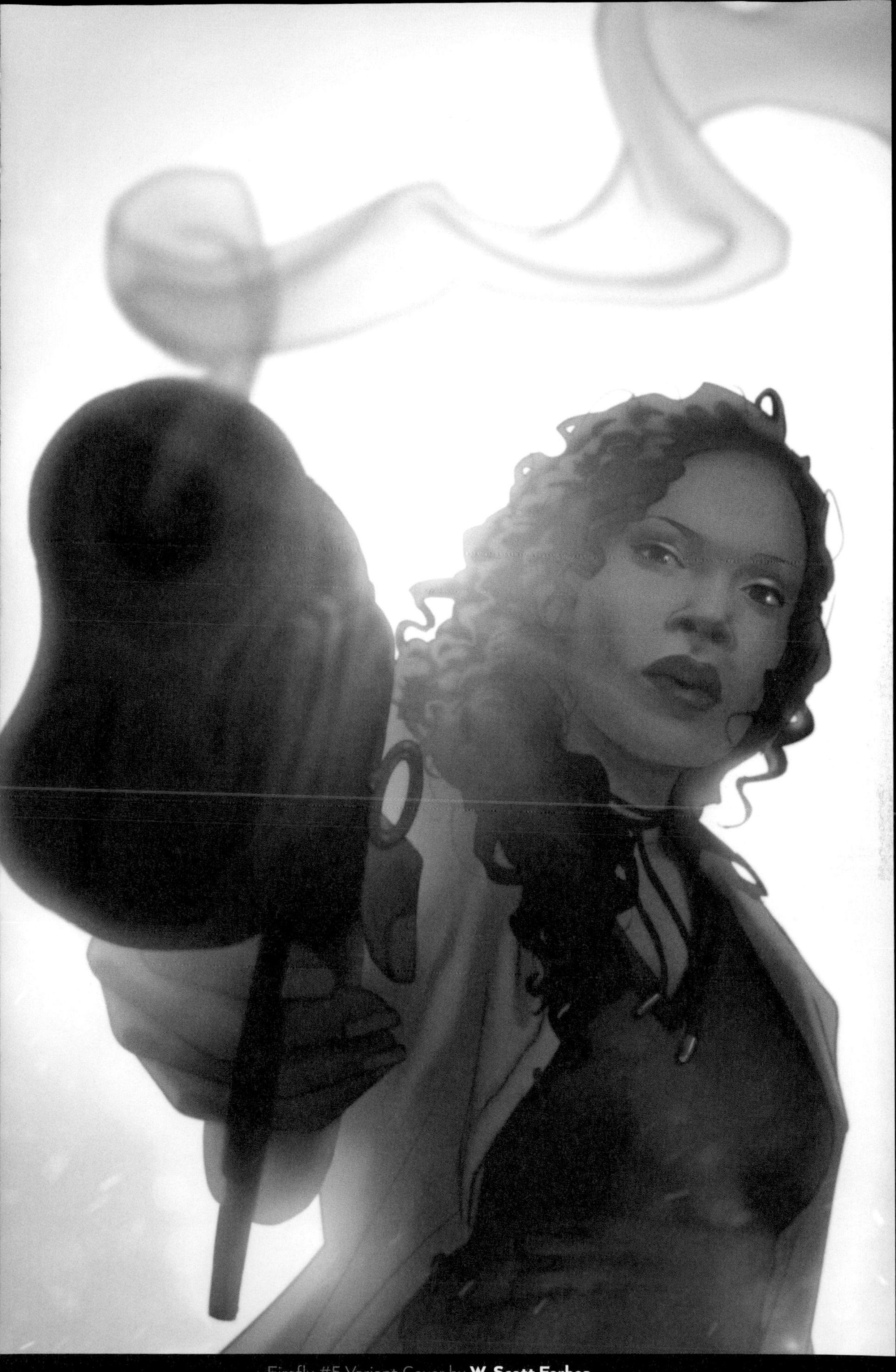

Firefly #5 Variant Cover by **W. Scott Forbes**

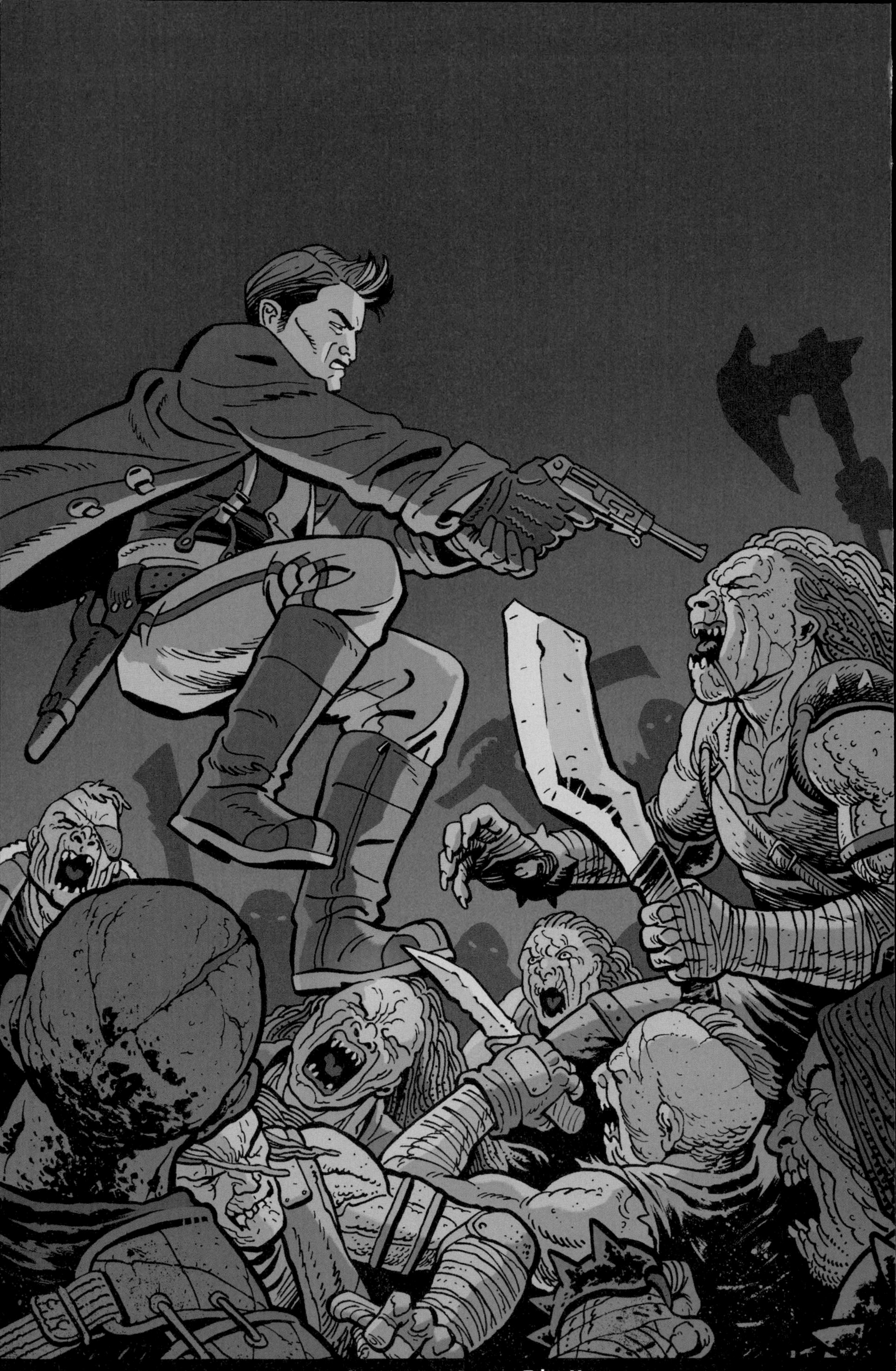

Firefly #6 Variant Cover by **Ethan Young**

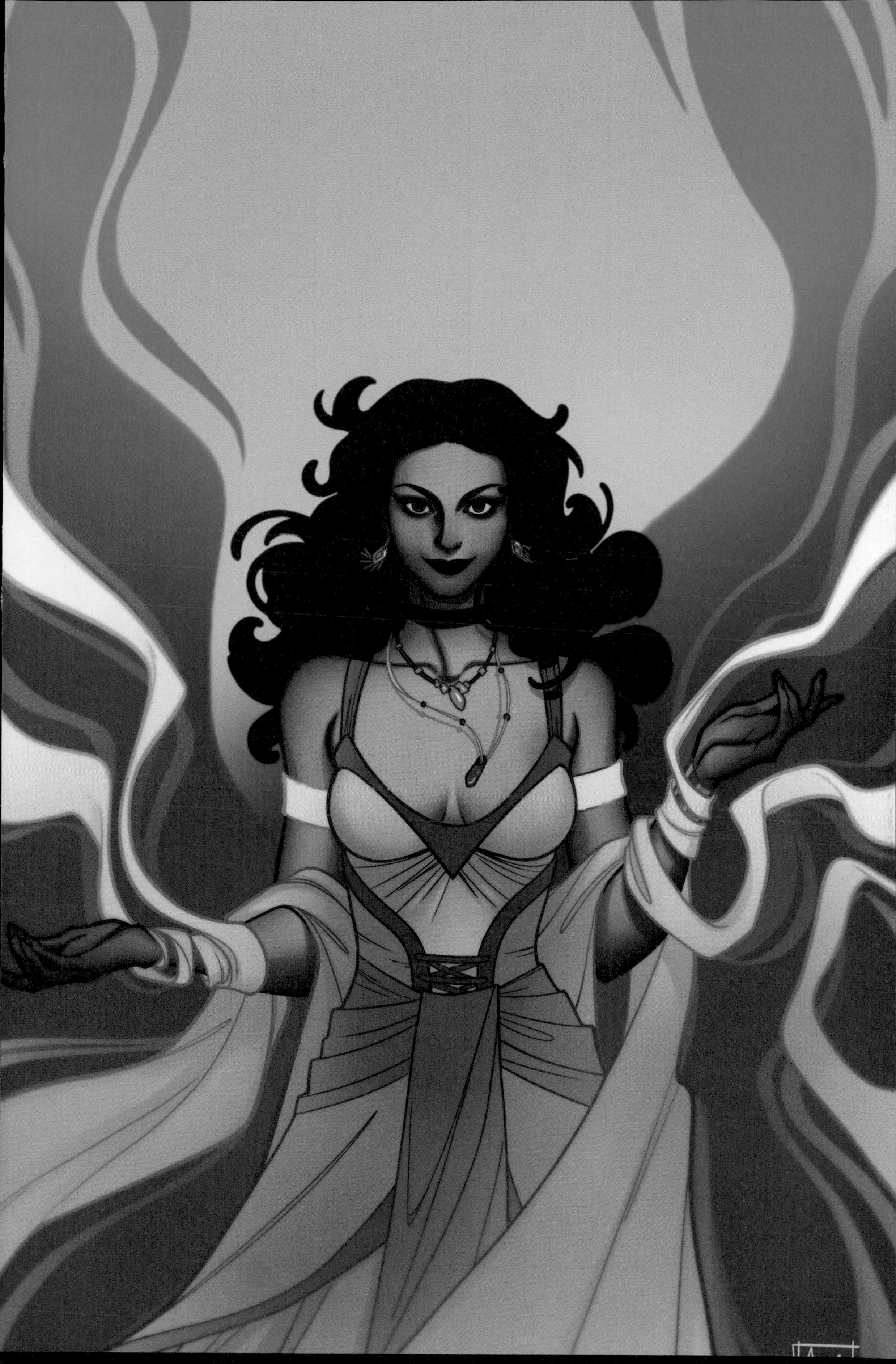

Firefly #7 Variant Cover by **Amelia Vidal**

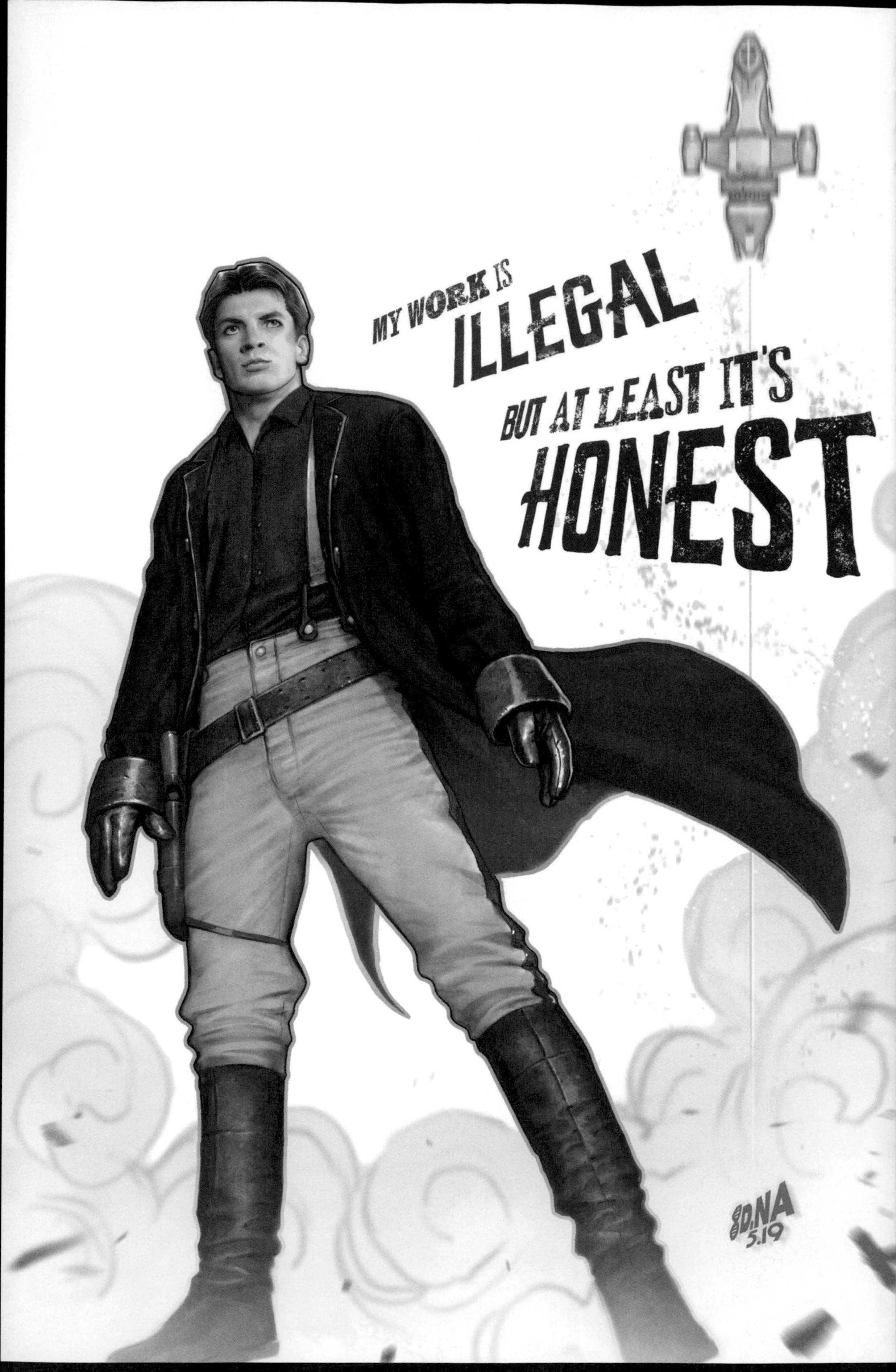
MY WORK IS
ILLEGAL
BUT AT LEAST IT'S
HONEST
D.NA
5.19

Firefly #8 Variant Cover by **David Nakayama**

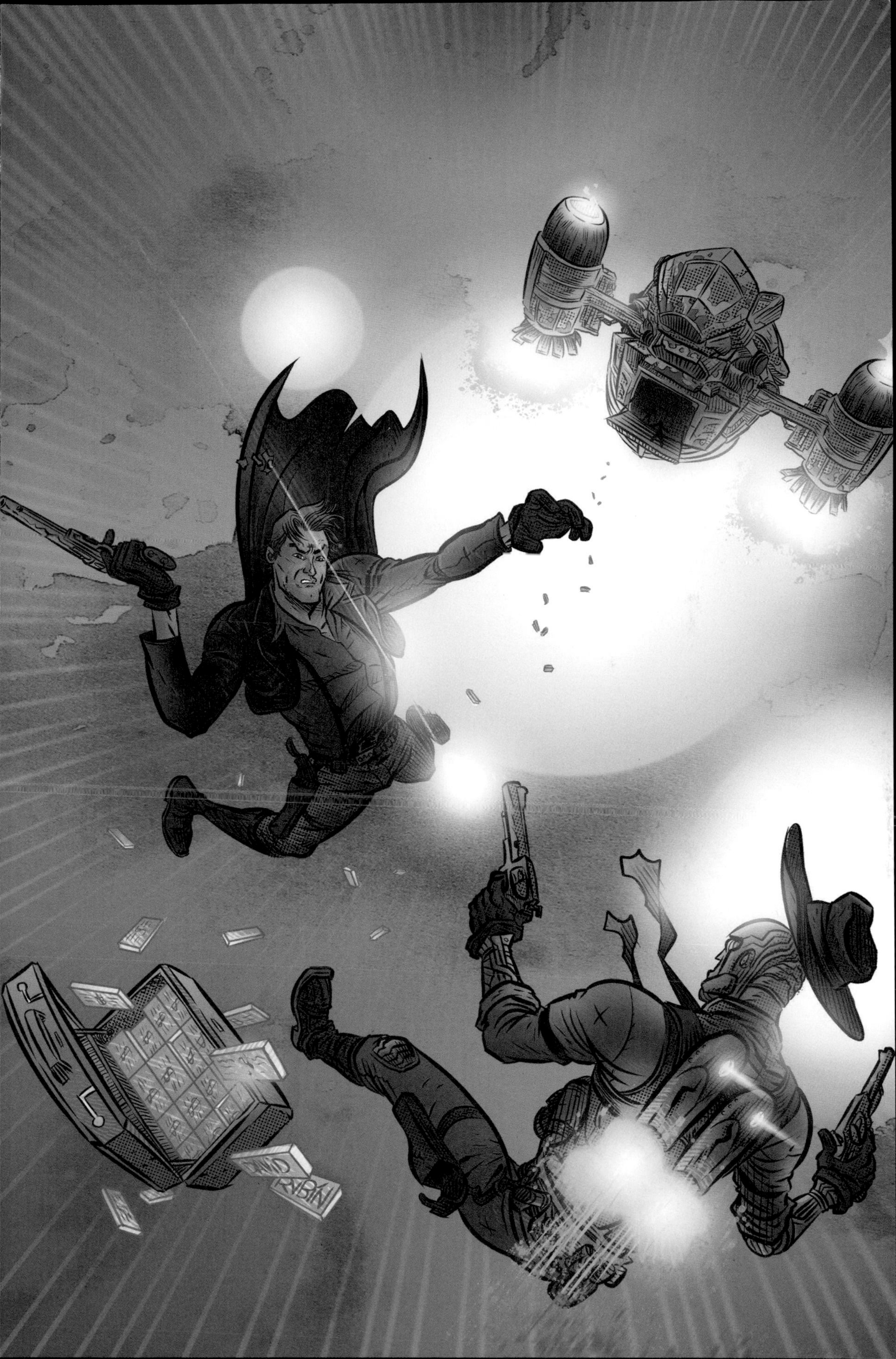

Firefly #5 Unlocked Retailer Variant Cover by **David Rubín**

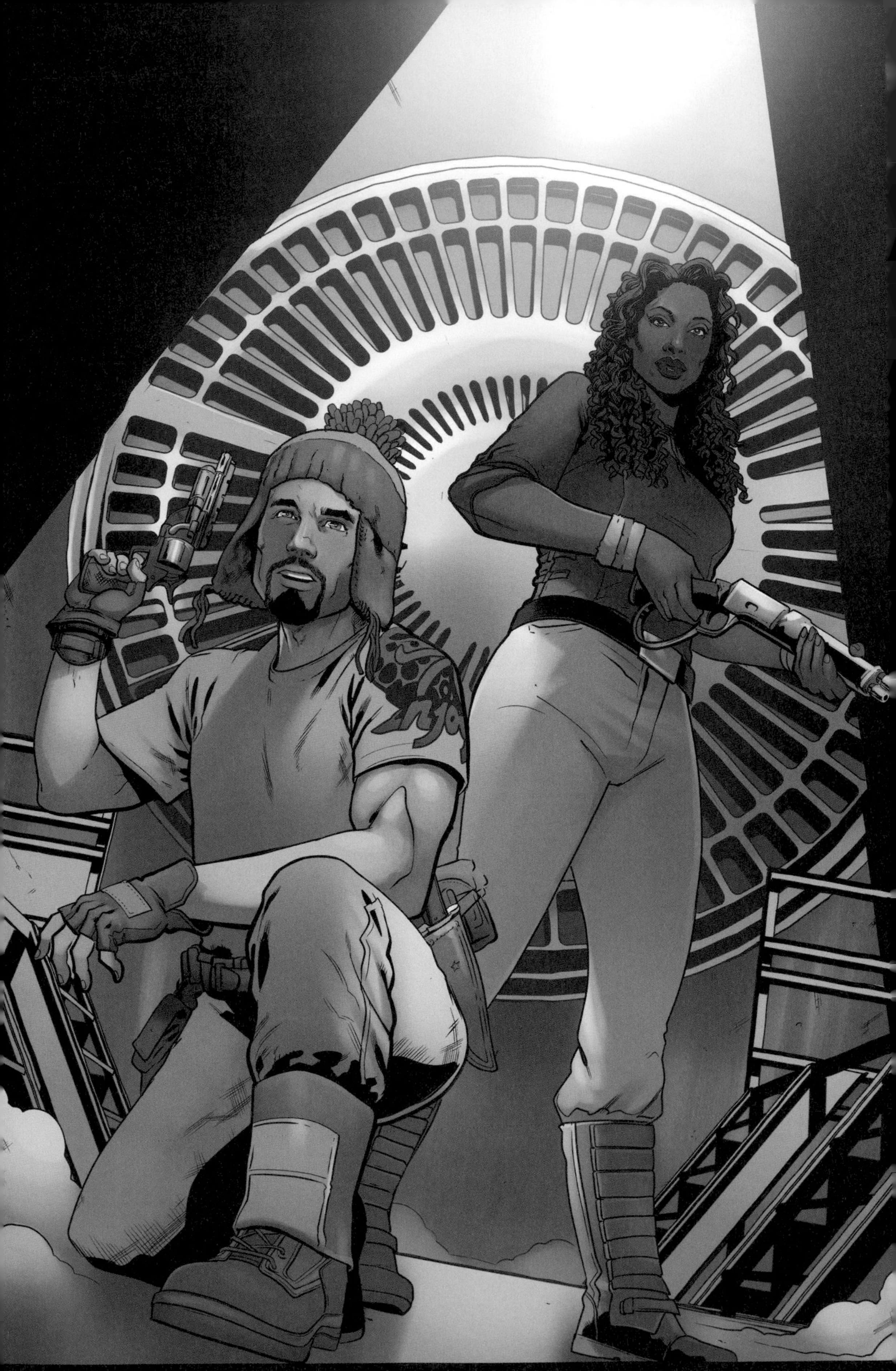

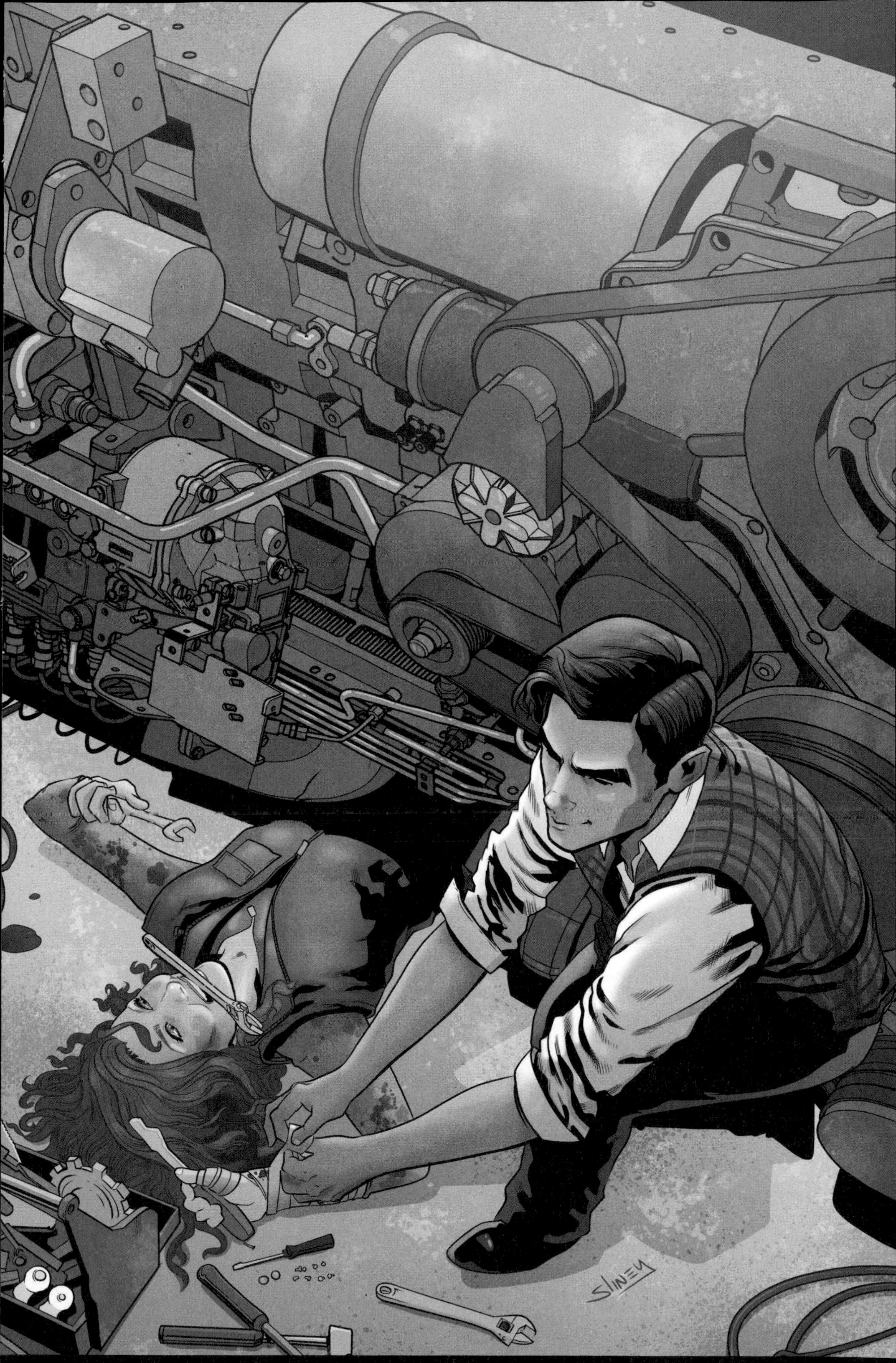
SLINEY

Firefly #7 Unlocked Retailer Variant Cover by **Will Sliney** with Colors by **Chris O'Halloran**

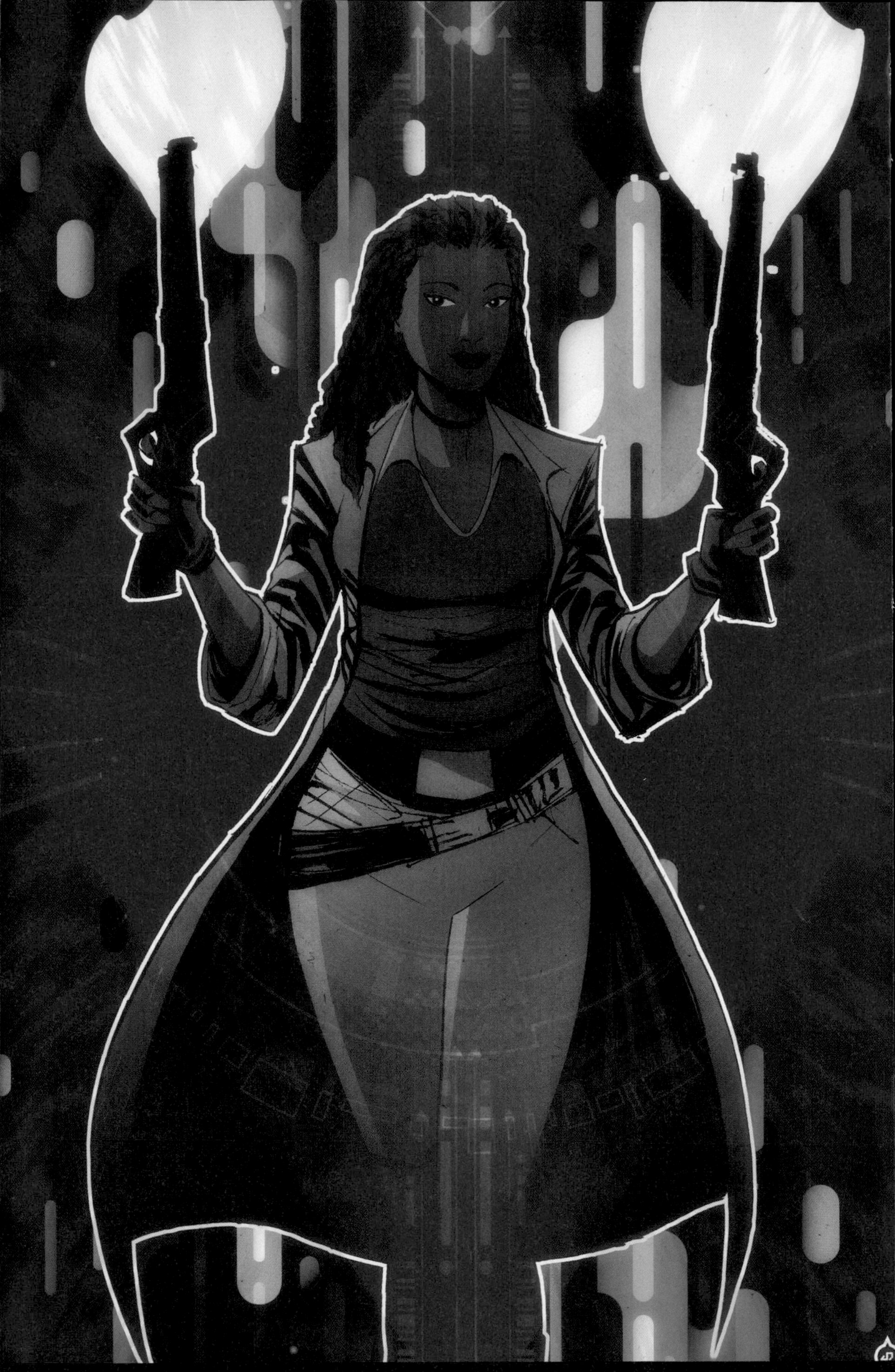

Firefly #8 Unlocked Retailer Variant Cover by **Juan Doe**

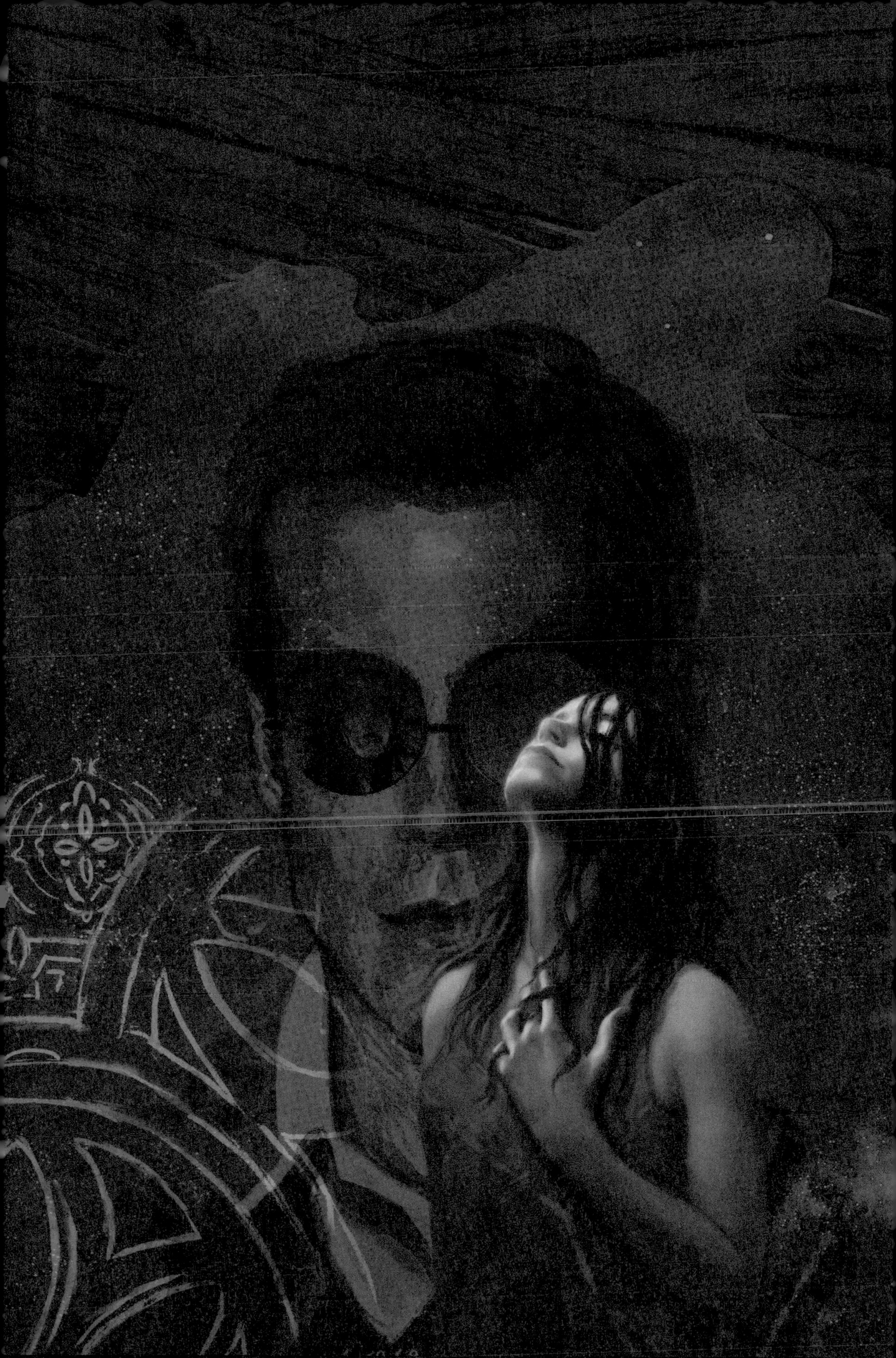

Firefly #5 Second Printing Cover by **Kirbi Fagan**

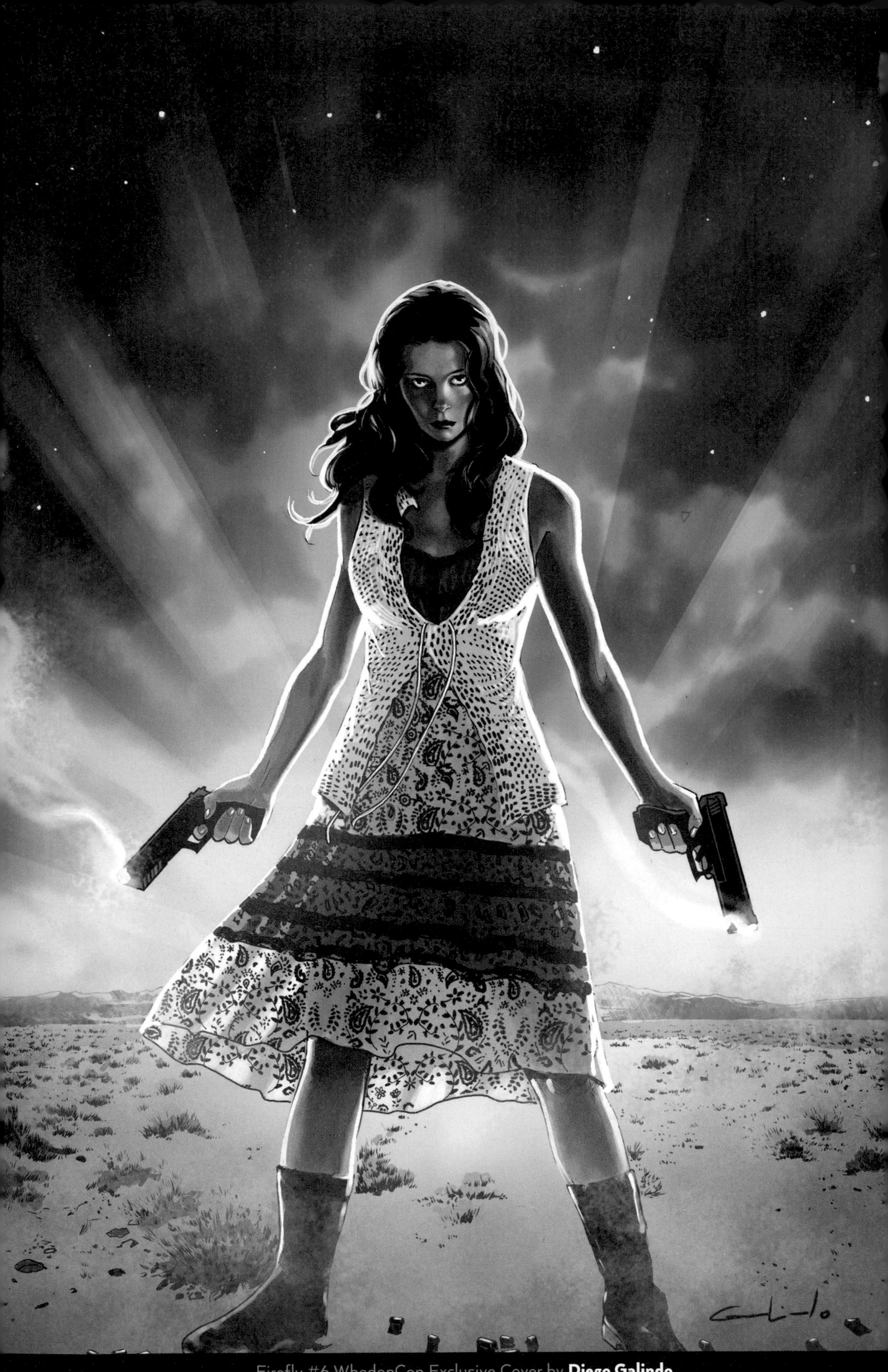

Firefly #6 WhedonCon Exclusive Cover by **Diego Galindo**

WHAT MAKES US SPECIAL

WE'VE GOT US SOME CRIME TO BE DONE.

...know why? Because we are so very pretty. We are just too pretty for God to let us die.

I don't believe there's a power in the 'Verse can stop Kaylee from being cheerful. Sometimes you just...

YOU'RE LO...

WE ALL A...

喧闹起来

And I'm thinking you weren't burdened with an overabundance of schooling. So why don't we just...

Ship like this will be with you 'til the day you die. That's 'cause it's a death trap.

Sir, I think you have a problem with your brain being missing.

Seems to me the last time there was a chance for a little palaver we were all manner of...

This ain't bad. There's a trick to it. Wood alcohol. Now we are favored guests treated to...

FINEST IN BEVERAGES THAT MAKE YOU...

喧闹起来

I brought you some supper. But if you'd prefer a lecture, I have a few very catchy ones prepped.

SIN AND HELLFIRE. ONE HAS LEPERS.

BETRAYAL. INEVITABLE.

WE'D BE DEAD.

Can't get paid if you're dead.

BEING RIGHT

MAN OF THE HO...

DEN OF...

SCRIPT TO PAGE
CREATING THE WORLD OF THE 'VERSE

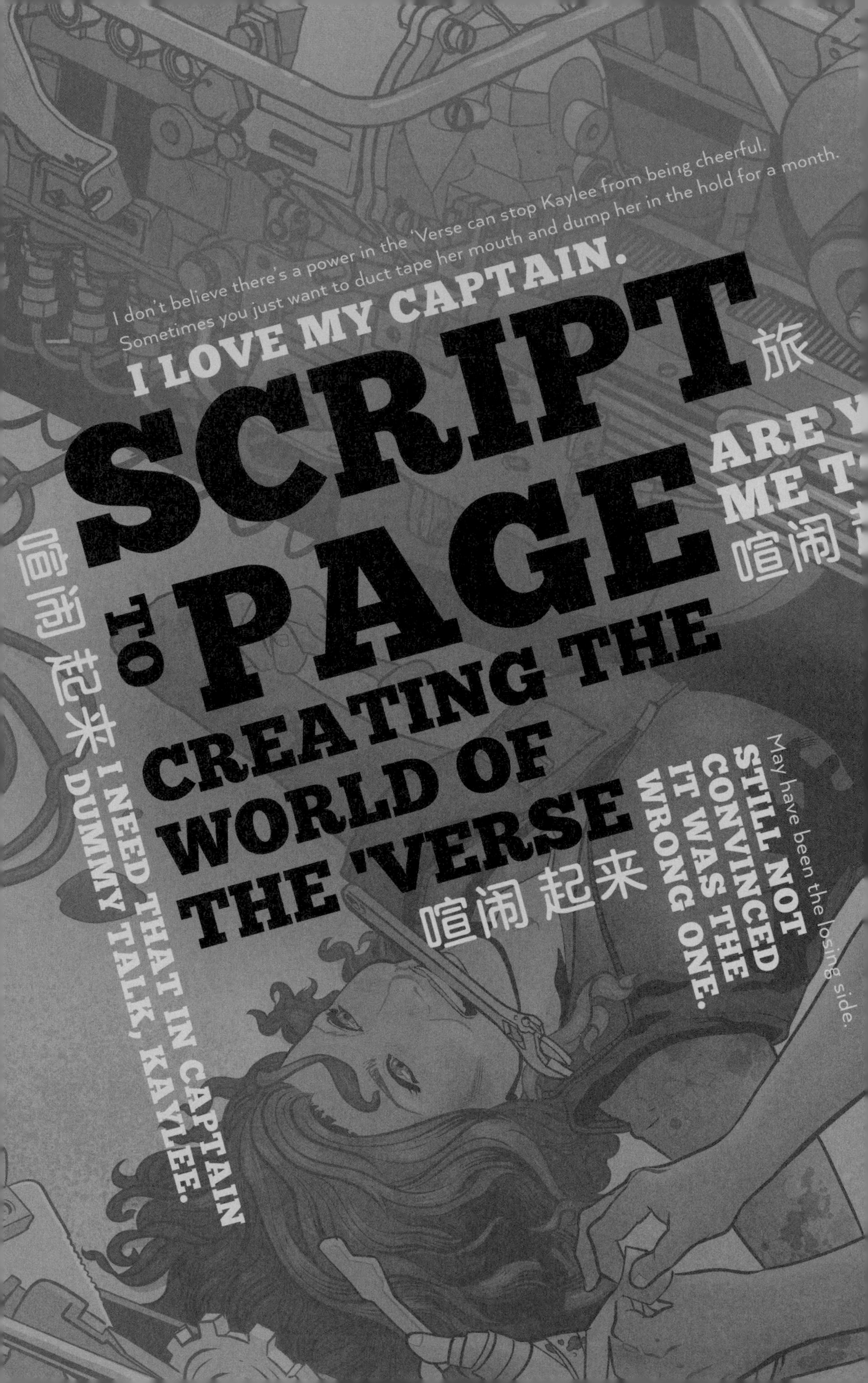

I don't believe there's a power in the 'Verse can stop Kaylee from being cheerful.
Sometimes you just want to duct tape her mouth and dump her in the hold for a month.
I LOVE MY CAPTAIN.
旅
喧闹
喧闹起来
I NEED THAT IN CAPTAIN DUMMY TALK, KAYLEE.
喧闹起来
STILL NOT CONVINCED IT WAS THE WRONG ONE.
May have been the losing side.

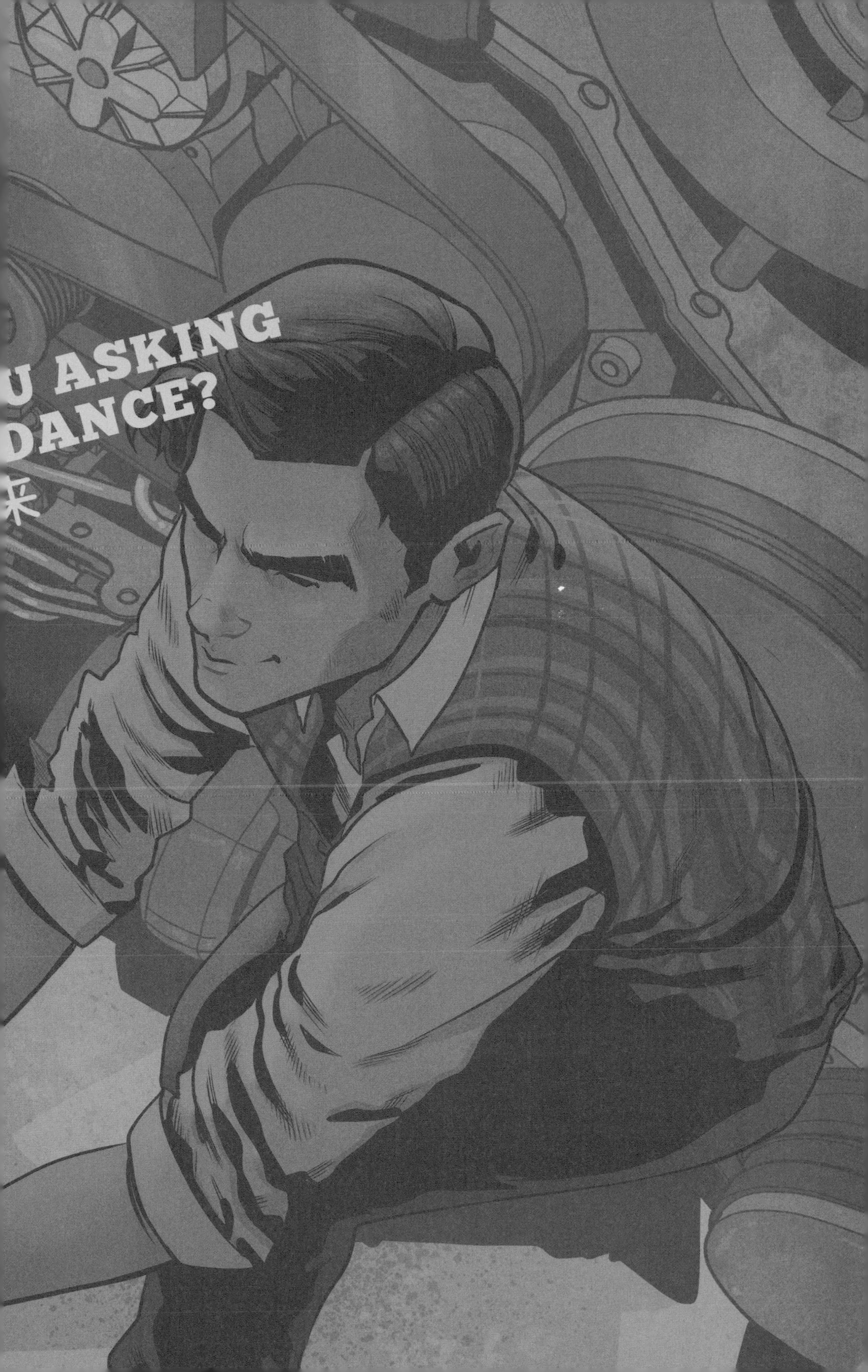
U ASKING
DANCE?

FROM SCRIPT TO PAGE

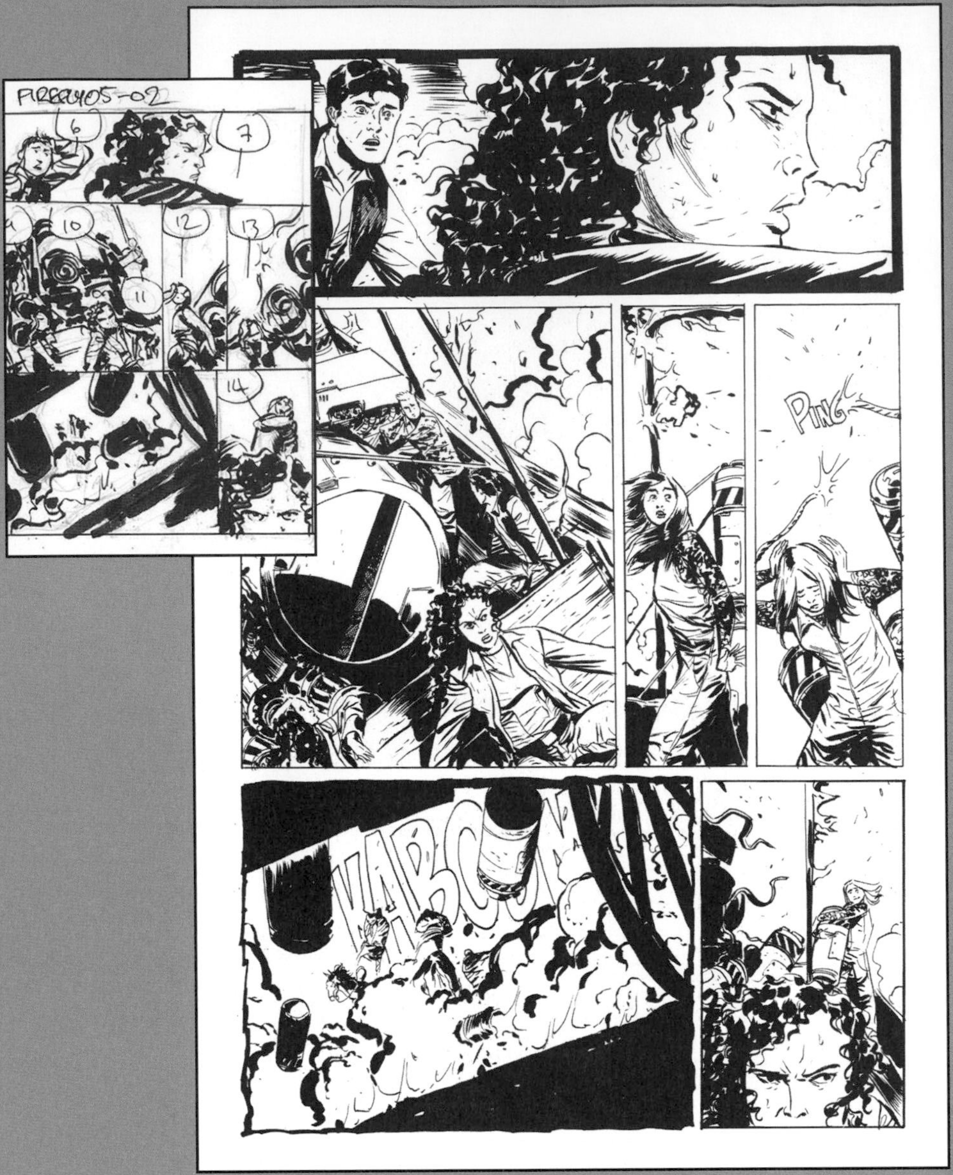
PING

ISSUE FIVE, PAGE TWO

Panel 1: Closer as they continue racing across the plains. Simon hunches by Zoë's leg, trying to attend to her wound. Blood's coming through her bandages.

1. SIMON: Zoë, you can't carry on like this! You're going to ***open up*** your ***wound***!
2. ZOË: Buncha ***pilgrims*** out there'll be happy to open up a bunch ***more*** if I ***stop***, Doc.

Panel 2: Zoë shouts back over her shoulder at Wash and Kaylee. Wash is inspecting the engine.

3. ZOË: Wash! Kaylee! You got what we need to get Serenity back in the air?
4. WASH: Well, we stole a whole ***engine*** from that ***Unificator*** wreck…
5. WASH: …lotta standard fittings here. Pretty sure I can retrofit this to replace our ***reaction thruster***--

Panel 3: Kaylee grins as she pats a stack of fuel cells on the wagon bed held down by ropes. The fuel cells are pretty big -- about two feet wide and one foot high and across.

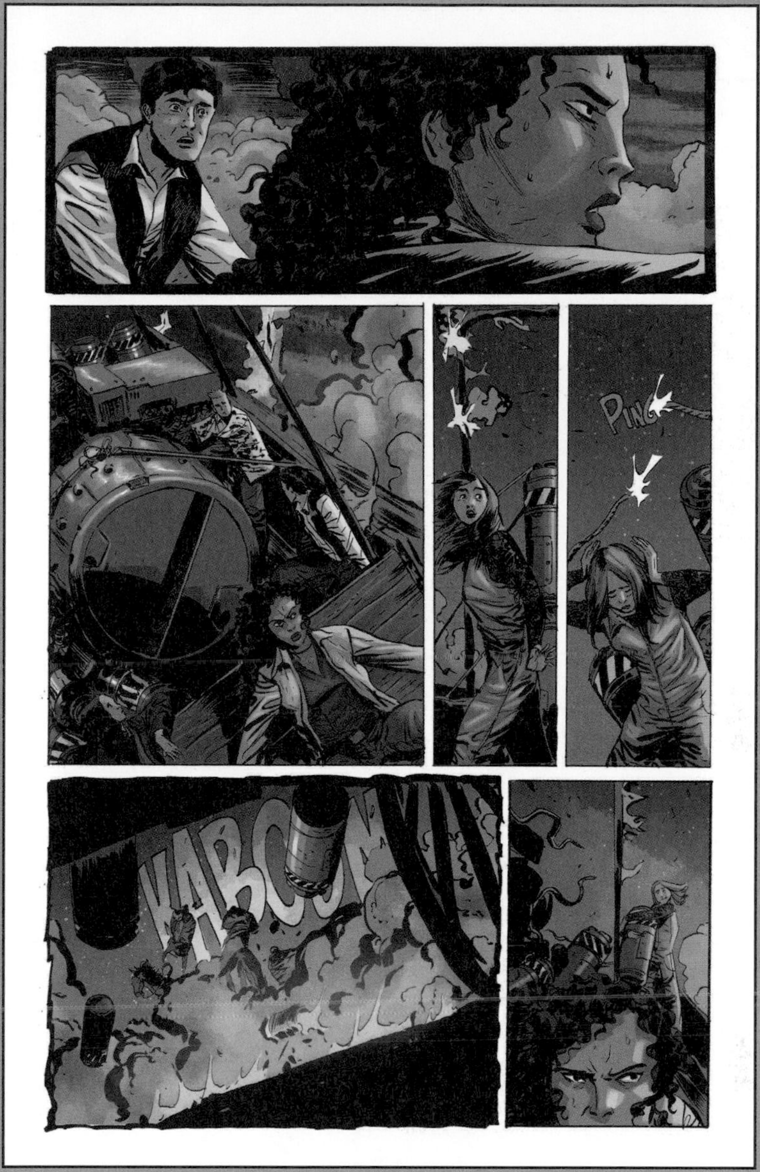
PING
KABOOM

6. KAYLEE: --and we got enough ***fuel cells*** to last us a month--

Panel 4: A pilgrim fires at her -- she ducks, but the spray of bullets hit the ropes holding the fuel cells in place, snapping them!

7. SFX: BLAM BLAM
8. KAYLEE: Whoop!

Panel 5: Fuel cells tumble off of the side of the wagon and EXPLODE, sending pilgrims flying!

9. SFX: KABOOOOM
10. PILGRIMS: Aaaaagh!

Panel 6: Kaylee turns, gives Zoë an apologetic grin. She's holding onto just a couple of the remaining fuel cells.

11. KAYLEE: Or a ***week***, anyway.

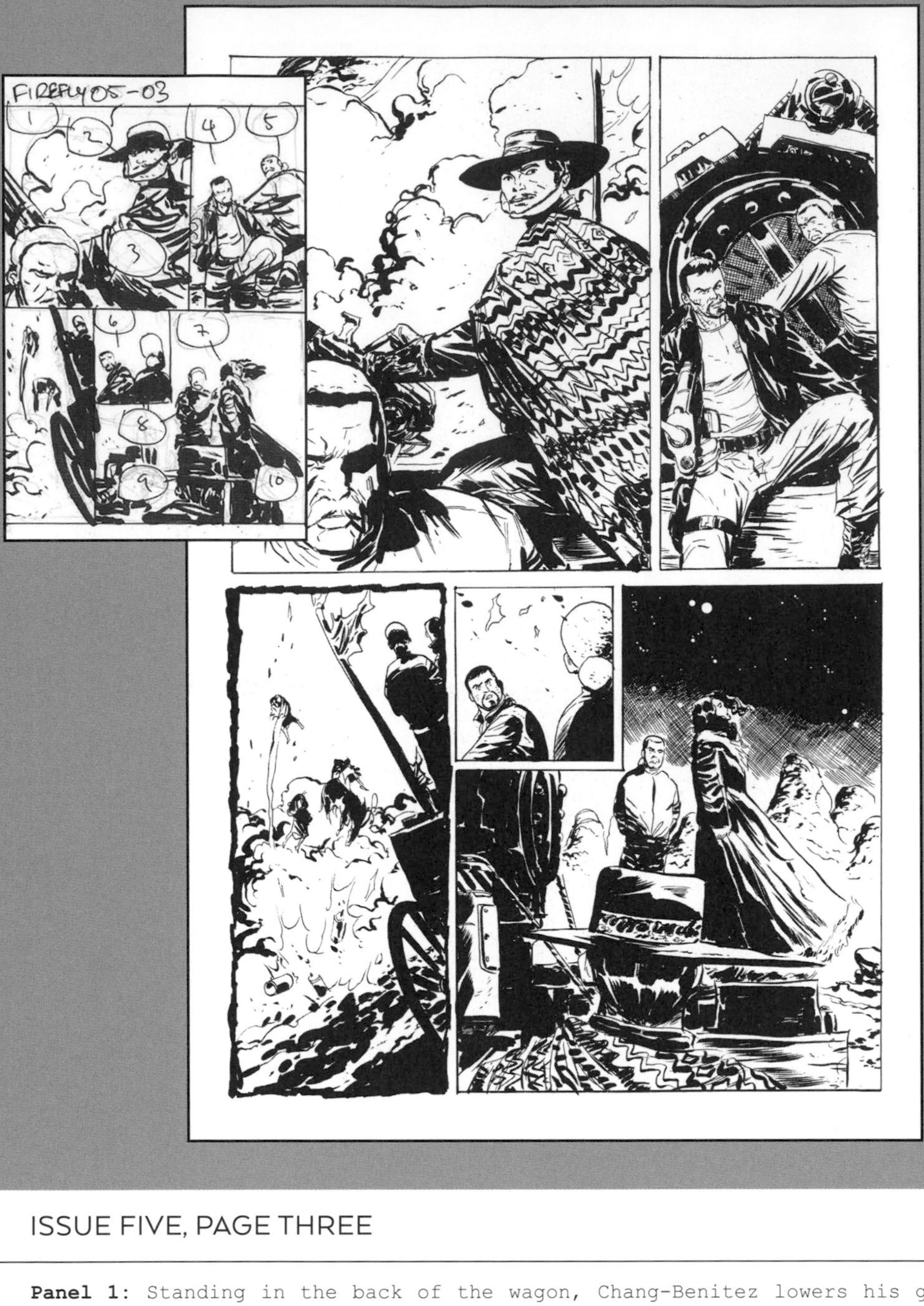
FIREFLY05-03

ISSUE FIVE, PAGE THREE

Panel 1: Standing in the back of the wagon, Chang-Benitez lowers his gun and turns back to grin at us, delighted. Behind him, pilgrims are scrambling, falling behind in the smoke and embers of the explosions.
Book is eyeing him grimly.

1. CHANG-BENITEZ: Well, that took care of them ***pilgrims*** for a while, anyway!
2. CHANG-BENITEZ: Wish I knew that trick when I was still a ***bandit***!
3. BOOK: God save their souls.

Panel 2: Jayne gives Book a look.

4. JAYNE: You praying for ***them***? They tried to ***cut*** our throats, Book.
5. BOOK: I pray for ***everyone***, Jayne.

Panel 3: They turn as another exploding fuel cell sends some more pilgrims flying.

6. SFX: KRAAAKOOOOOOM
7. PILGRIMS: Yaaaa!

Panel 4: Jayne eyes Book warily.

    8. JAYNE: Yeah, well. Don't pray for me.

Panel 5: Inara looks skyward. Book is following her gaze. Chang-Benitez is giving her a quizzical look.

    9. INARA: Yes. Just pray for **Mal**.
    10. BOOK: Believe me, I **have been**, Inara.
    11. CHANG-BENITEZ: Which one's **Mal** again?
    12. INARA: You know. The tall, handsome, **stupid** one…

ABOUT THE AUTHOR

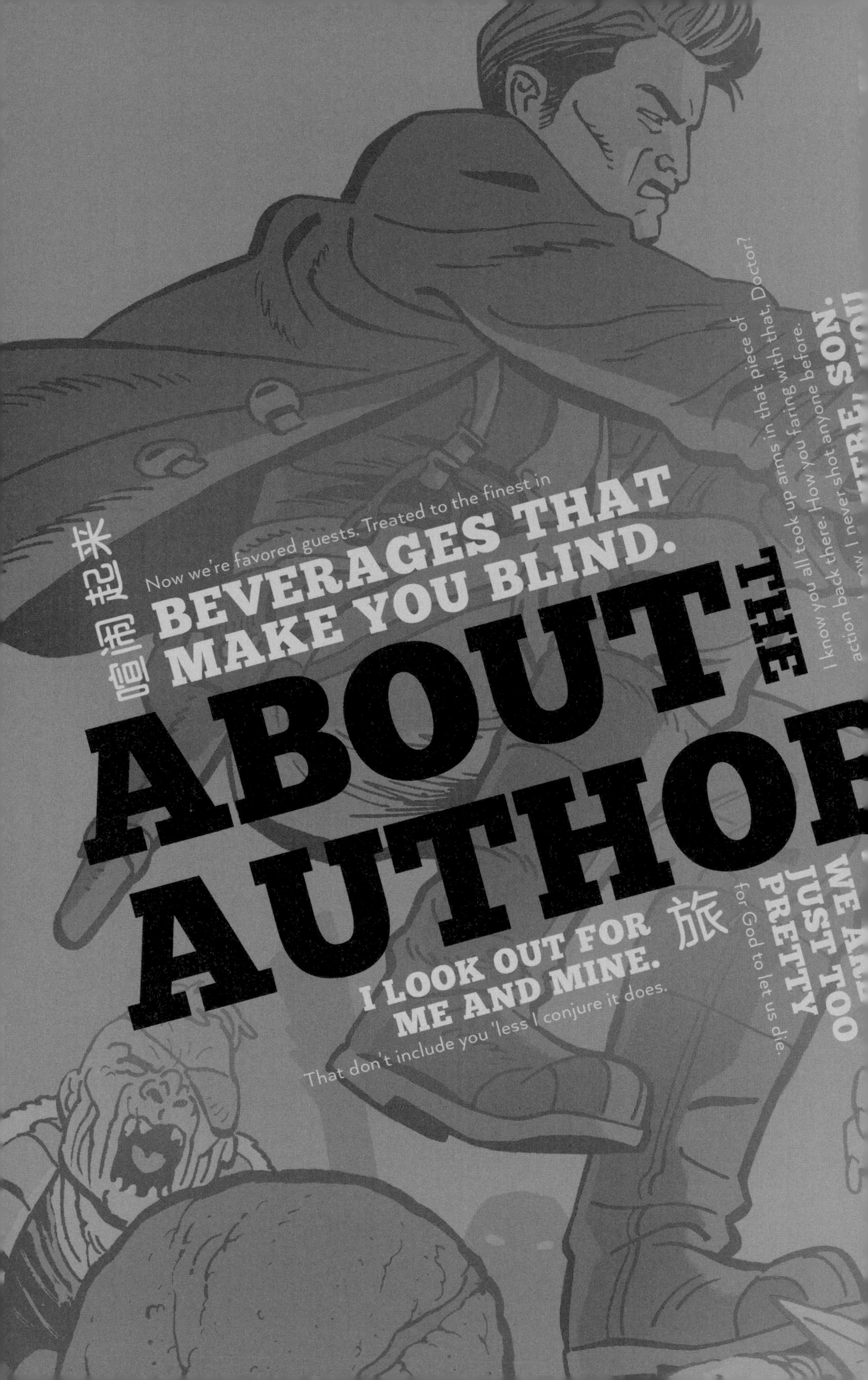
Now we're favored guests. Treated to the finest in
BEVERAGES THAT MAKE YOU BLIND.
喧闹起来
I LOOK OUT FOR ME AND MINE.
That don't include you 'less I conjure it does.
旅
I know you all took up arms in that piece of action back there. How you faring with that, Doctor?
I never shot anyone before.
SON.
WE ARE JUST TOO PRETTY
for God to let us die.

Joss Whedon is one of Hollywood's top creators, scripting several hit films including Marvel's *The Avengers*, which was a breakout success and became one of the highest grossing films of all time, and its sequel *Avengers: Age of Ultron*, and creating one of television's most critically praised shows, *Buffy the Vampire Slayer*. In 2000, Whedon garnered his first Emmy nomination in the category of Outstanding Writing for a Drama Series for his groundbreaking episode entitled "Hush," and he earned an Academy Award nomination for Best Screenplay with Disney's box-office smash *Toy Story*. Originally hailing from New York, Whedon is a third-generation television writer. His grandfather and father were both successful sitcom writers on shows such as *The Donna Reed Show*, *Leave It to Beaver* and *The Golden Girls*.

Greg Pak is a Korean American filmmaker and comic book writer best known for his award-winning feature film *Robot Stories*, his blockbuster comic book series like Marvel Comics' *Planet Hulk* and *World War Hulk*, and his record-breaking Kickstarter publishing projects with Jonathan Coulton, *Code Monkey Save World* and *The Princess Who Saved Herself*. His other projects at BOOM! Studios include the award-winning creator-owned *Mech Cadet Yu* and *Ronin Island*.

Dan McDaid is a British comics artist and writer with a lustrous head of black hair and a full, healthy beard. After breaking into comics with the UK's *Doctor Who Magazine*, he went on to co-create *Jersey Gods* for Image Comics and *Time Share* for Oni Press, as well as drawing cult favorites *Big Trouble in Little China* and *Dawn of the Planet of the Apes*. Following a well-regarded run on IDW's *Judge Dredd*, he launched his own webcomic, *DEGA*, and is currently drawing the new adventures of the Serenity crew in BOOM! Studios' *Firefly*. He lives in Scotland with his partner Deborah and a large gray cat whose name means "Dark Stranger".

Vincenzo Federici is an Italian comic book artist from Naples. After his Classical Arts studies, he started to work in comics for French publishers, like Soleil Éditions and on a creator owned project for the Italian publisher Noise Press, called *The Kabuki Fight*. He then moved to American publishers, working with IDW Publishing, Zenescope Entertainment, Dynamite Entertainment, BOOM! Studios and more, on series like *Army of Darkness/ Bubba Ho-Tep*, *M. A. S. K.*, *Star Trek*, *Firefly*, *Go Go Power Rangers* and more. He also is a teacher in different Italian Comic Art schools.

Marcelo Costa is a comics artist and colorist. As a colorist, he's best known for his work on *Power Rangers: Shattered Grid* and *Power Rangers: Soul of the Dragon*, and *Planet of the Apes Visionaries*. As an artist, he's worked on Zenescope's *Grimm Fairy Tales*, Action Lab's *Season 3*, and the episode "Star Trip", from the Society of Virtue YouTube Channel. Currently, Marcelo is also working on *Self/Made* and *Teenage Mutant Ninja Turtles: Shredder in Hell*, in a partnership with Matheus Santolouco.

Jim Campbell has been lettering comics professionally for almost a decade, before which he worked in newspaper and magazine publishing for even longer. He knows more about print production than mortal man was meant to know and has also scanned more images than you've had hot dinners. Unless you're ninety years old. If you're very unlucky, he might start talking to you about ligatures.

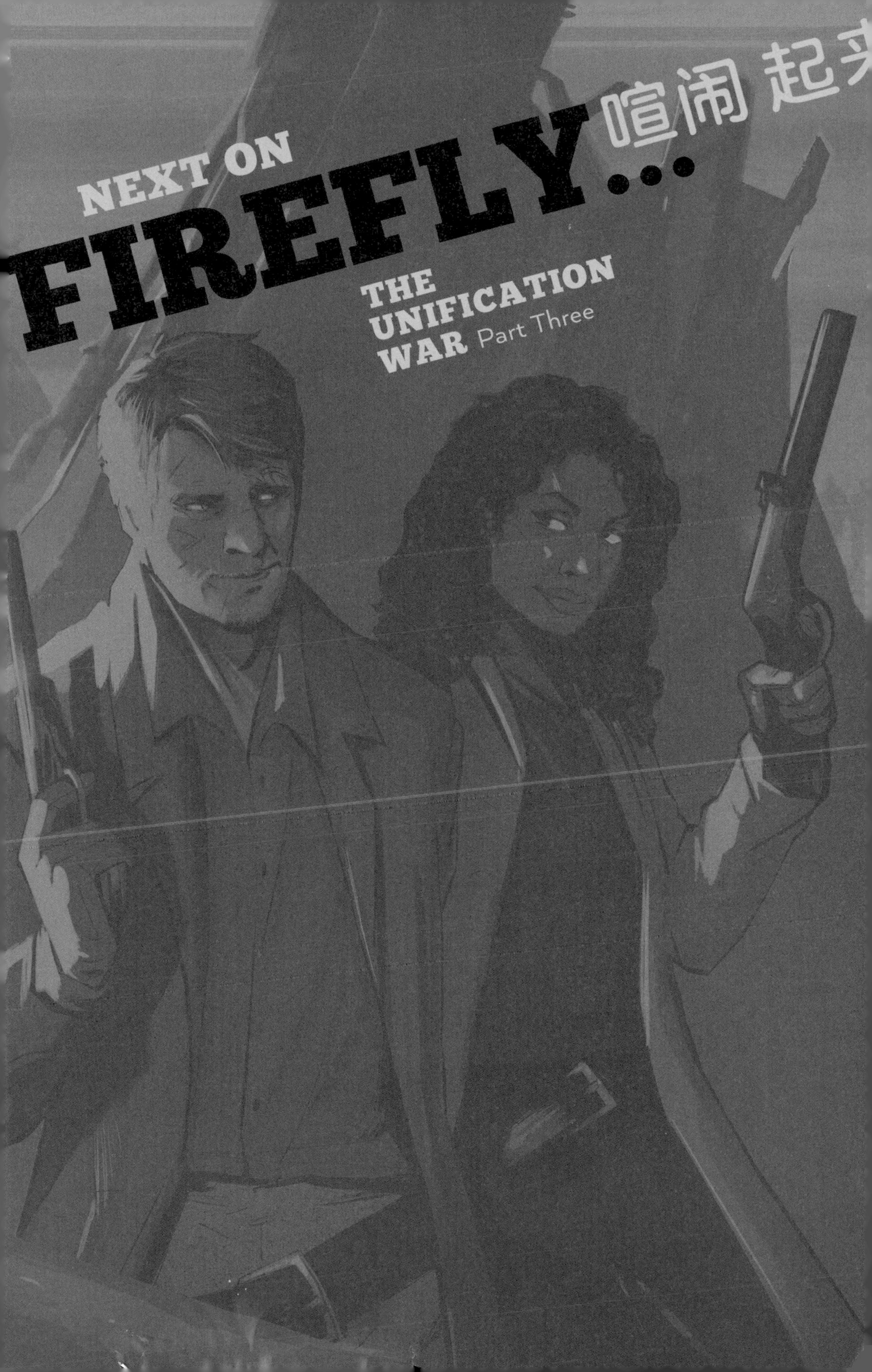
NEXT ON
FIREFLY...
喧闹起来
THE UNIFICATION WAR Part Three

DISCOVER
VISIONARY CREATORS

KIERON GILLEN DAN MORA
ONCE & FUTURE
VOLUME ONE

JAMES TYNION IV
WERTHER DELL'EDERA
MIQUEL MUERTO
SOMETHING is KILLING the CHILDREN
VOLUME ONE
SCOTT SNYDER

Brian Azzarello · Maria Llovet
FAITHLESS

GRANT MORRISON DAN MORA
Klaus
How Santa Claus Began

SIMON SPURRIER × MATÍAS BERGARA
CODA
VOLUME ONE
"This one is really special!"
—JEFF LEMIRE

matt kindt tyler jenkins
GRASS KINGS
volume one

BOOM!™ STUDIOS

AVAILABLE AT YOUR LOCAL COMICS SHOP AND BOOKSTORE

To find a comics shop in your area, visit www.comicshoplocator.com

WWW.**BOOM-STUDIOS**.COM

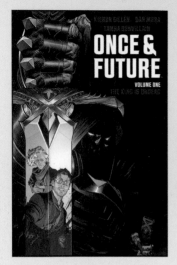

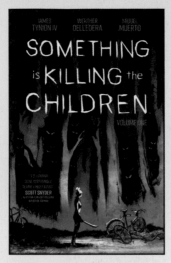

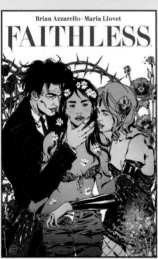

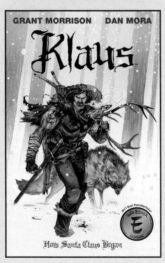

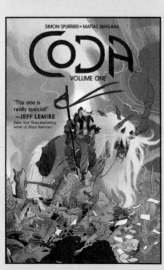

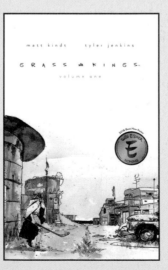

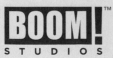

Once & Future
Kieron Gillen, Dan Mora
Volume 1
ISBN: 978-1-68415-491-3 | $16.99 US

Something is Killing the Children
James Tynion IV, Werther Dell'Edera
Volume 1
ISBN: 978-1-68415-558-3 | $14.99 US

Faithless
Brian Azzarello, Maria Llovet
ISBN: 978-1-68415-432-6 | $17.99 US

Klaus
Grant Morrison, Dan Mora
Klaus: How Santa Claus Began SC
ISBN: 978-1-68415-393-0 | $15.99 US
Klaus: The New Adventures of Santa Claus HC
ISBN: 978-1-68415-666-5 | $17.99 US

Coda
Simon Spurrier, Matias Bergara
Volume 1
ISBN: 978-1-68415-321-3 | $14.99 US
Volume 2
ISBN: 978-1-68415-369-5 | $14.99 US
Volume 3
ISBN: 978-1-68415-429-6 | $14.99 US

Grass Kings
Matt Kindt, Tyler Jenkins
Volume 1
ISBN: 978-1-64144-362-3 | $17.99 US
Volume 2
ISBN: 978-1-64144-557-3 | $17.99 US
Volume 3
ISBN: 978-1-64144-650-1 | $17.99 US

Bone Parish
Cullen Bunn, Jonas Scharf
Volume 1
ISBN: 978-1-64144-337-1 | $14.99 US
Volume 2
ISBN: 978-1-64144-542-9 | $14.99 US
Volume 3
ISBN: 978-1-64144-543-6 | $14.99 US

Ronin Island
Greg Pak, Giannis Milonogiannis
Volume 1
ISBN: 978-1-64144-576-4 | $14.99 US
Volume 2
ISBN: 978-1-64144-723-2 | $14.99 US
Volume 3
ISBN: 978-1-64668-035-1 | $14.99 US

Victor LaValle's Destroyer
Victor LaValle, Dietrich Smith
ISBN: 978-1-61398-732-2 | $19.99 US